...so received the Tony
...tors Under 35. After work-
ing as an editor for fifteen years, she became an agent and is currently a partner with Dunow, Carlson & Lerner Literary Agency. She lives in Connecticut.

'Through the alchemy of a grand game, Betsy Lerner has woven a universal coming-of-age story for both mother and daughter. A poignant, humorous and often painful struggle through the pageantry of playing cards; a woman's face on every one'

PATTI SMITH, author of *Just Kids* and *M Train*

'In the end what we want from our mothers – and what they want from us – is acceptance. "Our mothers have been always trying to fix us, which has given us the message that we're not OK," says Betsy Lerner. Meanwhile, we daughters have been trying to fix them. Betsy's book says, stop trying to fix one another. You're both OK as you are'

JOANNA MOORHEAD, *Guardian*

'A funny, tender, sometimes sad account of a mother–daughter relationship that is often painful but always honest . . . It's also a valuable piece of social history'

ANNE SEBBA, *Jewish Chronicle*

'An entertaining portrait of a group of wonderful women, growing older now and braving new battles, with sweetness, humour and sharp perceptiveness. This is a book with heart and feeling'   GEORGE HODGMAN, author of *Bettyville*

'*The Golden Girls* meets *The Sisterhood of the Travelling Pants* for a game of bridge and a plate of fishballs. I loved this memoir about a mother and daughter putting their differences aside'
SARRA MANNING, *Red*

'*The Bridge Ladies* reminded me of *Tuesdays with Morrie*, except that it takes place on Mondays and it has five Morries. In this exquisitely written book, there's humour, candour, no-nonsense wisdom – and portraits of five women whose like we won't see again. I devoured it in one greedy sitting, and started re-reading as soon as I finished'
WILL SCHWALBE, author of *The End of Your Life Book Club*

Also by Betsy Lerner

Food and Loathing

The Forest for the Trees

The Bridge Ladies

a memoir

Betsy Lerner

PAN BOOKS

First published 2016 by Harper Wave,
an imprint of HarperCollins Publishers

First published in the UK 2016 by Macmillan

This edition published 2017 by Pan Books
an imprint of Pan Macmillan
20 New Wharf Road, London N1 9RR
Associated companies throughout the world
www.panmacmillan.com

ISBN 978-1-4472-7252-6

1 3 5 7 9 8 6 4 2

A CIP catalogue record for this book is available from the British Library.

Designed by William Ruoto
Sketch courtesy of Chris Silas Neal
Printed and bound by CPI Group (UK) Ltd, Croydon, CR0 4YY

Visit **www.panmacmillan.com** to read more about all our books
and to buy them. You will also find features, author interviews and
news of any author events, and you can sign up for e-newsletters
so that you're always first to hear about our new releases.

For Roslyn and Raffaella,
my mother and daughter

CONTENTS

Contents

You get one mother in this world. Only one.

—Harvey Fierstein, *Torch Song Trilogy*

The Bridge Ladies

As a child, I was fascinated with the Bridge Ladies. They showed up regularly at our house, their hair frosted, their nylons shimmery, carrying patent leather pocketbooks with clasps as round as marbles. I loved greeting them at the door, hanging up their coats in our front hall closet, where I often played inside the folds of my mother's mink. I watched as they gathered around the card table, crowded with a twinset of cards, ashtrays, cellophane-wrapped cigarette packs, a scoring pad, and crystal dishes of candy. Eye level to the Bridge table, I greedily surveyed the candy and would plan high-speed kamikaze raids to nab some from below my mother's radar. Where my father would let me sit on his lap while he played Gin Rummy for a hand or two, the Bridge Ladies erected a square fortress with their backs as they played, communing in their strange language of bids and tricks.

As a teenager, I'd make myself scarce when the Bridge Ladies came over. As far as I was concerned, they were square. They didn't work, didn't seem to get that feminism was taking over the world. Billie Jean King had defeated Bobby Riggs in the Battle of the Sexes Tennis Match, Gloria Steinem had started *Ms.* magazine, and Helen Reddy roared. To me, the Bridge Ladies were conventional, their sphere limited to family, synagogue, and community. Their identities restricted to daughter, mother, and wife. On top of which their idea of fun was an afternoon of playing Bridge. *Seriously?*

I was after bigger game. I was already reading Anaïs Nin and Henry Miller. In other words, I was determined to lose my virginity as soon as possible and have many lovers. I hated our New Haven suburb and my high school for its devotion to conformity. As far as I could tell, the most creative endeavor for the girls was growing their hair as long as possible in order to qualify for the national "Long & Silky" contest. All I wanted to do was get out and stay out. I spent my time dreaming of escape to New York, specifically Greenwich Village, where I hoped to find like-minded people, poets, and writers. I moved there for college and stayed for graduate school. Though I didn't become a fixture at Studio 54 or Warhol's Factory, I'd made a life there: worked in publishing, eventually married, and had a daughter.

Then something happened. After twenty years of living and working in New York, my husband was offered a job at Yale University Press. You didn't need a Google map to see where this was going: New Haven, my childhood home and the crucible of my pain. I was supportive when he accepted the job; the reality of moving home took a little longer to fathom.

For me, the biggest challenge was having my mother become a regular part of our lives. When I lived in New York, we spoke once a week, perfunctorily on Sundays. Now I would be living 5.1 miles away from her. I told myself I could handle it. After all,

I was well into my forties when we moved home, I was a mother in my own right, yet my conflicts with my mother still flared brightly. Why was everything so loaded? Why was I reduced to my teenage self almost every time we got together? Was everything she said a criticism, or did it only sound that way? We circled each other like wary boxers. Once, she asked why I bought low-fat cottage cheese instead of fat-free and nearly set off a world war between us. It was cottage cheese, for god's sake! Translated through the mother-daughter lexicon: Was I ever going to be good enough?

When my mother was recovering from some surgery in January of 2013, I stayed with her to help out. We had been living in New Haven for more than a decade by then, my dad gone, my daughter a teenager in her own right, we had made new friends and were knitted in. I had become a partner in a literary agency and was commuting to New York twice a week, getting my city fix. On top of that, God shined down his light on our fair city and conferred an Apple Store upon us. Did I really have any reason to complain?

I wasn't exactly looking forward to staying with my mother, but I also knew the job would be made less onerous by the fact that she, even at eighty-three, was more comfortable refusing help than demanding it, best summed up in the well-known joke: How many Jewish grandmothers does it take to screw in a lightbulb? *You shouldn't worry . . . I'll sit in the dark.*

Every day, one of her Bridge Ladies visited, as if in an unspoken rotation. They were smaller now, some a little unsteady, but still decked out in color-coordinated outfits, accessories, heels, and bags. When they said I looked good, I wondered if they really thought I was fat, if my unruly hair was an offense. When they asked after my husband and daughter, it struck me that they had been there for all of the rites of passage in my life: they had attended my bat mitzvah, danced at my wedding, and sent gifts when my daughter was born. I had never really taken stock of their generosity; they likely had no idea how much adolescent rancor and disrespect I harbored. Or how I had clumped them all together like the presidents carved into Mount Rushmore, indistinguishable one from another.

As demographics go, the Bridge Ladies couldn't be more alike. They are all in their eighties, all Jewish, and they all attended college. They married young, married Jewish men, and stayed married to them. They had 2.5 children. None worked outside the home during the years they raised their children, except Rhoda, who shattered the stained-glass ceiling when she became the executive director at the synagogue. They did the shopping and cooked the meals; *The Joy of Cooking*, published in 1936, was their bible. They picked up the dry cleaning and cleaned their homes. (Eventually, each would be able to afford cleaning ladies, as they would all become upwardly mobile.) They decorated and planned vacations, from the Catskills to Puerto Rico to Rome.

They lived through the Depression and World War II. Some of their husbands joined the war effort. They witnessed the civil rights era, The Vietnam War, and the feminist movement, though they didn't shed their girdles or burn their bras. They were just a little too old or insulated to embrace *The Feminine Mystique* or articulate the problem that had no name. They saw interfaith marriage among their children and interracial marriage among their grandchildren. When they grew up, gay people were completely closeted, like movie star heroes Montgomery Clift and Rock Hudson. Today, they are witness to the legalization of gay marriage in every state in the nation.

Though they were not all born in New Haven, they have lived in the greater New Haven area for all of their adult lives, they raised their children here, four have buried husbands here, and one buried a daughter. They are all in relatively good health (knock on wood, poo poo poo). Their adult children are as great a source of pride as they are of aggravation. They don't like to brag, but their grandchildren are brilliant. And on Mondays at noontime, for the past fifty-five years, they gather for lunch and Bridge, the card game whose golden age coincided with their generation's coming of age.

Bridge was the HBO of its day. In the 1930s and 1940s, 44 percent of American households had at least one Bridge player. Matches were broadcast on radios, and popular movies like *Sunset Boulevard* and *Shadow of the Thin Man* featured scenes with Bridge games. Robert Cohn, a character in Hemingway's *The Sun Also Rises*, boasted about his winning streak at Bridge. The *New Yorker* published "My Lady Love, My Dove," a Roald Dahl story where a couple are caught swindling their hosts during an evening of Bridge. Charles Goren was a household name, the man who popularized the system of counting points still used today. His books have sold millions worldwide, clogged the best seller lists, and his Bridge column appeared in nearly two hundred newspapers. The guy was a rock star.

Enter television. By 1954, more than 80 percent of American households had TV. Evenings once spent listening to the radio and engaging in social activities like Bridge got crushed. Today, there are approximately three million active Bridge players, which puts the game on par with stamp collecting and fly-fishing. In 2015, after an eighty-year run, the *New York Times* cut its Bridge column. How long can the game exist? Not one of the Bridge daughters learned to play, not at our mothers' sides and not in college, where most of them learned in the parlor rooms of their all-girl dormitories.

When each one of the ladies braved that nasty winter to pay my mother a visit, I found myself inexplicably happy to see them, almost giddy as I took their coats, as I had as a child, hanging them up in our front hall closet. It was no longer stuffed like a dry cleaner's carousel with coats and slacks suffocated in plastic wrap. My mother's mink long retired, the closet now had a sad capacity. The wooden hangers clattered against each other like wind chimes before a storm. I held back an intense longing for my father, growing concern for my mother, and shame for how I used to feel about this small band of women. Each one brought a meal or brownies or cookies.

"I need those like a hole in the head," my mother would announce when they left, though we'd gobble them up after dinner while watching back-to-back reruns of *The Big Bang Theory*.

After my mother recovered, I couldn't stop thinking about her friends from the Bridge club and what seemed to me the vast distance between our generations. Even their names connoted a bygone era: Bette, Bea, Jackie, Rhoda, and my mother, Roz. (Though Bridge is a game for four, there are five women in the club. In case one can't play, they still have a game; this way the show goes on.) I had known these women my whole life and hardly knew them at all. I was deeply touched by their support and loyalty to my mother. According to her, the Bridge Ladies have grown apart over the years, their affection for each other is sometimes blunted, their lives diminished by the effects of aging. Despite differences and silences built up over the years, there exists a devotion to one another; these are dutiful women, their love flinty, but made to last. I knew that if I were to get sick, there wouldn't be such a steady stream of friends visiting. I'd be lucky to get a few texts with smiley face emojis and some messages on my wall. Facebook may connect us across the world and throughout eternity, but it won't deliver a pot roast.

I wondered what their lives would have been like had they been given our opportunities. Did they dream of having other partners? Were their marriages based on love, their husbands' potential as providers, or a combination of the two? Whenever I asked my mother if she loved my father, her answer was always the same: he is a good father and a good provider. I got the feeling her ability to choose was as important as his ability to earn. And, of course, it was. For my mother and for all of the ladies, their fate largely rested on one choice: the man they married. Their financial well-being depended on it. Without a doubt, the men set the stages on which they lived their lives.

"I deferred to your father," my mother explains, though I remain incredulous. "I wanted to."

"Mom," I reply, "no one *wants* to defer."

"I did, I truly did." She means it. Or she thinks she means it. I remember many days growing up when deferring didn't look all that great.

I wanted Hepburn and Tracy, Bogey and Bacall; I wanted big love for them, not something prudent, economical. But the ladies come from a different stock. In the first place, they accept their lot. They are grateful for it! The concept of loving yourself first is unheard of to them. Who had time, with a husband and family to take care of? They didn't dwell on their inner lives. They didn't stretch their spines on yoga mats, and they certainly didn't spend hours in therapy sessions complaining about their parents. Oh, the billable hours my friends and I have logged both condemning our parents and seeking their love. If anything, the ladies don't understand our self-obsession, our selfishness.

When I asked the ladies if I could sit in on the game, they invited me to join them for lunch and Bridge on Mondays, and eventually into their homes for one-on-one conversations about their lives. At the outset, I was interested in the mundane moments: carpooling, packing lunch boxes, or mixing up a batch of sour cream dip with Lipton's Onion Soup Mix. I wanted to know about Dr. Spock and Dr. Seuss, and what it was really like raising a generation of children more entitled and indulged than any other that had come before, my generation: the baby boomers. I was also curious how they felt about all they missed out on: the Pill, pot, and Jimi Hendrix. What was it like finding a joint in a teenager's jeans, or birth control pills in her purse? In the end, I wanted to know how the ladies felt about everything that mattered to me and to my generation. I wanted to see where we connected, if we connected.

I thought I'd go to the Bridge club for a few weeks but stayed for nearly three years. When they opened up to me, I found their stories moving and poignant. I once deemed the ladies not worth knowing; now I wanted to know all I could. This was especially true with my mother. I had no idea that by entering her world, I would begin to bridge both the generational gap and personal gulf that had defined our relationship.

A year or so in, I started taking Bridge lessons, a game that well acquaints you with your deficits. With little natural affinity for the game, I persisted, often at the encouragement of the ladies. My older sister, stupefied by my project, once asked, her voice thick with disbelief: Do you actually *like* Bridge? Do you like *them*?

These days, much of the conversation at the Bridge table re-volves around accidents and illness, death and dying, which hap-pen at an alarming rate. There was one Monday when the ladies talked about a two-funeral day earlier in the week. "You must think we're pretty morbid." Bette laughs. "But it's our life."

I get it. Death hovers over the Bridge table. How could they not fear taking that wrong step, that inaugural fall that leads to a broken hip, incapacity, or worse? Once, when I asked how a friend of theirs died, Bea looked me in the eye. "Old age, Betsy, have you heard of it?"

In part, this is a group portrait of the ladies, what they share with each other, but also what they keep to themselves. Like my mother, these women don't openly reveal their feelings. Pain is a private matter. Sometimes, watching the ladies play Bridge, I can see the girls they once were and the cards they were dealt; it's all there in their faces as they open a new hand of cards, each ripe with possibility, rife with disappointment.

In discovering the unsung lives of the Bridge Ladies, I also came to better understand the ragged path that connects me to my mother. This is our story, too.

CHAPTER 1

A Private Language

It was the Monday after the 2013 Academy Awards when I first sat down with the Bridge Ladies. It was Rhoda's turn to host. She lives in a tidy waterfront condo. You can tell that it's decorated with the furniture from her previous home in Orange, a residential suburb of New Haven, where she lived and raised her family for twenty-seven years. The dining room table is a little too big and formal for the space, and the two lamps flanking the couch in the living room are as big as third graders. But she loves it here; it was the perfect downsizing, the best thing she ever did, she says, turning around in her compact kitchen as if she were modeling a new dress. Best of all is the deck overlooking the water, where terns and osprey regularly visit, where the water reflects the light like foil.

Her table is set with linen and china. Napkins are gathered in silver rings, serving pieces are lined up like soldiers, and precut butter pats rest like a row of collapsed dominoes on a pretty dish.

A noodle kugel fills the house with a smell I have long associated with love. On the table, a wooden trough-shaped dish holds a salad. It is hand-painted, and along the rim I notice Rhoda's name and her late husband's in a pretty script. *Peter and Rhoda.* There are reminders of their life as a couple all throughout the house, but I become fixated on this serving dish with the folksy script yoking their names. I wonder if Rhoda sees the inscription, if it makes her sad, or if it is part of the scenery now: his absence nowhere and everywhere.

I don't know what I was expecting, but when the Bridge Ladies arrive at Rhoda's, they don't seem all that happy to see each other, greeting one another with a bit of forced friendliness. Over time, I will witness all manner of lightly veiled forbearance and exasperation among them in the form of eye rolling, sniffing, and dismissive body language. They never kiss or air-kiss hello. No hugging, no body contact whatsoever. I wonder if it has always been thus. As young women were they affectionate, demonstrative? Or were there rivalries and hidden alliances among them? Did they have fun? It's true that I can't stand some of my closest friends; why did I imagine anything different from the ladies?

When my mother sees me she does that thing she always does. If you blink you would miss it: the maternal once-over. Calculated in a few seconds, she inspects my clothes, my waistline, the sheen or lack of sheen in my hair. She will know if I've been getting enough rest, biting my nails, or picking at my face. Doubtless there are some mothers who gaze proudly on their daughters' figures and outfits, but for Roz and me what I wear and how I look have been a battleground from the time I began to dress myself.

Though none openly admit it, the Bridge Ladies, like most women of their day, groomed their daughters for potential mates. Yes, they sent us to college for an education but also hoping we would meet our husbands there. As recently as this past spring, 2015, my mother voiced her wish that my daughter choose a college with a good ratio, and she wasn't talking about teacher to student. Marriage was essential for our mothers. They feared for us going forward in life without the same protection they believed came with marrying a Jewish man.

One of the Bridge daughters put it this way: "They're from that whole generation of women whose prime focus was not career, but getting a man. So that's your capital."

I resented this pressure when I was in my twenties. I knew how badly my mother wanted me to marry, and it made me feel defective and unlovable even as I rejected her outdated values. I was pursuing a career; I wanted a soul mate, not a meal ticket. I once asked my mother what she would prefer: if I got married or won a Nobel Prize. "Don't be ridiculous" was all she said in response.

I posed the same questions to each of the ladies:

Did you always know you would get married?

Absolutely.

Did you ever consider marrying a non-Jewish man?

Never.

Did you know you would have children?

Absolutely.

Did you ever want anything else?

No (except for Bette).

Why not?

It never occurred to us.

Was it the cultural expectation or was it what you wanted?

Both.

In just one generation, the world they knew would radically change. Bridge daughters, collectively: some married Jewish men, some intermarried, some divorced, and some, god-forbid, did not marry. We would not return their serve. We got birth control and advanced degrees, slept with men we never intended to procreate with, moved to big cities, and lived on our own. If anything, I defined myself in fierce opposition to my mother, putting career and personal fulfillment over marriage and children.

I am well aware that for my mother how I appear before her Bridge club is as much a reflection of her as it is of me, and because I want to make a good impression with the women, I don't mind making an effort, though it's never quite enough for her. My mother wishes I would wear some makeup and accessorize with a bracelet, earrings, anything. She has been known to say, with just a hint of desperation in her voice, "Not even a little lipstick?"

I don't have to look at her to know what she is wearing. She could be a senior model for Eileen Fisher, with her wardrobe full of mix-and-match slacks, tops, and jackets. Her ensemble is rounded out with black Mary Jane shoes with fat Velcro straps, earrings, and a matching strand of beads, in all likelihood purchased at a quaint New England crafts fair or from one of the "funky" shops in downtown New Haven where all the jewelry vaguely resembles a model of the solar system. But I give my mother credit for putting on her beads and bracelets, her Bakelite earrings that look like miniature mahjong tiles, or the gold ones that resemble tiny wine casks.

I marvel at how much care all the women put into looking nice for Bridge, especially as they only have each other to impress. But it's not about that: these women do not leave the house unless they are pulled together. Going out without lipstick on was like walking outside naked. When I ask each Bridge daughter what she remembers from the Monday club, the first thing they mention is how the ladies dressed. They were elegant, grown-up, always wearing hose, heels, skirts, and pearls, their hair teased, curled, straightened, or frosted.

I can tell my mother is relieved when I show up at Rhoda's looking "nice." In this case: black jeans that aren't too shabby, a loose-fitting cream blouse ("anything but black!"), shoes instead of sneakers, and the only necklace I wear: a gold pocket watch with roman numerals finely etched like scrimshaw on its elegant ivory face. I had admired it since childhood, often hunting for it among my mother's many jewelry boxes. Once, when I was home after graduating from college, which in my case is a euphemism for barely graduating, having been felled by a major depression, my mother happened upon me in her dressing room admiring the watch.

"Take it," she said.

I was astonished. She couldn't possibly mean it? I felt I had been caught red-handed and declined her offer.

"I'd rather you enjoy it while I'm still alive," she insisted.

I always thought the gift, given in haste, was my mother's way of telling me something she could never say, something that would always remain unsaid.

"Take it," she urged. "I want you to have it."

♠

When the house was quiet on a Monday afternoon, it meant our mothers were out playing Bridge. For all we knew they could have been having an affair with the tennis pro or embezzling the Sisterhood's Scholarship Fund. If someone was murdered in New Haven on a Monday, the ladies had an airtight alibi. What the ladies actually did at the Bridge table was a mystery. Even the score pad divided into two columns was like a riddle out of *Alice in Wonderland*: We and They. *Who were they? Who were we?*

It wasn't a game you could learn in an afternoon, like Scrabble or Monopoly. It wasn't even like other card games. No, Bridge was complex and certainly not for children. Still, I loved everything about playing cards: the suits and their symbols, the red Hearts and Diamonds, the black Spades and Clubs one petal short of a lucky clover. I loved the backs of the cards: some with elaborate Spirograph designs, others with animals, flowers, or covered bridges. My favorite had a pair of winged cherubs on bicycles in the center of the card and bare-breasted mermaids in each corner. I was mightily impressed with a deck of cards my dad brought home from a trip. They had the Pan Am logo and he said they were complimentary. How could such treasure be free?

I loved playing War, then Spit, then Gin Rummy with my dad. I loved Spades and Hearts and was the mastermind of an after-hours game of Hearts at sleepaway camp where a small group of us played by flashlight on our counselor's bed behind a partition at the back of the bunk.

Before I was old enough to understand any card games, I invented my own called Card Mountain where I'd throw a blanket in the air and let it fall into whatever shape it would take. I would then set up the cards, by suit, in the folds and nooks of the blanket, creating my happy fiefdom of cold-eyed kings, scornful queens. Jack was the dashing prince, and the number cards their loyal subjects. Sometimes I would have to throw the blanket a few times to achieve maximum ramparts and parapets, and when I was finished I would collect all the cards and tuck them back into their box, the blanket left in a pile like the pale outline of a ruined fortress.

♠

As the ladies head over to Rhoda's dining room table for lunch, Bea makes a straight line to the far end of the table. "We're not rigid," she says, "but this is my seat." Today, decked out all in purple, her metallic tennies and crystal bracelets that throw rainbows when the light hits them just right, Bea could be a poster child for Jenny Joseph's famous poem, "When I Am an Old Woman I Shall Wear Purple," which celebrates old age as liberation from traditional conventions and expectations. The poem always grated on me, since the sad fact is that when you are old you are more likely to wear Depends and a Life Alert necklace. But not Bea, she is spry, sharp, funny, and the only lady outrageous enough to occasionally drop the *F* bomb. Bea isn't an old hippie or part of the counterculture, she just does her own thing and in this way stands slightly apart from the others.

Rhoda serves her kugel, and the ladies pass around a salad. She is the only one who has a "gentleman friend," her generation's term for boyfriend. There are framed pictures of them on the kitchen counters and scattered around the condo: at a benefit, on a cruise, with friends. It was unexpected this late in life, but I'm convinced it's responsible for the spring in her step.

I feel like an interloper. Do I participate or observe? Am I trying to impress them or they me? I am sitting next to my mother and it's as awkward as if we were strangers on a train. We are careful not to accidentally touch or make eye contact. Conversation starts with The Oscars. They all watched at least a part of the ceremony. The ladies are avid moviegoers, even though most movies today are "dreck" by their standards. Those who saw the foreign film *Amour* loved it; others avoided the all-too-real depiction of dementia. In a flush of civic pride, they were annoyed with screenwriter Tony Kushner, who portrayed Connecticut, their state, as voting against the Thirteenth Amendment in his movie *Lincoln*. They hated host Seth

MacFarlane. *Feh!* He didn't hold a candle to Bob Hope. Forget about the dresses!

"Actresses have been dressing like hookers for years," my mother says, capping the conversation.

Talk turns to a minor scandal at the Jewish Community Center over a zoning issue. As Rhoda tells it, the head of the committee called someone an "asshole" at an open meeting. She puts her hand over her mouth to muffle the expletive.

"Thank god he wasn't a gentile," Rhoda adds.

I'm confused. "You mean the guy who cursed was Jewish?"

All the women know this to be true and nod affirmatively.

I'm still confused. Isn't this man's outburst "bad for the Jews," as the expression goes.

No, no, the women explain. If a gentile had cursed, he would be accused of anti-Semitism and that would be far more incendiary. They are willing to take one for the team to avert even worse repercussions. Their logic seems warped to me until I realize that the goal is to draw the least amount of attention as possible, deflecting even the slightest whiff of anti-Semitism. I'm impressed with their diplomatic chops, their nuanced grasp of the issues; if only the Bridge Ladies could be sent to the Middle East. After all, who better understands the art of compromise than a person married for over fifty years. Rhoda concludes the conversation, as I will discover she often does, with her customary disgust of contemporary life: "The whole level of public discourse is in the sewer."

♠

The very fact of the Bridge club, its endurance, speaks in some ways to the ladies resisting change or upholding the status quo. If the Bridge Ladies said so, my mother tended to go along.

They were like city hall. One Bridge daughter said they were like the Supreme Court. Their decisions were treated as the letter of the law. They were mavens, advising on camps and colleges; they referred doctors and plumbers, mechanics and gynecologists. Where to get your rugs cleaned and dresses hemmed. What the golf course was to men, the Bridge table was to women, the de facto social networking of its time. You would sooner argue with Talmudic scholars than challenge their collective wisdom.

These days, the ladies shy away from controversy. I know my mother wishes the ladies would mix it up more. She religiously reads the *New Yorker, Harper's,* the *Nation,* and the *Atlantic.* She attends lectures on politics, Israel, art, and more recently Black Lives Matter. She has strong opinions, they all do, but the ladies hew to the truism that it's best not to talk about politics or religion. And I suspect for a long time, this suited my mother. After all, it was her great success as a Brooklyn-born socialist that she passed as a suburban matron who learned how to play golf and tennis, joined the Sisterhood and eventually three Bridge clubs.

Her socialism, her Zionism, all of this was shelved when we moved to Woodbridge, our affluent suburb northwest of New Haven. She traded in her Karl Marx for Emily Post, the high priestess of etiquette, as if adhering to her advice could spare us the kind of social disgrace that in an earlier era would have landed us in the stocks. The landscape appeared as a minefield where she could easily trip up not knowing how people were related, who went to school with whom. She was anxious about nearly every aspect of social life: what were the customs for entertaining, the protocol for extending invitations and reciprocating? Margaret Mead had an easier time in Samoa!

I didn't get it. She constantly harped on the fact that she felt like an outsider. Our suburban ranch, two cars, and membership to the synagogue and Jewish Country Club all looked plenty normal to me. Too normal! Her mother had emigrated from Russia without knowing English. How could my mother, coming from Brooklyn, via Stamford, to New Haven feel so alien? Only it wasn't about distances. I was much older before I realized my mother felt like an outsider because of how inadequate she felt about herself.

Sitting down for our first "official" talk, she is eager to tell me about her family's poverty in Jersey City as if it's a badge of honor. We are in my living room and she's all dressed up and made up like a Russian Matryoshka doll brightly painted with many shiny layers of varnish. She has always been like the tiniest doll, the one that's impossible to crack.

Only now, she enthusiastically recalls having lived in one tenement after another with the buckled linoleum floors and refrigerators cooled by blocks of ice, relatives arguing leftist politics like in a Woody Allen movie except it wasn't exactly funny.

"Is this what you're looking for?" she asks, wanting to please me.

I'm not sure what I want now that we're here. I feel awkward and embarrassed. Aren't I already supposed to know my mother?

"I had one doll," she proudly remembers, a gift from a wealthy relative, and a favorite red cable stitch "skating" sweater she knitted with her friend Cookie Ginsberg whose mother owned a yarn shop.

"What kind of a name is Cookie?" I ask.

"What kind of a name is Cookie?" my mother repeats. Her use of a question to answer a question is right out of the linguistic Yiddish playbook, and I understand immediately that she not only deems the question foolish, but has no intention of answering it.

"Do you remember that sweater?" she asks hopefully, "with the zipper."

I act as if I can't remember but I know exactly the sweater she's talking about—only I am ashamed because I never liked it, found its homemade stitches crude, the zipper hard to work. It was the sole artifact from a life I couldn't fathom, full of import like the red balloon, only I failed to appreciate my mother's girlhood handiwork.

"I know I kept it. You children wore it. I don't know what finally happened to it. Do you remember it, the red sweater with the cable stitch?"

"Sort of," I say, "yeah I think I do." And then I have a sudden longing for it—the embarrassing hand-knitted item of clothing—and I see myself skating as a little girl with a bright red face pushing off toward the middle of the pond in our backyard. But it's a manufactured memory, more a wish or an image I conjured from having heard a story many times.

"I remember every coat I ever had," she proudly tells me, most notably a taupe coat with a Persian lamb collar and cuffs she wore when she was engaged. When I question how she could afford it, she doesn't hesitate, "If I could only have one coat, I wanted the best and my mother would splurge for me." She adds, "I'm still like that."

She also makes the point that unlike today's clothes hers lasted for years and years, and more than that: she took care of them. Her veiled accusation/criticism is not lost on me, a citizen of the wasteful generation. "I wore that Persian coat for years, I gave it to my cleaning lady. And it was still in good shape."

The only time I glimpsed the residue of her impoverished childhood was when she yelled at my sisters and me for not taking care of our things. Once she found a blouse under my bed with its tag on. I thought her head would explode. We didn't know the value of a dollar! We could not fathom her life, nor were we especially impressed with her hardships. We were spoiled suburban girls who had multiples of everything.

"We didn't *feel* poor," my mother says now with a degree of wonder in her voice. "We just didn't."

They were all children of the Depression, the ladies, though they all claim it didn't affect them. They were too young, and their families were spared complete financial ruin. It wasn't about the "haves" and "have-nots," they tell me; everyone was a have-not. To hear the ladies talk about the Depression: no biggie. Still, they knew the value of a dollar and remembered when a loose cigarette cost a penny, a dime for a ride on the trolley, and twenty-five cents for a movie.

"Here," my mother would say, pushing the phone toward us to say hello to my grandmother. Talking to her mother always seemed like a chore, placed more out of duty than love. I always assumed my mother was embarrassed by my grandmother's Russian accent and Old World ways. She wore her hair in a bun held together by netting that, turned upside down, could have doubled as a bird's nest. She colored her hair black with a tube of something that resembled shoe polish. She gripped a sugar cube between her front teeth when she drank tea, and used Vaseline exclusively and liberally on her entire body, and then kept pennies in the empties.

Only now, she speaks with great pride about the young Russian immigrant who signed up for language lessons as soon as she came through Ellis Island. I suspect my mother is scrubbing her history. When she finally told us about my grandmother's violent and tragic past, it was impossible to comprehend the magnitude of trauma this sweet, gentle woman had survived. She and her two sisters discovered their parents murdered in their home during the Kiev pogroms of 1919.

I want to know everything, but all my mother will say is that she had nightmares her whole life and that she would cry out in her sleep.

"It was very, very traumatic."

When I challenge her about keeping all of this secret, she shrugs. "What can I tell you—protect the children. That's how I was raised. Was it right? I guess not."

"Mom, how could you not have told us?"

"It was the culture, Betsy. Go question culture."

"Did she long for Russia?"

"She loved this country, its ideals, everything it stood for. I was born on Washington's birthday and my brother was born on election day. My mother took it as a good omen."

When she first arrived, my grandmother worked in a millinery factory, but once her English improved enough she landed a job as a saleswoman at Russeks, one of Manhattan's first upscale department stores.

"She loved clothes and she would buy them with her discount. She loved I. Miller shoes, a very fancy shoe store, like Ferragamo today."

The next time I am in New York I attempt to find the store on West Forty-Seventh Street. I don't see it at first. The building is surrounded with scaffolding and looming cranes. I peek through the fencing and there it is, a once grand building made of white stone now almost completely black. The store had catered to actresses, and through the grime I make out the names Mary Pickford and Ethel Barrymore etched into the facade where their statues once stood, recessed into the building like Greek gods. A man on the construction site tells me it's coming down in a few days. I'm seized with panic; it suddenly feels as if this small detail from my grandmother's life is about to be demolished and with it every trace of her. I want to stop the flow of traffic on the busiest corner of New York City and tell everyone how she shopped here, a young immigrant extending her foot like a Russian aristocrat as a salesman removed a shoe from its tissue.

I knew firsthand that my grandfather's abuse was cataclysmic, epic, ruining many good times and almost every holiday meal. He once stopped talking to me for two years because I wouldn't give him a piece of bread from a fancy Italian loaf I believed my aunt was "saving" for a special dinner. I was probably ten years old when he shook his fist and thundered, "You deny your grandfather a piece of bread!" It was biblical! It was Moses at Mount Sinai finding the Israelites worshipping false idols and going ballistic.

"He came into conflict wherever he went." My mother's voice lowered, even though we are alone in my living room, sitting at opposite ends of my couch. "No one could tell him anything, no one was smarter than your grandfather." Her tone was sarcastic, angry.

His volatile temper could be triggered by anything: something as small as an empty bottle of milk in the refrigerator, a newspaper creased incorrectly. Our grandmother did everything she could to quell his outbursts, to keep him from making a scene, especially in public. I had no idea how desperate my mother was to leave home, how dark her thoughts sometimes turned.

My grandmother also longed to leave him, but what options did she have? She was twenty-nine when they married, an old maid by the standards of the day. He was a tall, blond American man, he had a job, and he asked her to marry him after a week. At first he seemed heaven-sent. They were married six weeks later. A woman in their building, also a Russian Jew, had left her husband and was raising two children on her own. "My mother both admired her and felt sorry for her. On the one hand, it could be done. On the other, better you should move to Siberia. It was a terrible *shonde*." A shame.

When my mother was still in grade school and they were leaving Jersey for Brooklyn, she overheard a teacher say, "We always lose the good ones." She wore this modest feather in her cap for years to come, providing some small ballast against her father's belittling. She wishes her mother had the conviction to end the marriage, end the bullying and constant insults he showered down on the family. More than once, her father berated his bright young daughter. "You have always been stupid, you are stupid, and you always will be stupid."

My mother could play Bridge day in and day out, laugh and gossip and swap recipes for quiche Lorraine, but it wouldn't change the fact that she was covering a raft of secrets and the crippling effect of her father's cruelty. Still, it's always there, at least to me, fear born of insecurities, dark moods that unexpectedly flare, and sadness that folds itself in silence.

I wanted to reach out to her, but her arms were crossed over her chest, her mouth puckered, the lines scored more deeply. I had always dismissed my mother's insecurities as shallow: Did we use the right decorator? Did the shoes match the bag? Everything had to match; I now see why. I disrespected her for only caring about how things looked. I never understood how much there was to hide.

I could tell that my mother was different from the other Bridge Ladies, from most of my friends' mothers. She was darker, moodier, and harder to know. By five o'clock or so, with a roast dutifully prepared and hissing in the oven, my mother would plop down, barricade herself behind her beloved

New York Times, and light a cigarette. I could see how tired she was, going through the motions of her grim duties. Driving car pool, she'd sometimes show up late, barely say a word of apology, and drive down the long gray roads of our town as if to an execution. Or ironing a stack of my father's handkerchiefs, pressing each one as if she were stamping out cholera.

Often, or so it seemed, he would come home from work and ask her if she had remembered to pick up the dry cleaning or run some other errand. Often, no, she hadn't. Identifying with my father, I made it my mission to correct the world of my mother's shortcomings in a game I invented and baldly named "Errands." I would navigate my bicycle around our circular driveway and over the bumpy lawn, doing the grocery shopping, going to the post office, etc. Our Dutch door became the bank teller, the garbage area was the dry cleaner, and so forth. I would happily chatter with the store clerks, thanking them while they made change.

Still, I wouldn't have traded my mother for the cookie-cutter TV mothers like Carol Brady or Shirley Partridge, who I'd watched in many after-school stupors. There were times she could be funny and outrageous and slightly out of control. In private, she would curse and be highly critical of people, lifting a single eyebrow in an arc of evil to put a fine point on things. It was thrilling to hear her unvarnished opinions instead of the photoshopped ones she gave in public. Sometimes I could make her laugh so hard she'd pee her pants; other times, I could barely get her attention.

At the end of those long days, my father asleep in front of the TV, my mother retired to her bedroom, and the kitchen long dark, I could hear the dishwasher running through its cycles, and see the steam rising from it like a pale ghost.

. . .

After lunch, the Bridge Ladies refresh their lipstick, each one holding up a small mirror and a tube of color in front of her face. I can't imagine how many thousands of times they have swiped their lips with pigment. They tilt the mirrors for a partial view of their faces, like looking in a rearview mirror. I wonder who they see—the young women they once were, or faces marked with the deep lines of age.

"Pony up," my mother says, and goes digging in her pocketbook. The "buy-in" is a buck and I will learn that every week, as the ladies retrieve their dollars, they briefly carry on as if the stakes are much higher. They drop their dollars on the coffee table, and if someone doesn't have a single they pretend she's trying to squelch.

Rhoda's folding Bridge table is set up, its legs as thin as broomsticks, as are four folding chairs. The twin set of cards decorated with peacocks, scoring pad, and pencil are neatly tucked into a corner of the table. Seated, the ladies look primmer than they are, elbows in, knees pressed together. As the cards get shuffled and dealt, conversation generally comes to a stop. They aren't fanatical about keeping quiet; they're more social than serious players. But they abide to some unspoken agreement about just how much talking constitutes too much. Then they go around the table bidding: *one heart, pass, one spade, pass, one no trump, three no.* I remember listening to this strange Morse code from my childhood.

At a certain point I become supremely bored and desperately want to check my phone. I've left it in the car for just this eventuality. I don't know much about the ladies at this point, but I sense that checking my phone and texting or doing e-mail would lower me in their estimation. A lot. It's hard to slow down and settle into Bridge time, especially on a Monday when the world is back at its desk, when I should be at mine, fielding e-mails from writers and editors. But it's soothing, too, being here as if nothing else exists. I sit back on Rhoda's couch. They will play like this for a few hours into the darkening afternoon. I listen to the sounds of cards being shuffled and dealt, not quite a lullaby but a soporific nonetheless.

At the conclusion of a hand, the ladies conduct a casual post-mortem of how the hand played out: they decry a bad split, praise a good strong second suit, sometimes, they say, the cards fall just right. I have no idea what they are talking about, their game a private language all its own.

CHAPTER 2

The Manhattan Bridge Club

I arrive early. The place is empty except for an older man sitting at a card table doing Sudoku. He doesn't look up when I come in. Taking in the vast space crowded with Bridge tables and chairs, I am once again reminded that New York City has a million hidden pockets where enthusiasts gather to folk dance, bake pastry, make pottery, and in this case: play Bridge. I know I'm in the right place, but I never expected to find the club here among a suite of nondescript offices in a Midtown high-rise. There is a plain plaque outside the door with black lettering: THE MANHATTAN BRIDGE CLUB. Though not always in this location, the club has been around since 1977.

Like an old deck of cards, the place feels worn around the edges. The tables each have four red plastic boxes on them that hold laminated cards, larger than playing cards, with tabs for each of the suits. I will come to learn that these are bidding boxes. I've never seen them before. The Bridge Ladies don't use these. A soda machine directly inside the entrance sells soda for fifty cents; have I gone back in time? Is Bridge that much of an anachronism? Along the hallway leading into the main room is a long table with bubble-shaped plastic candy dispensers that bob forward like toy drinking birds to dispense pretzels, M&M's, Mike and Ikes, Oreos, and pretzel logs. Make no mistake: Bridge noshing is serious business.

There is a buffet area toward the back. I hear some rumblings and eventually a woman emerges with a large tray and starts to set up a buffet. There is a counter for coffee and drinks and more candy dispensers. If I could I would put my mouth to the one with M&M's and Hoover them. These candy dispensers will taunt me for the duration of my Bridge lessons, but that is an old story.

I am flooded with anxiety. It has been a long time since I have tried to learn anything new. I tell myself it's only natural to be nervous. I stand next to the reception desk and attempt to look nonchalant, reading and rereading the signs about tournaments and standings affixed to the wall. Finally, a few people trickle in and greet each other. All middle-aged and older. Some sit, others claim tables and head over to the dinner buffet. Then more come and there is an easy camaraderie among the assembled, forming little hives around the tables. A man steps up behind the reception desk, starts counting money, and gives off a vibe not to bother him. More people come, and the room gets loud. It's too hot in here, like a lot of old Manhattan office buildings with their old radiators hissing and spitting. I want a cookie. I want to bolt. Only then a woman comes over and asks me if I'm here for the beginner lessons. Yes, I brighten, I am.

There are two glassed-in rooms used for teaching, lectures, and my favorite term: "supervised play," as if we were kindergarteners in an enclosed playground. We are set apart so as not to disturb the serious players and various tournaments going on in the main room. I'm relieved to set down my things and take off the coat in which I am now marinating. Two other people join: a British woman who barks "pleasure" when you introduce yourself, and a plump man who looks guilty of something, perhaps stuffing his pockets with cookies. He and I are both rank beginners, and the English lady used to play but she insists she has forgotten all of it!

Over time, I'll meet many people at the Manhattan Bridge Club who are coming for a refresher, or are starting all over. It sounds like Weight Watchers where, defeated, you periodically return, hoping once again to get it right, hoping something will stick. Some people played when they were young and want to take it up again. Some people have a spouse who plays and they want to get in on the action. Though they are quick to add that it's very intimidating, they worry that they'll never catch up to their spouse's level, as if they could more easily awaken all seven chakras and make passionate love than play a single hand of one no trump.

I can tell right away that our teacher is no-nonsense. Barbara is tall and attractive and all-business. She mixes the cards with precision, keeping them in a tight arch when she reverse-shuffles. As she deals the first hand, dropping a card in front of each of us, going around in a clockwise circle, she explains the big picture.

"The object of the game is to take tricks. We are here to take tricks. Do we understand?"

Yes, we dumbly nod.

"Have any of you played Hearts?"

Yes, we have!

"Good! It is based on the same principle."

In Hearts, as in Bridge, there are four players and the cards are evenly dealt out, thirteen cards per player. In both games, each player must discard in the suit that has been led. The highest ranked card in the suit takes the "trick" and leads the next card. This is the principle of "following suit." Hearts is easy because you are simply trying to discard your Hearts when you can't follow suit, which explains how I was able to dominate the game at summer camp. And that's where the comparison ends.

In Bridge, Barbara explains, there are two components to the game: bidding and playing the hand. Bridge bidding is referred to as an "auction," and there are elaborate rules that govern the bidding. Barbara starts out slowly enough for small children. The first order of business, she tells us, is to organize our cards by suit and then count how many points we have. Face cards, also known as honors, are assigned numerical worth: ace = four points, king = three, queen = two, and jack = one. *Easy-peasy.* Only then, she explains, there is a hierarchy in the suits themselves, ranking from the bottom: Clubs, Diamonds, Hearts, and Spades. Hearts and Spades are the "major" suits. Clubs and Diamonds are considered the "minor" suits. *Sorry, Clubs and Diamonds.*

Barbara moves to the board and writes the number 26 on it, tapping it with her chalk for emphasis. We are looking for a "fit." Bridge is played with partners, you and your partner try to determine, through the bidding system, if your combined hands have twenty-six points and at least eight cards in the same suit, which will become the trump suit. If that isn't complicated enough, you can also play in "no trump." Bridge just isn't happy unless it messes with your head.

Barbara suddenly looks like a hawk bearing down on us. She is very clear in her message: twenty-six is the number of strength-points needed *between* you and your partner to hopefully take ten out of the thirteen possible tricks and thus win a bonus score. *Bonus score?* Now she's furiously writing more numbers on the chalkboard to show how many tricks are necessary to get a partial score. *Partial score?* Then the numbers start coming faster; it's like a conveyor belt that speeds up without warning. I copy them all in my notebook, but they might as well be computer code. Worse, I am too intimidated to ask questions and betray my lack of math skills. The Brit seems to be keeping up. The other man is truly clueless and keeps smiling like one of the Keebler Elves while stuffing cookies in his mouth. I am somewhere in the middle, leaning toward Elf.

Now Barbara places a rectangular metal tray in the center of the table with four slots, each containing thirteen cards. It also shows the four directions of the table: north and south (who are partners), and east and west (who are partners). The tray also designates the dealer with an arrow. I've never seen this contraption but come to learn that it's a duplicate board and is used in duplicate Bridge, where each table competitively measures itself against other tables. But for the purposes of teaching, these duplicate boards are set up so that the hands are simple, and if all goes well we should be able to grasp and execute the most rudimentary bidding.

All does not go well.

As dealer, Elf must bid first. (I am greatly relieved to be off the hook.) He stares at his cards. Then he looks around the room as if following a fly doing loops. The British woman fans her cards, then herself. The lack of air is oppressive, but there is something vaguely hostile in her gesture. I will discover that there can be a lot of waiting around at Bridge tables, especially among beginners, and it seems exceedingly rude to hurry anyone along. Only now the Elf is chewing the inside of his mouth, a glaze of perspiration visible on his forehead.

Finally, Barbara intercedes. "How many points do you have?" she asks the frightened man.

He counts his high point cards again, pointing to each one with his index finger in an audible whisper.

Now the British woman exhales loudly.

"How many?" Barbara repeats, urging him on.

"Thirteen?" More question than an answer.

"And do you have five of a major suit?"

The Elf nods yes, trembling with uncertainty.

"And what suit is it?"

He looks as if he might be peeing his pants.

"Are they Spades?" Her tone becomes gentler and paradoxically scarier.

"Yes." Now the Elf looks astonished, as if The Amazing Kreskin had taken her place. How did she know he had Spades?

I realized soon enough that the teachers were so well acquainted with these teaching boards that they basically knew what each student had in his hand. Still, it was always a little unnerving when a teacher would ask from across the table why we didn't make a particular bid or drop a particular card, as if they were mind readers. If they could see into our hands, what else could they see?

I went home that night thoroughly discouraged and completely energized. I could tell right away that this game would not come easily to me: too many numbers and too much memorization. When asked for my phone number I'll often mistakenly give one from a previous address. I still have to look up my Social Security number when requested. I am password-challenged beyond belief. And I still count on my fingers for the most basic addition. I was more than challenged: I was handicapped. But I also had fun, felt stimulated. I don't have hobbies. I've never dug my hands down into soil. Never took pleasure in reducing a soup stock. I was struck that this was something I might actually enjoy doing now and into my senior years, like the ladies. Plus I had already taken the plunge, and suffered the anxiety of attempting to learn something new.

But there was something else, too. I felt an immediate affinity for the game itself. Not that I would be good at it, but I sensed, even that first night, that Bridge was a metaphor for many things.

CHAPTER 3

The Athenian

When I first sat in on the Bridge Ladies' games I was hoping to find the remnants of a 1970s encounter group or rap session where the women openly shared details about their lives. I didn't expect any of them to be inspecting their vaginas with handheld mirrors, mind you, but I thought they would be more forth-coming, more open, and, hopefully, a little gossipy. Instead I discovered that they never trash anyone, never talk about some-thing that bothers them, and never share a deep feeling. Three unspoken commandments are etched in stone:

Thou shalt not pry.

Thou shalt not reveal.

Thou shalt not share.

"Why is it all such a taboo?" I ask my mother after having observed how taciturn the women are after a few weeks.

"It is what it is." Her catchall for life's conundrums.

"Why can't you talk about things that bother you?"

"We just don't."

"What could happen?"

My mother shrugs, though some time later Bette will tell me that in the past women had been flushed from the club for failing to adhere to the unspoken decorum. Talking too much or saying the wrong thing could get you booted. The worst offender was a woman who had gotten caught up in the vitamin craze in the 1970s and proselytized their healthy benefits to the girls. Worse, she tried to rope them into selling the vitamins in a pyramid scheme. I ask Bette how they voted her off the island. She's embarrassed to tell me: they just sort of stop calling.

Was my presence inhibiting them or were Bridge clubs a lot like long marriages where you learn to keep quiet for the sake of the greater good? No one is going to change, not after fifty-plus years. One of my Bridge teachers told me that she and her husband had to stop playing together for the sake of the marriage. She liked to play by the book, he from the seat of his pants. At first it was exciting; for god's sake they met cute at a Bridge tournament. But after a time it created more conflict than any partnership can withstand.

In time, I will observe husbands and wives publicly shaming each other for mistakes. They know they're in public, but tensions can run that high in Bridge; a single mistake can cost a game and bidding incorrectly puts your partner in jeopardy. The only Bridge table murder on record occurred in Kansas City in 1929. A husband and wife were having a bad night. She overbid. He lost the hand as a result. She called him a bum. He slapped her. She shot him dead.

The ladies are at no risk of emotional outbursts where Bridge is concerned. They keep their game and themselves in check. Thought bubbles often hang in the air. What would happen if the ladies gave voice to their fears and frustrations, if someone rang a bell and they stepped inside the ring instead of dancing around the ropes?

♠

When it's Bea's turn to host Bridge, she treats the ladies to lunch at the Athenian Diner, then it's back to her condo for cards. The diner is right out of *Saturday Night Fever* with purple leatherette booths, mirrored walls, and cut-glass chandeliers. It hasn't changed much since I went to high school. It was the place where most of the school's clubs hung out after sports games or debates or choir concerts. After a win, the entire football team and cheerleading squad would take up residence. I half expect to still see them when I arrive to meet Bea. It's also one of her regular breakfast spots and she tells me to meet her there for our first talk. She is already seated when I arrive. Before saying hi, she points out her booster seat, "I'm shrinking, Betsy, what can I tell you?"

Bea waves over our waiter, "Omar, my friend would like to order and I'll have my usual." Omar winks in response. Maybe he is just playing along, but I get the feeling he cares about Bea; she is probably the only customer in the greater New Haven area who has bothered to learn his name. I guess that he is in his thirties, handsome with jet-black hair, easy in himself. He takes my order and collects the menus. Bea reminds him that she likes her rye bread seedless. "Got it, mama," he says, clearly not needing reminding, then whispers to me from behind the menu, "Cougar," and winks again.

When I ask Bea to tell me about her hometown, she wearily says she can't remember what she had for lunch the day before, as if bringing up memories is as heavy as the famous green limestone quarried in Bedford, Indiana, where she tells me she is from.

"They used that stone for the Empire State Building, you can google it," Bea adds proudly.

Though she claims she can't remember, Bea begins to describe the town's central square, looking upward at the fluorescent lighting, her eyelids fluttering. "There was the courthouse, the hotel, a grocer, a feed store, and a five-and-dime." Pleased with herself and her powers of recollection, Bea perks up and says, "How do you like that, Betsy?"

Bea often ends a sentence with a question, but that first day I didn't know if she was looking for an answer, or just making a point.

As I sit down with each of the ladies, they also claim they can't remember anything, as if struck by a case of collective amnesia. Memories don't flood back exactly so much as dangle like the letters on an eye chart glowing on the wall, some within reach, some still too blurry to make out. For Bea, the dusty town of Bedford turns Technicolor as memories come back to life, like the Bantam rooster that got into the nuns' chicken coop and fertilized the whole lot!

"They thanked my father," Bea says, still amused. "Those nuns never had so many chickens in their lives."

A teacher called Craigy Gunn preached that you don't make fun of people's names. "And with a name like that you can see why! It's still good advice," she says, thumping the table the way a doctor checks a knee for reflexes. And every Friday night during basketball season she cheered on the boys who were invariably defeated by the team from Gary, Indiana.

"Gary was a town of steelworkers," Bea tells me. "Those kids were gigantic!"

A little girl in the next booth, maybe two years old, pops up and stares at us. When Bea waves hello she quickly ducks, then reemerges a few moments later like a periscope in a submarine. The mother looks over at us, apologetic.

"She's adorable," Bea says as the girl nearly hoists herself over into our booth, her mother pulling her back by the ankles. I realize then that Bea has turned the Athenian Diner into Bedford. I would learn that she does this wherever she goes: the Soup Kitchen, the senior center where she plays cards twice a week, the pool at her condo. If there are people around she wants to get to know them, at least to say hello. *You want to go where everybody knows your name.*

"We were just one of three Jewish families in Bedford. And with our name: Bernstein! How do you like that, Betsy?" Bea's parents came to this country as teens through Philadelphia and settled for a time in Cincinnati, where they met, picked up some English, she some sewing skills, and headed west to the limestone capital of the world. Somehow the Romanian immigrant and his young wife with their thick accents and dark curls made a go of it, eventually opening a clothing store off the square, Bernstein's Ladies Ready to Wear.

Bea can't remember how they were able to open a store without a single connection or relation.

"I don't know. I was little."

I wager that her father might have started selling fabric from a pushcart, as so many immigrants did. Bea says they had the store for as long as she can remember. Her mother dressed the mannequins, like life-size dolls, in the store windows according to the seasons. Her father had carved out a niche selling clothes from New York. The dresses were more expensive than the "*schmatas*" from the newly opened department store J. C. Penney, and less expensive than the dressmaker's.

She's emphatic that she never experienced any anti-Semitism in Bedford. The only thing that separated her father's store from the others in town was that they closed on Rosh Hashanah and Yom Kippur, when they headed out to Louisville for

High Holiday services. Then she lowers her tone, so as not to appear bragging. "We had a car, Betsy. Not everyone did."

"Fifty cents down, fifty cents a week." Bea thumps her fingers on the table again explaining how her father started a lay-away plan. He figured out how to manage cash flow before they called it that and as a result made it through the Depression. He could do no wrong in his young daughter's eyes. They had a two-story house with hardwood floors and Oriental rugs. Bea had a pretty room with balloons on the wallpaper.

"I had everything, Betsy."

The Bernsteins also had live-in household help, and her father treated the young women who worked for them over the years fairly, they were on a first name basis and they lived in the house with the family.

"It wasn't *The Help,* Betsy," Bea says. "If I eat steak, you eat steak. If I eat cake, you eat cake. That's how it was in our house."

♠

The following Monday it's Bea's turn to host. The ladies arrive at the diner and claim their seats. Bea is busy going from table to table greeting nearly everyone who has come in, many on walkers, some in wheelchairs, one with a plastic tube snaking from a portable oxygen tank into his nose. Some are here with home aides, slumped over, or shrunken as gnomes. The Bridge Ladies grow restless, complete with deep sighs and shoulder shrugs, as Bea continues to make the rounds. I get that the ladies are impatient. They want to order lunch and get to Bea's to start playing. I also get the feeling that they are a bit squeamish about all the infirmity. The ladies are in very good shape. They still drive except for Jackie, who had a fall and is unsteady on her feet. They go to New York for operas, Broadway shows, and museums. My mother traveled to Israel last summer for a wedding and danced the horah in her Ferragamos. Looking over at these less fortunate folks who have been felled by strokes or illness is difficult. You want to empathize, but you also want to distance yourself. Old age isn't contagious. Still, you don't want to catch it.

I'm also beginning to worry about my mother, who is uncharacteristically late. All the ladies remark on it, a collective concern rising around the table. My mother is extremely punctual, always early to appointments and performances. This is because she leaves roughly thirty to forty-five extra minutes to get anywhere, factoring in traffic, a possible restroom stop, time to park, and the outside chance of Armageddon. Choosing a time to meet or leave has become a constant negotiation with her. It took a while for me to realize that she wanted more time because she *needed* more time. She has always had the energy of ten men. I either couldn't or didn't want to fathom her slowing down. Now, I've learned to accommodate it, do things on her timeline. I get it. Plus, there is nothing worse than driving with her when she perceives that we might be late. She drums her lacquered nails on the car door and exhales heavily, like a stoner after taking a monster hit off a bong.

When my mother finally arrives, she doesn't offer any explanation, but she has a funny look on her face. When I question her later, she says, embarrassed, that she fell asleep on the couch, reading the paper. Once, when she didn't hear the doorbell, I let myself in and made my way down the long front hallway of our house to discover her on the couch, her head pitched forward. I instantly imagined the worst. I didn't want to call out "Mom, Mom" and shake her shoulder. I didn't want her gone. Then, just as I'd gathered the courage to approach, she roused. Trying to shake off the fright, I told myself that this would be the best possible outcome. My mother going gently into that good afternoon with her beloved *New York Times*, reading a Ben Brantley review for a new play that she'd rush out to see based on his recommendation. My mother talks about Ben Brantley as if she knows him and has been having an ongoing dialogue with him for decades. If she hates a play he touts, she wants to throttle him. "I'd like to throttle that Ben Brantley." And if she likes one, all is forgiven.

When the waitress returns with our drinks Rhoda asks for a Splenda, and the waitress takes a limp yellow packet out of her apron. When she leaves, the ladies explain that the customers steal the artificial sweetener, so they no longer keep it on the table. I confess that I steal my Sweet'n Low from Dunkin' Donuts. After a brief silence, Bette confesses that her husband does, too. I can't even begin to calculate how many pink packets have been pilfered worldwide.

"Are you girls ready to order?" The waitress sinks back into her hip.

Girls?

After the waitress takes our orders I ask the ladies how they feel about being called girls. My mother doesn't like it one bit. Bette and Rhoda don't mind. Jackie says it makes her feel young. Bea doesn't care. That's it. No discussion of aging, of how they feel, or what it was like becoming invisible past fifty and now, well into their eighties, infantilized. My question doesn't go any farther than a flat rock that skims the surface of a lake then sinks.

♠

The level of intimacy between my friends and me is anathema to the Bridge Ladies. I once asked Bette if she has any idea how open we are with each other, and she imagined it was like *Sex and the City*. Okay, we're not *that* open. We don't talk about bleaching our assholes, but we talk all the time and about everything. We are obsessed with work, obsessed with our iPhones, obsessed with ourselves. We are obsessed with our kids and our "parenting," which wasn't even a verb when our mothers raised us. We talk about meds, moisturizers, and mammograms. We talk about Lena Dunham, a lot. At a recent overnight with three women friends, there was a graphic description of a colonic and a lively conversation about what constitutes cheating. We discuss books and movies and aren't afraid to disagree. We talk about Hillary and the possibility of having a female president.

We compare notes about therapy and our "issues" as freely as we would a new restaurant or a yoga studio. Casual conversation at a cocktail party can often begin: "as my therapist said," or "as I said to my therapist." When you discover a person has never been to therapy it's as if they are somehow lacking in self-awareness. I have a friend who once said he never cried in therapy. Well, I smugly countered, I guess you're not doing the hard work.

Now, and with more regularity, we talk about the indignities of middle age: back problems and colonoscopies, hair color and the horror of finding brown spots on the back of your hand. We don't feel bad about our necks yet, but the scarves and turtlenecks aren't far behind.

I've cried my way through plenty of therapy sessions on the long road to getting my shit together, where I alternately blamed my mother for all my ills, felt compassion for her, judged her, hated her, and accepted her. For the most part, I thought I was done, but moving home reactivated every button and not gradually. It was simultaneous with crossing state lines. I might as well have been the man in the game Operation with his vital organs exposed: the Adam's apple, the wishbone, the broken heart. Every time you touched the sides trying to fish out an organ, an angry buzzer went off.

It struck me as more than a little ironic that I was the daughter moving home, the middle, the black sheep. I told myself I could handle it, tried to convince myself it would be good, repeating the plusses like a mantra: It was a great job opportunity for my husband. My father was ailing and I could see him more. It would be good for our daughter! We'd save money!

No matter what I told myself, I was totally freaked out. I was afraid all those landmarks, like the Athenian, from my difficult teen years would trigger memories of how I slowly fell apart in high school. I couldn't believe so many of my high school haunts were still there: Claire's, the one vegetarian restaurant with ostensibly the same menu from the 1970s still chalked in pastels on the blackboard; Group W Bench, a 1960s relic named for Arlo Guthrie's song "Alice's Restaurant" and go-to for hippie paraphernalia; and Toad's, the dive bar where you could get in with a fake ID and make out with a Yalie on the sticky dance floor. Would it all feel like some hideous déjà vu? Would I start to spiral?

But my biggest concern returning home was the proximity I would now have with my mother. We had never been close and were reliably caught in a classic mother–daughter dynamic: whatever she said I took the wrong way. Every comment she made felt like a referendum on how I lived my life. I wear my jeans on the long side and they tend to fray at the heel. She begs me to get them hemmed, offers to take them into the tailor herself, that's how badly she wants it done. Likewise, the fringe on a small rug I keep in front of my kitchen sink has frayed. She knows a carpet man who can repair it. Why won't I let her take it in? *Why won't I?* She says she is going to "kidnap" the rug and get it repaired behind my back. She is so upset that I don't have paper hand towels for guests in my downstairs bathroom that she brings me her own paper towel holder and a few packages of pretty towels to "get me started," like a box of Kotex pads when

I first got my period. When she leaves, I throw the whole lot of it under the cabinet.

Would there ever come a time when I wouldn't feel judged? Did everything have to come under scrutiny? My homemaking? My work? She wants to know why I work so hard. She doesn't think I *should* work so hard. Do I really *need* to work this hard? she asks in an accusatory tone, as if I'm *creating* work for myself. The judgments implicit: first and foremost, if I'm working so hard, how could I be spending enough time with my daughter? Equally important: I shouldn't *have* to work. In the rubric of my mother's life, the man is supposed to be the provider. This is nonnegotiable. When I mention that many of my friends' husbands are stay-at-home dads, my mother says with a dismissive chill, "Good luck to them."

Sometimes I sense envy in her. I work in a field she wanted to be a part of. My mother wanted to write, and once she confided in me that she had selected the pen name Lynn Carter. I made fun of the hypocrisy in choosing a name that disguised her Jewish identity. And I teased her for coming up with it before she wrote a page. I couldn't see then that her desire to write was something that connected us; instead it struck me as another reason for me to find her lacking.

Since I've moved back to New Haven, my mother has been kind enough to point out that I don't stack the dishwasher efficiently, that I have to run cold water, not hot, when I run the disposal, that I need to iron clothes if I "fail" to pluck them out of the dryer after twenty minutes and hang them up. I waste money on Starbucks and magazines off the rack instead of saving with a subscription. I put too much salt on food, wear bulky clothes that make me look bulkier, my couch needs to be reupholstered, the tablecloth for my dining room table doesn't precisely fit, and yes, I know, the napkins don't match.

If you were to put my mother on the stand and ask her to take an oath, she would swear on a Bible that she doesn't criticize me (or my sisters), especially where my daughter is concerned. On the contrary, she would say she marvels at how I do it all. Who is telling the truth? In Deborah Tannen's book about mother-daughter relationships, *You're Wearing THAT?*, she reports that the number one complaint grown daughters have of their mothers is that they are always criticizing them. Conversely, as one mother puts it, "I can't open my mouth, she takes everything as a criticism." Tannen explains that what mothers see as caring, daughters take as criticism. Or in my case, multiply that by moving back home and living a few miles away from the source.

Tannen goes on to point out that the smallest comment a mother makes carries with it the ever-present question: Do you see me for who I am? And is who I am okay? One Bridge daughter talks to me for over an hour about how much fun she had growing up. But when we get on the subject of appearance, the tenor of the conversation changes. "My mother is very, very concerned about appearance. She's more concerned about appearance than substance. Her first question would be, what do they look like? as opposed to, what do they do?" We're about to say good-bye when I ask her what she wishes from her mother if she could ask for just one thing. "Could you accept me for who I am?"

Even when my mother was trying to help, we somehow missed. Once, she offered to take me to a special shoe store in Manhattan and treat me to a pair of shoes when I needed heels for some occasion. It was always difficult to find shoes that fit my wide foot. She told me they made fashionable custom shoes for all kinds of feet. They were expensive, and this was a generous offer. When we finally arrived at the store on the East Side,

I looked into the window and immediately saw it for what it was: not a shop of fine handmade Italian or British shoes, but a repository for all the world's freakish feet. It was like the line at Lourdes, people desperate for a miracle for their gigantic bunions. *Really, Mom, this place?* She urged me to be open-minded, go inside, at least look at the shoes. The salesman was a log of a man in an ill-fitting black suit who grunted his welcome. I watched how he fitted a woman whose feet dangled like flippers. It was classic us: my mother trying to do something nice for me, me feeling like more of a freak because of it.

Thousands of dollars of therapy were thrown out the window one fall afternoon when my mother arrived at my house with silver polish and rags. I didn't see it coming, still can't believe that it was a small pink tub of Gorham Silver Polish that took me down.

She knew I was having a dinner party and it "killed" her that my serving pieces were tarnished. My mother brought her own apron and was tying the strings at her back in preparation of her work. She enlisted my daughter, who was spreading out newspaper on our kitchen table as instructed by the master polisher. When I came downstairs and saw this project in process, it felt as if I had been stung in the face by a hundred bees.

Why couldn't she leave my silver (me) alone? Why did her help feel like a judgment on how I chose to live my entire and apparently tarnished life? Why, when I told her I didn't want her to come over and polish, didn't she listen? Why was polishing the silver more important than doing as I wished? Why was polishing the silver more important than anything? More to the point: Why wasn't I a sparkly daughter who *wanted* to polish her silver with her mother, who would happily hire a "lady" to do the dishes— something else my mother constantly nagged me about—after all,

I was so tired from working too much. She insisted she had a "very good lady" to do the dishes for god's sakes! She offered to pay for it! Why was I so stubborn? And while we're at it: Why didn't I love to shop and decorate? Why didn't I "do something" with my hair? Why didn't I wear bright colors and sashay around in Belgian slippers and velvet headbands like you-know-who? And for that matter: Why couldn't I just be happy? Why was I dark and moody and difficult? Why was everything a battle?

I grabbed the newspaper my daughter had lined the table with and started balling it up. I think I started screaming then, too, or maybe I had only raised my voice at that point. I saw my mother start to take off her apron but think better of it and just leave as quickly as possible. Now I'm sure I was screaming because she was getting in the car with her apron on and my daughter was crying and I had to go to bed for a while afterward, my whole being exhausted with rage and shame, especially for having exploded in front of my daughter, who adored her grandmother.

When I told a good friend about the incident, expecting an ally, she said, "God, I wish my mother would polish my silver."

The following Monday, I placed a call to a new therapist.

♠

Anne is tall and dresses monochromatically in neutral colors. Her hair is white and cropped short. She is calm. I like her voice. I like the office, furnished with modern furniture, a gray carpet with thin black lines around the border like Etch A Sketch. There are thick wooden beams and casement windows with brass pulls that look like teardrops. However modern the room, there is no hint of technology, not a computer or phone charger anywhere in sight, which I imagine is deliberate. Though it is against my nature, I trust her almost right away.

I tell Anne that I need to get along with my mother, now that we live twelve minutes apart. I can't keep letting her get to me. And more, I say, I don't want to repeat these patterns with my own daughter, though I already hear myself sounding like my mother: begging her to trim her split ends (It's healthier! Your hair will grow faster!), and freaking out when all the clothes I've laundered and folded are in a heap on the floor. I tell Anne about the silver incident, only now I am trying to entertain her, be funny and ironic about the whole thing. But my efforts are hollow. I am like a comic about to get the hook.

I am tired of myself and this same tape loop and the inexplicable ways in which it involves my mother. I am tired of therapy, that obligatory first session with a new shrink when you empty the rocks from your pockets. Mine begins when my mother took me to my first shrink when I was fifteen, ostensibly for help, only she seemed angry that I had gone off script; her bright precocious girl turned dark and moody, reeking of pot smoke, grades tumbling. I tell Anne about a major depression in college and complete breakdown in graduate school. And how one psychiatrist after another prescribed whatever new antidepressant was on the market, all leaving me more lethargic, more depressed. I felt there was a scrim between the world and me. Sometimes, in college and later, out of desperation, I would call home and then not be able to speak. I could hear my mother's voice cycling through worry, distress, and aggravation. *Are you there? Are you there? Betsy, are you there?*

I assure Anne that I've been well for a long time, stable for over two decades. How I eventually found a doctor who suspected I was manic-depressive and treated me with lithium. I stress to Anne that I never go off my meds. In fact, I'm a model patient, a straight-A student in the school of mental health. I don't want her to think that a jagged pile of psychiatric shards is sitting in front of her. I still feel a wave of shame admitting my illness, as if I am defective, unreliable, could suddenly bug out. I still resist the label, though the medication has worked for over two decades: I've never bottomed out again, never felt my brain on fire. Even though I have come to Anne for help, I don't want to admit I need it.

I tell her that more than once my mother has given me all the credit for getting well, for not giving up, for doing it on my own. I know she means it as great praise, but it makes me angry. Why did I have to do it all on my own? Then guilt sets in: my mother did the best she could, I say. Right?

Anne doesn't say anything.

I describe how I was afraid to have children, especially a daughter. I didn't think I could tolerate any more mother-daughter drama. My worst fears dissipated when I got pregnant and even more when I found out I was having a girl. Almost overnight, I embraced everything I had rejected, mainly home-making and domesticity. I took months painting a raw wooden dresser for my daughter's room with bold colors on the trim, hunting down antique glass pulls decorated with kittens that I had seen in a magazine. When she was little we baked! From scratch! I bought cookie cutters for every holiday. We'd decorate cats and witches for Halloween, wrap them in black and orange tissue paper with ribbons of the same color, and bring them to the neighbors. *Maybe I was manic?* Sometimes I would stand back and look at my little girl decorating our cookies covered with icing and sprinkles and marvel that she was mine. Or see myself: Where was the girl with the Doc Martens and unquiet mind? Was she in remission or gone forever?

Only now, I couldn't understand why things weren't better with my mother. Would I have stabbed her to death with the fork she was polishing? No. But I thought having my daughter,

having our relationship, would reset my compass. Wasn't I lav-
ishing her with the love I craved? Wasn't our closeness proof that
some cycle had been broken? Hadn't I gotten anywhere in the
mother-daughter wars?

I start to cry. It comes on suddenly. I have to take off my
glasses and reach for a tissue. I tell myself to get a grip, that this
is pathetic, only I can't stop crying. I can't even look at Anne.
Then I feel giddy and nauseated at the same time, as if thrown
from a swing.

Finally, I look up. Anne's expression remains unchanged. I
find this intensely comforting. This will be the beginning of a
few years of work. Over the course of our sessions together, I
will try every trick in the book to distract, entertain, and antag-
onize Anne, but she will not flinch. She will not be my mother,
much as I throw myself against her walls. She asks if I'd like
to come back. I nod that I would. Anne takes out her planner,
which looks more like a teacher's attendance book, and opens it
on her lap. We agree on a time for the next session. She marks
it with a pencil.

♠

Like Rhoda's, Bea's place is furnished from a previous lifetime.
There is a heavy credenza, couch and chairs covered in dark
fabric. The ladies play in a breakfast nook in her kitchen with
corner windows and a Tiffany-style lamp hanging over the table, decorated with a slot machine's bright cherries. There's a
small TV off to the side.

As I've observed, talking subsides once they start playing. The
game requires total concentration. Rhoda takes a long time to
lead and Bea mutters, "Play it. You're not going to sleep with it."
She rarely needs time to ponder which card to play and flicks it

insouciantly into the middle of the table. Her speed is intimidating, dealing quickly and scooping up tricks in one quick motion.

Between rounds, Bette reports that a good friend had a fall. She has a black eye, a gash on her head, and a sprained wrist. It could have been worse, the ladies say in unison, as if in reading responsively at services. It also comes out that a friend is down to ninety-three pounds and is in so much pain she can't make it upstairs to her bedroom. They've transformed the dining room into her bedroom. I know my mother would rather die than set up camp in a hospital bed in the dining room for all to see.

Now that the subject of death has been broached, I ask the ladies if they fear death. Rhoda, first, emphatically says no. Jackie and Bette look down, stricken. "Yes, I do," Bette finally says, and Jackie commiserates. I have pushed them to talk about something difficult and yet I suddenly don't want the responsibility of holding up an unwanted mirror. Do they think about how many days of glorious sunshine are left? How many more winters will wash through their bones? Just hearing them admit fear scares me. Of course, we all think our mothers will never die, that cord never cut.

More than death, my mother fears becoming a burden. She's also concerned about the availability of a good manicurist and electrologist in the nursing home, should it come to that. Bette's doctor told her if she falls it would be the end of her.

"You need to get a new doctor," Rhoda chimes in.

Then I ask Bea, who has been uncharacteristically quiet, if she is afraid of dying. "You're dead, you're dead," she barks back.

♠

Bea's father died when she was eight years old some years before penicillin could have cured him. She cocked her head when she told me this, as if to say: *thems the breaks*. I figure it's her way of pushing it off; what else can she do? It was a long time ago. She has been fatherless for many decades. At eight, do you even understand the magnitude of such a loss? And at eighty, do you still long for him?

I suspect Bea's life was irrevocably changed when she lost her fun-loving father, an only child left with a mother she never quite connected with.

"Every year we lost at least one teenager," Bea told me that first meeting at the diner. She was tired by then and was no longer animated. "The kids were warned not to go swimming in the quarries," she said, disgusted that the warning wasn't heeded. Her class lost a beautiful young boy called Millard Fleetwood, age sixteen. The cliffs were as beautiful as they were treacherous; the sheer rock face rose as high as it plunged beneath the blue-green water, irresistible to teenagers who believed themselves impervious to danger, indestructible. It was easy for a swimmer's arm or leg to get caught between the crags of limestone invisible to the eye. There was nothing abstract about the death of a classmate, a boy you might have danced with or had a crush on, or watched playing basketball among a welter of other beautiful young men whose futures just as easily, cruelly, could have been cut down.

Much would be left behind in Bedford: the ready-to-wear dress shop owned by a young Jewish family, a yard full of deflowered chickens, and the last bounce of a basketball on a gymnasium floor after a crushing defeat. When I ask Bea where her father is buried, she tells me the Jewish cemetery in Louisville. I ask if she ever visited the grave with her mother. She looks at me and doesn't answer right away, as she usually does. "No," she finally says, shaking her head, "we never did."

CHAPTER 4

A Thousand Bette Cohens

Bette's perfectly appointed living room could be the set of an Edward Albee play: handsome 1960s-style furnishings, the paintings and knickknacks placed just so. There is no wet bar with carafes of scotch and bourbon, crystal rocks glasses, and a silver ice bucket with claw-shaped tongs, but it's easy enough to imagine. The room is immaculate; a vacuum cleaner has left a wide wake in the carpet. When I first arrive, Bette leads me into this room once filled with friends and cocktails and hors d'oeuvres being passed on silver platters, but whatever ghosts mingled here have long faded. The room isn't gloomy, but the house feels lonely with three grown children long gone. A daughter in Hartford practicing law, another in Paris for more than twenty years, and a son in Baltimore, an emergency room doctor.

Arthur and Bette bought their house in Woodbridge as a young married couple and have lived here for sixty years. "My parents thought we were crazy," Bette says. "It was like the wilderness. There were no streetlights. No stop signs." All of New Haven's suburbs had once been agricultural; Woodbridge was known for dairy farming. In the 1950s and 1960s, most of that farmland would be divided into two-acre plots where young families would raise their kids in ranch houses and colonials.

The rest of the ladies would also settle in the surrounding suburbs. If White Flight was a national phenomenon in the sixties, New Haven was its poster child. Its policies for public housing and urban renewal were so misguided as to insure a tale of two cities. Racial tensions played out on a national stage when Black Panther leader Bobby Seale was tried for murder in the New Haven courts. Bette's neighbor prosecuted the case. He and his family had bodyguards for the duration of the trial. "It didn't affect us all that much," she says. "We still lived our lives."

The ladies were not oblivious, but they were insulated. Woodbridge had everything they needed: good public schools, country clubs, a synagogue, and the nearby Post Road for shopping. It's not that they weren't aggrieved by the world around them, but within it they had constructed their own.

Outside their kitchen windows, each shared a view of Connecticut's hardwood trees, which change with the seasons like the set of a Chekhov play. It's where they've washed a million dishes, wiped the counter a million times. This is where you could find them at almost any hour of the day, making a meal, filling the dishwasher, emptying it. And when they were younger, smoking a cigarette while talking on the phone, the curlicue on the cord stretched tight, watching the evening sky as it went from indigo to navy to black, or the red tail lights on a husband's car, garishly reflected against the asphalt in the New England night.

Of all the Bridge Ladies, I've always felt closest to Bette, in part because of her friendship with my mother. When the weather is good, they walk together on a path, a half-mile loop around a cornfield. Our families also celebrate some of the Jewish holidays together, now that we've all got skeleton crews. Her husband, Arthur, is my favorite of the Bridge husbands. He was loyal to my father in the aftermath of his stroke and long past the point when most friends fell away. And after my father died, he'd readily volunteer to help my mom with things around the house, often "fixing" an appliance by just plugging it in, always more amused than chagrined.

Bette also comes to all of my daughter's plays. She comes in part because of her friendship with my mother, but her fidelity to these fledgling productions isn't a chore; she loves watching ninth graders attempting *The Tempest*, or hoofing their way through *Thoroughly Modern Millie*. Bette had been the star of the drama club at Hillhouse High. When the cast list was put up, she was confident that she would land the lead in all the school plays, and she always did. "I thought I was the greatest thing going!"

Bette isn't at all reticent to talk with me, says she's been looking forward to it, clears her throat and leans in.

"So when did you win your first Oscar? When did it all begin?"

Bette laughs, settles back into her chair, but she doesn't need to search her memory. She might as well be telling me about something that happened that morning.

"Well, actually, it started in the second grade. I was playing the part of Mrs. Upper Lip, and I opened my mouth and out came this wonderful voice, and I remember looking around and having everyone pay attention to me. I decided then that drama was going to be the thing that I would do with my whole life."

Bette has a deep sonorous voice and perfect articulation. When she speaks it's as if she is reading a short story aloud, speaking in full sentences with well-placed pauses. No *ums*, no *ahs.* All of this dates back to a Chapel Street studio in downtown New Haven where Bette first took elocution lessons.

Enter Julia Jacobs. Masculine like Joan Crawford and angular like Katharine Hepburn, she was the embodiment of the young actress's dream. "I loved her. As a matter of fact, I would imitate her when I got home. The way she pronounced certain words, I would pronounce certain words. I just worshipped her. And I was her star."

Elocution lessons were popular in the 1930s and 1940s for people who needed professional coaching and for new immigrants hoping to shed their accents. Most of the kids in Bette's class were there to work on "self-presentation," which basically meant manners, but not Bette Cohen. She was there to hone her craft. Her dream solidified when she saw the movie and performance that would change the course of her life: Bette Davis in *Dark Victory*. From that day on she changed the spelling of her name from *Betty* to *Bette* in homage to the great actress.

"You were just a kid. How did your parents let you do that?"

"I just did."

Bette's father had no use for his daughter's fancy lessons. When she was old enough to drive, he refused to let her take a car from the lot. A tight-fisted used-car salesman, his constant refrain was: If you crack up the car we'll go broke. Bette didn't care; she even enjoyed the two-mile walk to the studio, rehearsing the monologues in her head, preparing to recite them for Julia, or incorporating her feedback on the walk home. When Bette's father threatened to renege on the dollar for lessons, Julia cut the price in half.

"I still think about her to this day, sometimes I even feel myself leaning in the way she would, the angle of her body."

Bette admits that she befriended Ginger Bailey because her grandfather owned the storied Shubert Theater. All the

Broadway-bound shows previewed there, including Rodgers and Hammerstein's *Oklahoma!*, *The King and I*, and *Carousel*.

"I felt so guilty at the time, but Shubert's had all the opening shows. Everything started here. Oh, I used to just drool over it." *An actress has to do what an actress has to do.* It isn't hard to imagine Bette playing the part of Ginger's new best friend, sharing the family box with its gold-leaf garlands and plush red seats, waiting for the curtain to rise while off-kilter notes filled the air from the orchestra pit below. "They were always the best two hours of my life."

When it came time to go to college, most kids from the 1949 graduating class of Hillhouse High were on their way to the University of Connecticut. Not good enough for Bette. She convinced her mother that Skidmore was the place where her youthful goals would be realized, and Sylvia Cohen made it so. She had lost a six-year-old daughter, and when Bette was born a year later, she arrived as a miracle. Her mother called Bette her charm and maneuvered around her husband to find the money to send her. She would do anything for her bright, beautiful, and talented girl. And Bette rewarded her throughout high school with one successful show after another, and to cap it all off, delivering the senior class speech. Bette was poised to step onto that college stage and shine.

Freshman year, the theater department staged *Our Hearts Are Young and Gay*, the very play Bette had just starred in during her senior year. She thought she had the lead sewn up.

"Oh my god, that's an easy one for me." But she got the second lead. She had no idea then that it would be the best part she would get during the next four years, when she was uniformly cast in one insignificant role after another. And with each defeat came eroded confidence. Every rejection was followed by days of dejection.

Her first year of college had brought with it the single, debilitating fact that would inform the rest of her life. All of the girls at Skidmore who had been the stars of their high school were now competing for the lead parts in the plays. "I was no longer the star, and I also was no longer getting straight A's because the competition on the curve put me further down." Bette lowers her head, closes her eyes, and takes a beat, only she isn't acting. It was the awakening that would come to define all of life's disappointments, only this one the first and most crushing. Bette looks up, shrugs. "There were a thousand Bette Cohens."

Of course I know that Bette didn't go on to become an actress; instead she became a wife and mother and, as I always knew her, a Bridge Lady. Only sitting with her now, in her spotless living room, I feel her disappointment as if it happened days instead of years ago.

"The whole thing was such an awakening to me that I shiver when I think about it. I would try out for parts and not get them. And it broke my heart."

"My poor roommate," Bette says. "I was so glum, trying to get it into my head that I wasn't going to be an actress."

The Importance of Being Earnest was the final play of her college career. During tryouts, the all-too-familiar feeling of dread crept in. Once again, anxiety conquered confidence, and Bette left the audition utterly devastated. Driven by despair, the clock on her college career ticking down, she did something she didn't know was in her: she went back to the director and pleaded for the part. "It was a huge risk. The audience would be full of parents. I was an unknown quantity for a lead as pivotal as Lady Bracknell."

"You begged her?"

Bette knew the director couldn't take the risk, but desperate not to see this last chance fall away like all the other roles she'd lost during her four years, she went back and begged, and astonishingly the director relented. Bette would play the part, reprising the high falsetto of her second-grade performance as Mrs. Upper Lip. The performance was a smashing success. The director found Bette after the show and apologized for having never cast her in any significant parts. She had no idea how good she was.

"How did it feel?"

Bette falls silent.

They were crumbs for a girl with a heart already broken.

♠

It's early April, and Connecticut is still refusing to warm. It's the first Monday of the month and Bridge is at Bette's. She wears perfectly fitting slacks and a sweater that doesn't match so much as goes with it. Matching is for amateurs. The way Bette puts clothes together is intrinsically correct; it's the mark of a woman confident in her looks and taste, and this poise extends throughout her home. It's as if all the energy she had once put into performance has been channeled into the presentation of self and home. Like all of the ladies, she took the road more traveled; her decision alone seems tinged with regret.

As the ladies filter in, Jackie remarks on the repaired skylights, which instantly triggers irritation in Bette. A tree had crashed through their den during a recent storm, and Bette is not happy about the repairs. Apparently the trim on the old skylights was flush with the ceiling but not so with the replacements. Bette points this out to the girls, disgusted. The ladies can't tell the difference, but Bette insists that it's not right. Arthur stops in for a minute to say hello and overhears Bette complain about the moldings. He throws up his hands. *There is nothing wrong with them!* Arthur is about as good-natured as they come, but everyone has a breaking point. You know that if he hears one more word about the moldings, no, if he so much as sees Bette glance skyward and register disdain, he might blow. But for now, he just leaves. No scene.

Bette and Arthur have been together for nearly sixty years. I know the trim on the skylights is not about to topple a marriage of this duration. These marriages are built to last, like the appliances from their era, made of cast iron and steel. Put another way: divorce was not an option. At different times, the ladies have asserted that marriage "forces" couples to stay together, and that this is a good thing. "You're forced to work out your problems, to stick to it," Bette says. Rhoda agrees; people divorce too quickly. I don't know that I agree or disagree, but like a high school debater assigned the affirmative position, I'd feel the need to defend divorce and choice in general. I'd argue that the deeper commitment is staying together when you're free to go.

This is my first lunch at Bette's, and I feel a little faint or nauseated. Her dining room has that darkly quiet, unused look, the table only set for holidays and special occasions. *Does anyone ever open a window around here?* Everything that might be needed is anticipated and already on the table: a pitcher of water, a tidy dish for Sweet'n Low packets and another for a selection of teas, condiments, and serving pieces for every dish. Bette has delicate bone-white dessert plates with round depressions for the matching teacups to nestle in. They put me in mind of a dollhouse tea party. Leaf-shaped dishes, smaller than actual leaves, are set out for the used tea bags, later to be choked to death by their own strings. A kettle quietly chugs along on the stove. Of the ladies who still prepare lunch, Bette, Rhoda, and my mother, none has relaxed their standards. This is most evident in the parade of napkin rings I've come to witness gracing their tables: silver, porcelain, tortoiseshell, bamboo, and Bakelite. I marvel at the care taken. Bette's table could be on display at the Smithsonian: MID–CENTURY NORTH AMERICAN DINING ROOM, CIRCA 1958.

The ladies tell me they are likely the last bridge club in the area that serves lunch, the last bastion of civilization. And it might be. Everyone is punctual, everyone is dressed, and no one checks her phone throughout the meal or, god forbid, during Bridge. Most of them never use their phones (flip phones), and I don't think any of them know how to pick up voice mail either. All of the Bridge Ladies have computers, only they are a greater source of consternation than information (except for Bea, who loves to google, send e-mails, and play Bridge on it). Bette and Arthur's computer is at least a decade old, but they don't see the point in getting a new one. "One minute it's working, the next not," Bette says, frustrated, as if it were a toaster you could smack to get going again. (Of course, my teenage daughter mocks me for not knowing how to write on someone's wall or for using hashtags incorrectly.)

Every generation has a technology threshold. The ladies have missed out on a lot of developments, only they believe they are better off. They abhor the sight of people bowed over their phones. Rhoda saw an attractive couple over the weekend at a very nice restaurant. She claims they were on their phones the *entire* time, not a word exchanged between them.

"Why don't they just stay home?" Rhoda asks the women, her voice laced with a mix of disgust and indignation.

Everyone agrees. The ladies can't stand iPhones. They see progress as negative. I have a low tolerance for conversations that glorify the past. At no point in history have people had more freedom and access to information. The world is still a violent and dangerous place, but it's not the Middle Ages when a third of the population was killed, or World War II (a so-called good war, their war) when more than sixty million people were killed. Was childhood ever innocent? Not too long ago children were born to work the fields and clean the chimneys. All these thoughts race through my mind when the ladies decry iPhones and the Internet and the horrible manners of people today. I want to blow a thick stream of pot smoke into the face of anyone that thinks the days of wine and roses were preferable to today. But I stay silent. This isn't my lunch and these aren't my battles. For the ladies, the last innovation they embraced, as far as I can tell, is the Cuisinart, introduced in the 1970s, virtually cutting in half the time it takes to make latkes, which isn't nothing.

Bea's been to the movies. She goes with the same friends most weekends and refers to them as the "flicks." She's outspoken about liking or disliking a flick, though she doesn't get into it. She'll tell you to see it for yourself. Rhoda loved *42*, the Jackie Robinson story. It was about her era and it was a good old-fashioned story where justice prevailed. My mother found it too sentimental, and they "agree to disagree."

"That's what makes horse racing," my mother says, a slightly more polite version of "there's no accounting for taste."

Jackie's husband doesn't like going to the movies, but they've happily discovered On Demand. She mentions that they watched *Les Miz* in bed. I imagine them propped up in their bed of sixty years, Fantine's melody washing over them. I've always felt that shy of unbridled passion, having someone to watch *The Wire* with is about as good as it gets.

Over the weekend my husband and I ran into Bette and Arthur coming out of the movies. We had all seen Woody Allen's *Blue Jasmine*. Bette was electrified by Cate Blanchett's performance. Jasmine was the role of a lifetime. Another couple hovered nearby. They looked tiny and infirm, the man pulling an oxygen tank behind him. As they came closer, I realized they were *with* Bette and Arthur. Of course I know that Bette and Arthur go out with couples all the time, but I felt a sudden pang for my mother, who often joins them for a movie. They insist she's not a third wheel, though she can never shake that feeling. Seeing the two couples made it tangible to me that my mother's life in the coupled lane was over. She always said of my dad that he was a great date, and a big part of losing him has been ending that era of their social life and adjusting to going solo. John and I don't mind going to the movies alone. We've taken separate vacations when our schedules didn't mesh. My mother wouldn't have dreamed of going it alone, or breaking ranks if she didn't like my father's choices. She thinks all of this independence is bad, her judgment unveiled when she says things like "if that's how you want to live." For her generation, all of these activities required a companion.

When my father first died, there was a swarm of widows for my mother to fall in with, but she hoped to find a man friend. She went on a date or two, but nothing ever panned out. My mother, all the women, are highly aware that the male to-female ratio in their age range wildly favors the men; women generally live longer than men by five years or more. So that when a man becomes a widower, he's usually snapped up pretty quickly. After a successful businessman in town lost his wife to cancer, the women speculated how long it would take before he was remarried. Bette: a year. Roz: six months. Bea: a New York minute.

In fact, if a man isn't snapped up right away, my mother suspects something "pretty bad" must be wrong with him.

"Like what?" I once asked her.

"Like anything."

"No really, like what?"

"I don't know." Her voice was weary and wanting me to stop this line of questions.

"Come on, like what, you must mean something."

"Who the hell knows," she said, exasperated with me. It was a familiar exchange. When I was little I'd ruthlessly question my mother, hounding her for answers, as if she were in the witness box and I could get her to crack by hammering her nonstop. *Why were we having a late dinner? Why did I have to go to Hebrew School? Why did my older sister get to watch the entire Oscars? Why! Why! Why!* My mother's answers were weak and unsatisfying: *just because, because I said so, everything doesn't have to have an answer.* And the one that infuriated me most of all: *Who said life was fair?* I was a child and as such still believed in justice, even if it only meant my sister and I getting the same size portion of ziti. Not so for my mother. She had known for a long time that the world wasn't fair. She had to live in it whether she wanted to or not.

When it's time to play cards we move into Bette's bright kitchen. The table is next to sliding glass windows, beyond which a weeping cherry's long tentacles stir in the wind. Outside, there's a picnic table with an umbrella cinched at the hips. The deck is bleached from years of sun. I can easily imagine Bette bringing a tray of hamburgers out to her husband to grill, her legs strong and tanned beneath a tennis skirt or crisp culottes and her three kids playing in the yard.

A large painting dominates one wall. It's of a woman in a flowery dress and floppy hat. Her eyes are somewhat vacant, and I can't tell if she is bored or sad, or if I'm projecting. My mother deals. Each lady picks up her thirteen cards and arranges them by suit except for Bette who sits this one out, loading her dishwasher. You get the feeling no dish has the chance to get comfortable in her pristine sink or on the clutter-free counter.

In lieu of the women opening up, I become convinced that the way each one arranges her cards betrays an aspect of character. Bette makes a tight fan of her cards, evidence of her mania for order. Rhoda holds her cards like a prayer book. Bea quickly snaps up one card at a time more like Blackjack than Bridge. Jackie remains impassive as she organizers her cards. If she had a pair of Wayfarers, she'd be cooler than Bob Dylan. My mother makes a wide fan of her cards and loudly grouses if she doesn't like them. Sometimes I think this is a big act on her part; but with my mother you can never tell. Her lack of poker face *is* her poker face. She has hidden her scars well. I imagine they all have.

♠

I ask Bette why she didn't pursue acting after her big success senior year and go to New York to audition.

"Well," she said, crossing one slim leg over the other, "I didn't have the guts, I suppose." I remind her that she had the guts when she pleaded with the director for the part. "I guess I did," she says, suddenly weary. "Where would I have lived? I didn't have any money. I wouldn't have known how to go about it."

Jackie also harbored a fantasy of being an actress, but she was more practical than Bette. A season or two of summer stock in New Hampshire was enough to satisfy her. After graduation, she won a radio contest and the prize was getting to be on a radio show with Zero Mostel. The show was broadcast from Sardi's, the famous New York restaurant known for its celebrity clientele and wall-to-wall framed caricatures of the greats. It must have been overwhelming for Jackie, her own nascent dreams of joining the theater already shelved. As she was leaving the restaurant, Mostel called out, "You find some guy to get married. Don't, don't go into this business." Doubtless, he would forget having said it no sooner than the words left his lips. Jackie, however, had already taken them to heart.

Bette mentions that she still looks at the audition notices in the paper.

"Really?" I can't believe it.

"I would never do anything about it." She waves off the admission.

"But you still look. Why?"

"I don't know. I just like to see what's out there."

"Bette," I say, "you must be looking for something."

"No," she says. Everything gets stony. Fun at first, talking about her youthful career now seems full of sorrow.

Finally Bette breaks the silence, she is curious if Julia Jacobs, too, had aspirations as an actress. Were they crushed all at once, or chipped away at slowly, over time, until she finally gave up, opened the studio, and proceeded to instruct a ragtag group of students how to open their mouths and speak? Bette would never find out how far Julia Jacobs had gotten, how far she had fallen. Did she sacrifice marriage for her art? Was she single because she missed the boat or because she was the captain of her own ship?

Bette looks at me. "I guess we'll never know."

CHAPTER 5

Bingo

Jeff Bayone, I learn, is the owner of the Manhattan Bridge Club. I'd seen him around. You can't really miss him. He is well over six feet tall, has a slouch as good as any detective on *Law & Order*, and a mustache from the 1970s. About this man I think you could safely say: he's been there and done that. I imagine that if he calculated all the time he has spent waiting for beginners to discard he could easily add a few months to the end of his life. He's filling in for Barbara and the level of intimidation is intense. He has no time for pleasantries and can seemingly size up a person with or without any Bridge potential. I fear he already has me pegged.

He tosses a duplicate board on the table.

"Let's get started, yeah?"

The Brit and the Elf are back, plus a new woman has joined us. She looks like a banker, wearing a navy-blue suit, the skirt pleated after a long day trading derivatives. When she unravels her turquoise Pashmina, I notice she's wearing a double strand of pearls with a diamond clasp in the shape of a butterfly. Stunning. She says she used to play, claims to have forgotten everything, the usual blather from returning students. Jeff has instructed her to join our lesson and take it from there. She can always move up to Beginner Two or Intermediate if she's more advanced than she gives herself credit.

It's been a few weeks of lessons and by now we should be able to grasp the basic concepts:

How many points and how many cards do we need to open a bid in a major suit?

How many points and cards to open in a minor suit?

How many points to open a "one no trump" hand?

How many points to respond to your partner's opening bid at the one level?

What does it mean when we bid "up the ladder"?

Folks, I am clinging to the first rung. Memorizing all of these numbers is beyond me. You are looking at a girl who sometimes confuses the number of states in America with the number of cards in a deck. *They are pretty close.* I once took a class with a woman who was so completely frustrated by all this bidding mumbo-jumbo that she whined, "Why can't we just say what we have in our hands?"

It's not that I didn't sympathize, but that would be like taking off all your clothes before you started a game of strip poker.

Jeff is staring at me.

"Are you the dealer?" He knows I'm the dealer. "Did you want to bid?"

I have thirteen points, but I don't have a five-card major.

"Pass?"

"Are you passing?" asks Jeff, and I immediately suspect I should have bid.

"I think so." My voice quavers. I half expect Jeff to tell me to drop and give him fifty for my mealymouthed response.

"Do you have four Clubs?"

"I do."

"So bid one Club."

"I thought you had to open with a major suit."

I've forgotten that we can also open the bidding in a minor suit; apparently we learned this during our second class. Jeff explains that the cheapest bid is one Club. Like at Sotheby's, you can't underbid someone. If you want to get involved in the bidding, you must bid higher than your partner, or outbid your opponent. Until now, my greatest accomplishment in the world of games was using a Q on a triple-word score in Scrabble.

Pashmina is my partner, and when it's her turn to bid she says, "One Heart."

I am supposed to know what her bid means, what she is trying to tell me. Jeff cocks his head toward my direction. I stare so hard at the cards they melt into each other like a cubist painting. The clock is ticking. The banker stares at me, perhaps she thinks I've had a small stroke. The Brit nibbles the salt off a pretzel log. (Take a bite for god's sake!) The Elf looks at me with big encouraging eyes and I kind of want to slap him.

I feel Jeff's impatience.

"You know," he says, "they play Bingo on Forty-Second Street."

It will take some time, if not an entire lifetime, to shake off the insult. Only instead of more humiliation, he pulls his chair in closer and looks each of us in the eye. His tone changes, his voice lowers. He is interested in imparting the idea that Bridge goes beyond rote memorization. There is a kind of beauty in deciphering the language of bidding and mastering the play of the hand. Though still numb from the insult, I detect a spark in him. "It seems like you're not getting anywhere, and then it gels," he says, his encouragement sincere. I see that he loves the game beneath his world-weary demeanor. He may even love us.

Pashmina has to leave early and makes a huge show of winding her scarf around her torso like a sari. Jeff tells her she should probably skip to Intermediate. This doesn't come as a surprise; she was obviously ahead of us. She smiles and nods knowingly, annoying as a teacher's pet. Jeff takes her place at the table. He seems like a magician so deft is his handling of the cards, the deck disappearing in his large hands.

"Okay," he says, "who can tell me what the finesse is?"

I don't dare open my mouth. Like a mother who sees her toddler heading for the corner of a table, Jeff sees every mistake long before we do.

The Brit jumps in. "Isn't it when you win a trick with a lower card whilst a higher card is still out there?" *Whilst?*

Jeff won't go so far as to say "good job" or offer a compliment of any kind, but he looks pleased, and the Brit glows. Oh, to get a nod from Jeff!

What I lack in skill, however, I make up for with enthusiasm. I get right away how complex Bridge is, how competitive and addictive. By my fourth lesson, I've bought two books on bidding and a Bridge app called Bridge Baron. Instead of doing my work reading manuscripts on the train, I've taken to playing hand after hand. *Just one more*, I tell myself. For the first time, I understand how the game has kept the ladies coming back over all these years. Yes, the comradeship, yes, the de facto support system, but I realize they also really love to play Bridge. It's incredibly fun.

People talk about how Bridge keeps the mind sharp, and I get this, too. You cannot play Bridge frivolously, yapping the whole time, or like my friend's poker game where the men get stoned and play half-baked into the night. Total concentration is required. This absorption may be the most intoxicating thing about Bridge: when you are playing you can't think about anything else. Hours pass imperceptibly. The known world slips away: work hassles, marital dry spells, my daughter's college applications.

Lesson over, I gather my things, still smarting from the bingo sling. Jeff must sense my bruised ego and says not to worry, keep coming back.

"I'm terrible at math," I say, offering this flimsy excuse.

"It isn't really math," he says, "it's logic."

Now I'm really fucked.

"You might want to repeat Beginner One. It's not a bad idea."

I get it. I need to repeat the grade. No child likes to hear it, but sometimes it's for his own good. The only thing I had been successful at was staying away from the snacks, but I took a fistful of Mike and Ikes on the way out that night and chewed the sweet gummy capsules to the exclusion of all other feeling as I made my way to the subway through the cold, dark night.

CHAPTER 6

How I Met Your Father

"Gosh, there were so many. I can't remember them." Jackie is referring to all the boys who hoped for a date with her: the girl with the size-four figure, wide-set eyes, and porcelain skin, alluring as a portrait of a nineteenth-century noblewoman, and almost as aloof. There was never a shortage of young men who called the Brody household in hope of a date.

This is our first visit, and Jackie has led me into her formal living room. It's beautifully furnished with exquisite antiques, but it also has a ghostly quality, not Havisham-esque, but long untouched. It's a great room and has likely seen its share of lavish parties; today it's more of a museum without the velvet cordons and security guard shuffling in the doorway.

Jackie grew up in Morris Cove, a spit of land on the Connecticut shoreline. As a girl, she and her classmates visited the Morris House, one of the oldest homes in the area, built around 1750. For some children, it was just an old house filled with a lot of old stuff, a butter churn, a chamber pot, and a fireplace big enough to roast small children. Jackie admired the austere yet elegant furnishings, the many-paned windows with rippled glass, and the shiny black hansom cab in the garage. She comes by her love of all things colonial honestly. "It's where my love of eighteenth-century furniture started," she tells me, and I can see her taste on display all around me. The house, Jackie tells me, is still there.

I offer to take Jackie for a "field trip" to the Morris House and also to her childhood home, hoping to jog some memories. She agrees, and a few weeks later on a cold April morning, we set out. Townsend Avenue is a wide boulevard where ordinary houses are washed out in the weak sun and American flags, once symbolic of this proud Revolutionary battleground, now hang slack and tattered. The first place Jackie spots is her grammar school, named for Connecticut war hero Nathan Hale. ("I only regret that I have but one life to lose for my country.") She and her brother walked a mile to and from school every day and again in the middle of the day for lunch. I marvel that they had time. More astonishing, her mother prepared a hot meal every day: pot roast, roast chicken, sometimes liver.

"No Hot Pockets? Lunchables?"

"No," Jackie says, a small smile.

It's the same brick building she remembers except for a new wing off to the side that probably houses the gym and cafeteria. It's a huge modern thing, and predictably Jackie doesn't like it.

We pass the Morris House. I pull into the driveway, closed for the season. It looks more like a farmhouse than the grand mansion I expected. It takes some backtracking then, but we finally find Jackie's house. She is shocked to see the yard covered in lawn ornaments and junk, all of it coated in some white material that looks like asbestos or the fallout of a nuclear holocaust. An awning hangs off the house, sneering in a malevolent grin. Jackie remains silent. When I ask her if she wants to leave, she nods yes.

This excursion was a bad idea. What was I expecting? That we would bond on our little adventure, that she would open up and show me where she smoked her first cigarette or made out with a cute boy? And what about Jackie? Had she expected to see her home as if preserved in a Norman Rockwell painting? Maybe that's how we all remember our childhood homes.

She wants to go home, but I push to see the famous carousel at Lighthouse Point Park. Originally built in 1916, it has been restored to its former grandeur. Jackie remembers riding on it as a girl on special occasions. Only now there are stand-alone barricades blocking the entrance. The road down to the carousel is too far for her to walk. No one is around, and I take a wide turn around the fences.

"You can't do that," Jackie says, alarmed, her hand pressed up against the window.

"It's okay, just for a minute."

"No, please, turn around." I can tell she's upset, but I'm sure that when she sees the carousel it will be worth it.

"No one's here. It's fine." I try to reassure her, but her eyes are wide with fear.

I'm not sure what emboldened me. Usually I follow rules like a Girl Scout. I'm also not sure why I disregarded Jackie's wishes; was I that desperate to make her happy, convinced I could? Jackie is the most difficult of the Bridge Ladies to get to know. I can't tell if she's shy and reserved, or just shy and reserved around me. She is also the most alluring, her allure born in part from her reticence, a quality I have never managed, though wished, to cultivate. I've even nicknamed her The Sphinx. She had been clear about not wanting me to bypass the gates and I crashed right through anyway. I realized later it was no longer about Jackie. My need trumped hers. I don't know what I expected to happen: that the sight of the mighty carousel would bring Jackie's childhood back in a warm bath of nostalgia? That I would make her happy? Was I trying to do this with all of the ladies, my mother most of all, the Uber-Sphinx?

I pull up to the octagonal structure that houses the great carousel, keeping it safe from the elements and vandals alike. I jump out of the car and press my face against the Plexiglass. Inside, dragons with scales dipped in gold, horses set four abreast brightly painted to a high gloss, at the top a frieze of the Connecticut seashore, and a Wurlitzer that pumps garish waltzes from the core. Jackie stays inside the car, staring straight ahead. I open the car door and ask if she wants to take a look, even though I know she isn't going to budge. I take one last peek again through the Plexiglass; the huge flared nostril of a horse and its angry eye black as a marble stares back at me.

Pulling out of the parking lot, I ask if she'd like to get an ice-cream cone.

"That would be fine."

I flash on Jackie as a young girl just then, atop her favorite horse, her mother waving as she came around, her father digging in his pocket for loose change as the bells on an ice cream truck tinkle in the distance.

♠

When Jackie hosts Bridge she also treats the ladies to a meal out in a diner near her home in Bethany. It's the most rural of New Haven's suburbs, a place where farms unfold like quilts, and horses stand still as plastic toys. The only signs of spring are the garish forsythia bushes, their buds exploding yellow like movie-theater popcorn, and early tulip shoots peeking up out of the earth like hungry beaks looking for food. The sky is overcast with gray bunting; the roads are bleached from salting.

When I pull into the parking lot, I see Jackie getting out of her ancient station wagon with wooden trim and side panels. She no longer drives and her freedom is hugely curtailed. Dick, who doubles as a chauffeur, does a three-point turn in the parking lot, slowly maneuvering the wide car like a yacht in a harbor. Jackie takes small, worried steps toward the entrance. She is bundled up, her pocketbook resting in the crook of her arm. From a distance, she looks like a doll, her hair coiffed and her lips painted coral. When I bound up to her in the parking lot, she looks frightened at first, as if startled by a deer. Then she recognizes me, "Oh, hi."

As we walk up the ramp into the diner, Jackie says, "I have to tell you something. I didn't like that trip at all. It depressed me." I open the door for her and we go inside. I feel terrible but I don't know what to say. I decide to shelve the other field trips I had started to contemplate.

The Country Corner Diner is a lot less "jazzy" than the Athenian. More homespun. A handwritten white board announces the specials: chicken and rice for soup, roast beef and mashed potatoes for a main. Goulash!! The ladies arrive and find their usual spot at the table. When my mother greets me, she says, "Well, hello there," as if we are casual acquaintances instead of mother and daughter. She likes to keep up this charade as if she were just another Bridge Lady.

A beautiful young woman gives us our menus and will be back for our order. She is slim, has high cheekbones, and her shiny brown hair is pulled back into a ponytail. She is a source of speculation among the women. Supposedly she has an advanced degree and at one time had a high-paying job in Boston or New York. Now, she works here, in an ordinary diner, on an ordinary country road. What is the story here? The ladies can't fathom how a girl this beautiful *and* educated is waiting tables. I speculate that she embezzled funds to support a cocaine addiction. The ladies do not brook such foolishness; my imagination is too vivid for them. Still, the ladies feel sorry for her. Didn't she have any options? Was there no one to catch her? Waitressing is not streetwalking, but the ladies' pity suggests as much.

For them, marrying and staying married kept dangerous waters at bay. None of the Bridge Ladies fell through the cracks like Lily Bart. None wound up in a polyester dress and white wedgies. Whatever opportunities they missed out on by *not* working, they were also protected *from* working. Why hadn't our lovely young waitress been protected thus? No one says it, but it's in the air: this wouldn't happen to a Jewish girl. Though of course it could and does.

♠

On the morning when I come for my next visit, Jackie is just waking up. Dick insists I come in and keeps me company while I wait. From then on, he always stays for some part of our visit. I can't tell if he and Jackie are inseparable or if he simply doesn't want to be left out. I ask Dick if he ever had any doubts about marrying, or if he ever questioned whether he would get married.

"Absolutely not. I never doubted it. Never. It's like it was ordained." I am always wary of people who go through life with absolute certainty, but when Dick says this I know he is speaking for the Greatest Generation, a time when men did the right thing: they fought for their country, they tipped the shoe-shine boy, and they hung up their hats before sitting down to a meal.

No baseball caps, bills back, at the dinner table. They worked forty hours a week, took out insurance policies, and married good girls. Being a man meant getting married and having a family and supporting them. *Girls were girls and men were men. Mister, we could use a man like Herbert Hoover again.*

For Dick the choice was simple: he wanted the most beautiful woman in the room. "Never had a flicker of a doubt." It was Dick's senior year at Yale and Jackie's junior year at UConn. She had come home for the weekend of the Yale–Princeton football game, for the social whirl. It was at a cocktail party where she and Dick first met. Only Jackie had come with a date, *obvs*. No matter. Dick marched right up to her and asked her out. I ask him how he had the chutzpah to approach her; she had come with a date after all. Wasn't he dissuaded?

"Nope."

"Really?" I pressed. "Weren't you, you know, kind of poaching?"

"Every man for himself." Dick doesn't blink. It is downright Darwinian. I look at the man across from me, now in his eighties, in leather slippers and a tartan plaid robe, and I think: *you devil.* Still, Jackie had to consult her calendar. For all his confidence, Dick didn't get a date with Jackie until Christmas. *Get in line.*

Dick points to a house through the woods. "That's where I grew up," he says proudly. "That's where we got engaged." Apart from living in an apartment for two years while their house was being built, Jackie and Dick have lived here for their entire married life. The mailbox is rusted, a long-abandoned nest under an eave hangs on precariously, and a step between the foyer and den is swayback from daily use. They raised two children here, a successful son who, like Dick, became an engineer, and a highly accomplished daughter, who works in communications. Dick swears they never had to push or prod; the kids understood what was expected academically, and life went according to plan.

Jackie comes into the den in a mauve robe and slippers. A small silver clip has become dislodged and hangs by a thread of hair. I want to reach out and refasten it, but that would be too familiar.

I want to know if it was usual to date a few guys at time.

"Oh, yes."

"Were you ever dumped?"

"No."

Then, excited, Jackie does remember one time, "I had the German measles and my boyfriend came to visit along with one of my girlfriends, and I never heard from either of them again. They eventually married, and I later learned divorced. Subsequently, I met her daughter and she was divorced as well." *Snap!*

The dating scene was centered on weekly dances. It was the era of the jitterbug, Lindy, and swing, even more outdated now than Bridge. The men uniformly wore white shirts and black jackets, narrow ties fixed with small clips, and hair pomaded off their faces. The girls favored long gowns with cinched waists or dropped waistlines, skirts billowed, light as a Mallomar cookie.

"There were a lot of dances. It was important to have a date and I always did," Jackie says nonchalantly.

"Were you happy to go out with any guy who asked?"

"No, I was choosy."

Lest Jackie get too big a head, it was her mother who harshly dropped her back down to earth, always withholding a compliment of any kind, especially where her beauty was concerned.

"She always said, 'That is for other people to say.' And she said it more than once." As if great beauty could also invite great tragedy.

When her father suffered a financial setback and temporarily moved the family into his sister's house, they had to tiptoe around Jackie's aunt, nicknamed Lady. Jackie remembers listening with her mother to the morning radio show "Breakfast with Dorothy and Dick." It portrayed a Park Avenue couple reporting on their glamorous New York life from their penthouse apartment complete with a butler and chirping parakeet. It was either a fabulous distraction or a ridiculous charade for Jackie's mother, her elbows deep in dishes, tiptoeing around Lady and her formidable airs. Still, when it came to dances, Jackie's mother always had money for dresses and nylons, bags and shoes. But it was her father who was fussy about her looks. He wanted her to look different from the "hoi polloi" and made sure she had well-tailored clothes and wore her hair in a demure fashion, unlike the pompadours and updos piled high with victory rolls like a surfer's perfect wave.

Dick took Jackie to the cozy Fireside Restaurant for dinner on their first date. After that he drove up to UConn on weekends to see her, though they still weren't exclusive. I ask Jackie if she was keeping her options open.

"A little bit."

When she spent a summer in New Hampshire doing summer stock, Dick followed her there, pretending that he shared her love of theater and painted flats all summer just to be around her and to ward off other suitors.

I ask Jackie if she fell in love or was it more that she could imagine seeing herself with Dick for the rest of her life.

"A little bit of both."

"Do you think women of your generation were more pragmatic choosing their husbands?"

"I suppose."

Why didn't the Bridge Ladies feel they had a choice? Ruth Bader Ginsberg is a contemporary of theirs. She grew up in Brooklyn. For all I know she could have been Israeli folk dancing at the

East Midwood Jewish Center with my mother. She probably plays Bridge! Yet nothing stopped her from pursuing her dreams of social justice all the way to the Supreme Court. The ladies marvel at her, but it ends there. They would not pursue careers; it wasn't in the cards.

I vowed that I would always work and bring home my own paycheck. I craved the independence my mother forfeited—at least that's how I saw it growing up. Once a group of junior high friends were talking about what we wanted to be when we got older. All of us wanted careers: doctors, lawyers, writers, and artists. Only one girl said she wanted to get married and make babies. That's how she put it: make babies. It sounded like a factory. It sounded like the 1950s.

Jackie's wedding album is big and heavy, almost like a piece of furniture, the photographs mounted on heavy stock, the black-and-white pictures creamy. Jackie was married in the grand ballroom of the Taft Hotel. It was a New Haven institution and was *the* place to get married. The lobby had seventy-foot Corinthian columns and a rotunda with a Tiffany stained-glass dome. (Bette also got married there. It was "the place" to get married in New Haven. An underground tunnel connected it to the Shubert Theater where Bette had been mesmerized as a girl. The most famous actors of the day traversed the tunnel from hotel to stage door. A key scene from *All About Eve* was filmed there, where the manipulative Eve Harrington plots to usurp the great Margo Channing, played of course by Bette's hero and self-appointed namesake, Bette Davis. The proximity must have been bittersweet for Bette; her alternate universe a minute and a million miles away. Neither she nor Jackie can remember how their parents could afford the Taft or the dresses they shopped for in New York, only that they did.)

Dick looks more like a bar mitzvah boy than a groom in the pictures, each one a familiar tableau from every Jewish wedding throughout the ages: the bride and groom beneath the chuppah, the groom breaking the glass, the first dance. Jackie looks somber on her father's arm. She reminds me that he had been sick in the months leading up to the wedding, steadily declining. Still, he would walk his only girl down the aisle—a father's sacred duty. Though he would be gone within the year.

Dick follows us into the dining room but stands off to the side. Jackie turns a few more pages: tables of guests stare out, one indistinguishable from the next. When she turns another page a Polaroid slips out of the album and wafts down to the floor. I pick it up.

"Whoa. Is that you?"

Jackie nods. "That's right."

She is in a high-waist bikini sunning, her body draped over some huge rocks. She looks like Rita Hayworth.

"Where was that?"

She looks at it more closely. "Summer stock, I think, New Hampshire."

It had been the summer Dick painted flats and didn't let her out of his sight.

I am more knocked out by the photograph than the entire album. It's so . . . sexy.

"How does all this make you feel?" They shrug at each other. Then Dick says something about it all being a long time ago.

The last picture in the album is kitschy in the extreme. Dick and Jackie peeking out of their hotel room with a sign dangling from the doorknob: DO NOT DISTURB. It's adorable. Still, I can't help but wonder what those wedding nights were like for nervous couples possibly having sex for the first time. All that pressure and inexperience.

"What if it's awful?" I once asked my mother.

"You try again," she said, "and again."

"Do you recognize yourselves in these pictures?"

"Of course," Dick says, his certitude back in full force. Only it's not exactly what I meant.

I want to know what lasts: if some piece of Jackie is still that girl on the rocks. And Dick the man who would follow her anywhere.

♠

Rhoda's husband, Peter, strikes me as something of a prince. Like Dick, he, too, was determined to build a house in his hometown of Roanoke, Virginia, when he and Rhoda moved there as new-lyweds. Rhoda didn't want to; she didn't think they were ready for such an undertaking. They didn't have a family yet!

"I just did not want to do that, but he did, and so we did."

"How could he do that? How could you let him?"

"I did not want to make waves. That was definitely not my style. That was not in my nature at all."

Rhoda is by far the most outspoken and confident of the Bridge Ladies. It's almost impossible to imagine her as deferential about anything she didn't want.

"Really, you couldn't confront Peter?"

"No, I could not."

The house that Peter built was a contemporary ranch with a sunken living room, three bedrooms, glass-fronted cabinets, and radiant-heated floors.

"It was all Peter. I think I picked out the color for the kitchen cabinets."

Her parents didn't question the move, even as they were dev-astated sending their only child so many miles away from their home in Salem, Massachusetts.

"My parents said that's where you're going to live. Where your husband is, that's where you live. I knew how painful it was for them. They were happy that I was happily married, but the separation was very painful."

Rhoda tears up remembering saying good-bye to them and uprooting. She was an only child and the center of her parents' lives. She never felt deprived, never hungered for siblings, never lacked for friends. Her father had lavished attention on her and she was proud to watch from inside his Ford while he went from door to door collecting insurance payments, handsome in his suit and tie. Unlike Willy Loman, her father was a success-ful salesman. No small feat for the son of a Russian immigrant to land a job with John Hancock, the prestigious nationwide insurance company. "He was a very social creature. He knew everyone and everyone knew him. If you were late with a pay-ment, he would extend the deadline, do what he could before canceling a policy." Then he'd take her for a favorite foot-long and a walk by the sea.

Rhoda confides that she was closer with her father. "My mother loved and adored me, but it was my father's love, I don't know, he was very protective and caring. If there was a raindrop in the sky, he'd be there in his car waiting for me."

"Ain't no sex!" Rhoda is emphatic when I pry into her college years. "Kissing, yes. But no sex." She crosses her arms over her chest and stares hard at me, lips clamped, when I ask about col-lege life.

"Nothing beyond kissing?"

"Maybe a little."

"Like what?"

I want to push. *Did you go to third? All the way?* But I've clearly entered a no-fly zone with her. Maybe it's for the best; Rhoda and I aren't in the girls' locker room sharing a smoke instead of here in her perfect home with a place for everything and everything in its place.

At Russell Sage, the all-girls college she attended, you could get bounced for getting caught with a boy in your dorm room, let alone getting pregnant.

"I don't remember a lot of complaining about it. We accepted it. I sort of took it for granted. Those were the rules. You know, if there was a rule, I had to obey it. I remember in school you would hear so and so did such and such, and I would be totally shocked out of my shoes."

"Shocked?"

"I was!"

"Are you telling me that all of the women at Russell Sage were virgins?"

"Why do you think they married so young!"

Until that moment, I thought women married young because it was the social norm, because their career path was as wife and mother. It really never occurred to me that they were raring to go. Bette remembered weekends at Skidmore when the girls were "let out of their cages," and went wild. They had largely come from private girls' schools and hadn't had much contact with boys. "They were breaking crazy." Bette reported. "On Thursday nights it was the Four S's: shit, shower, shine, and shampoo." *Shine?*

Rhoda met Peter at a Hillel party in the fall of Rhoda's junior year. Peter had come with a date, but when he saw Rhoda, he apparently told his date, "I do apologize, but that's the girl I'm going to marry!" Apocryphal or not, he pursued Rhoda and she eventually fell for the young man who had enlisted in the navy at seventeen, was in Officer Training School, and had come back to Rensselaer Polytechnic Institute for a second degree. An officer and a gentleman, *and* Jewish! *Love lifts us up where we belong.*

Still, Rhoda made Peter wait until she finished school. They were engaged by March and married right after she graduated.

"Do you remember how you felt that day?"

"Nervous."

"Nervous because . . . ?"

"Just nervous. I think most brides are, were."

"I just can't get over all of you women marrying at such a young age," I say, still incredulous.

"And I can't get over all of you women marrying at such an old age," Rhoda witheringly returns. Advantage: Rhoda.

♠

Bette was in a bind. She had met and started dating Donald, a young doctor, during his residency in New York when she was a junior at Skidmore.

"We had a very passionate thing going on between us that was overwhelming. I thought I was the luckiest girl in the world."

I'm imagining Richard Chamberlain as Dr. Kildare, but Bette says he wasn't very handsome. His attraction was his personality.

"He was as bright as can be, very smart, charismatic, very exciting."

Bette desperately wanted to marry Donald. She was twenty-two and soon to become the last single girl on the face of the earth, or so it felt. Only Donald kept presenting obstacles. Bette suspects that he wanted a woman with means.

"Between us we had very little. I think he wanted his companion to come from a wealthy family. I was not that person."

She also knew that beyond his charisma he was a man wired with insecurities.

"First of all," Bette says, leaning forward in her chair, as if the revelation were still somehow taboo, "he was an illegitimate child."

The story Bette proceeds to tell is outright Dickensian: Donald's biological father never accepted him; he absolutely renounced any part of his parenthood. Part of Donald's drive to become a doctor, she says, was to show his father that he had done something important with his life, with no help from him. This desire culminated in a long-anticipated journey to his father's law office.

"He walked in and said, 'I am your son and I am now a doctor and I have a residency at Mount Sinai Hospital.' The father turned to him and said, 'I have no son. Please leave.'"

"Oh my god. How does a person recover from that?" I ask.

"I think there were a lot of reasons for him to have great insecurities."

In retrospect, Bette can see that the chemistry between them was all mixed up with that anger and disappointment. "And the relationship reflected that."

"What did you do?"

"I finally realized that there was not going to be a future with Donald."

Enter Arthur. He was a local boy working in his family's thriving fabric business. Smart as well, he was educated at the University of Chicago, where he was recruited at sixteen. A friend set them up on a blind date.

"I sensed someone who had both feet on the ground, wasn't a dreamer, was gentle and kind." Bette could tell that Arthur went into the family business under some duress; he was too smart to be behind a counter cutting fabric. Bette was also aware that her parents were hoping for a match.

"My family thought, oh my god, if she could ever marry into that family. And I sensed that."

The break with Donald wasn't clean, and Bette saw him on-again, off-again when she started seeing Arthur.

"Did he know that you were also dating the doctor?"

"He did," Bette tells me, "but he never said a word about it."

"Did the doctor know about Arthur?"

"He did," she says. "He could be quite snide, saying things like, 'What are you going to talk about at night, yards of calico?'"

Two male egos couldn't be more different. Donald: cocky, argumentative, arrogant, and insecure. Arthur: kind, laissez-faire, humble, and stalwart. After five months of dating, Arthur asked Bette to marry him. When she said no, he stopped calling. No drunk dialing, no just-happened-to-be-in-the-neighborhood ruses. Arthur took his lumps and kept his distance.

Every time Bette and Donald had broken up, Bette became more and more distraught, but after two months of near constant fighting, she finally broke it off for good. "I finally realized that there was no future with the doctor. I knew it was over." All the gray area cleared. Bette saw a future with Arthur and she knew she'd be a fool not to try again.

"Okay, I think it's time for me to marry Arthur Horowitz. I went down to the store on a Saturday, which was the busiest day, and I remember walking into the store and saying, 'If you'd still like to marry me, let's go to New York—leave the store right now—and buy an engagement ring, and get married.'"

Arthur dropped everything, and they went to the city to buy a ring.

"I bought this ring—*he* bought this ring."

Bette also admitted that she would have never married a poor man, couldn't fall in love with one. She remembers buying furniture as a newlywed in New York, Arthur writing a check for the couch, the chairs, and the dining room table. This was amazing to Bette, having grown up under her father's constant penny-pinching. Suddenly, here was a man who could write a check for anything she picked out. "I wasn't grabby. I was amazed, and grateful." Bette's father, upon first coming to his daughter's spacious three-bedroom house in Woodbridge, broke down in tears standing in the living room. "It was the first and only time I saw him cry."

Betty twists her engagement ring around her finger to show me the diamond. "I've worn it to this day."

♠

"I've told you about Eugene."

Yes, my mother has told me about Eugene Genovese a hundred times, the Italian boy she had a huge crush on. It's her West Side Story without the snapping. He was smart, outspoken, and a leader in the socialist movement American Youth for Democracy.

"Do you know what a Red Diaper baby is?" my mother asks in a pointed, accusatory way. She always assumes that a "young person" can't possibly know anything about the world pre-the-year-they-were-born.

"Yes, I know what a Red Diaper baby is," I say, full of annoyance.

"Okay, I didn't know. Just asking."

When Carl Bernstein published *Loyalties*, his memoir about being a red diaper baby, my mother, nearly sixty at the time, first divulged her youthful allegiances.

"I felt if a journalist of his stature could divulge his background, why couldn't I?"

There has always been some version of this war going on inside my mother: should she do what she really wants or conform, say what she really thinks or keep quiet, not risk offending anyone?

Of course, by then no one really cared.

I like to imagine my mother handing out leaflets like Barbra Streisand in *The Way We Were*. Or eschewing marriage and going to work on a kibbutz in Israel as she once dreamed, picking oranges from high up on a ladder in khaki pants and a cotton blouse tied in a knot at her midriff.

Like all of the Bridge Ladies, she would marry a Jewish boy— not a Chava among them, Tevye's youngest daughter in *Fiddler on the Roof*, who defies her father and marries a gentile. The first time I saw the musical I was stunned when Tevye refused his last chance to say good-bye to his beloved youngest daughter when they were forced to flee Anatevka. What kind of father would do that to his daughter? The Bridge Ladies would not test this. (Predictably, I would.)

Eugene Genovese went on to become a highly respected historian known for his Marxist perspective. My mother would sequester herself away with the reviews whenever he published a new book, nursing what I imagined must have been the delicious, unanswerable question: *what if?* But my mother is pure pragmatist, never once indulging my fantastical childhood questions: *What if you married Eugene? What if you didn't marry Daddy? What if I wasn't born!* No matter how much I begged her to wager an answer, contemplate an alternate scenario, to make believe just one time, she was unwavering, refused to play along, was wholly dismissive of the enterprise. Now, she shows me his picture in her high school yearbook, small as a postage stamp, and remarks on how handsome he was. All I see is a boy with an exceedingly high forehead and a tiara of curly hair. His inscription was deflating at best: *Dear Roz, You better come to more meetings. Best, Eugene.*

"Mom, were you hurt?"

"I can't remember."

"What do you mean you can't remember?"

"What do you want me to say?"

"It's not exactly a nice message. He's scolding you for not going to more meetings."

"What do you want me to say?"

We are different, my mother and I. She's not interested in the past, while I've nursed every romantic disappointment since the third grade when a boy raced by my desk and dropped a tiny, promotional bottle of Shalimar on it, only later confessing that he meant it for the girl sitting at the desk next to me and wanted it back.

Years later, when my mother discovered that Genovese returned to his Catholic roots, she was bitterly disappointed. He was no longer the man she remembered. My mother, down to her core, is a socialist and atheist, no matter how bourgeois she appears or how many tennis bracelets she wears.

We're in the kitchen, finishing our turkey sandwiches, when I ask my mother if she was a virgin when she married. She puts down what's left of her sandwich, disgusted, the crust like a crude smile.

"Why do you have to know that?"

"I want to know."

"Do you ask the other ladies?"

"Not directly."

"Then why me?"

"C'mon, Mom," I whine, my finely honed reportorial skills in full force. She clams up.

I had lost my virginity in high school on a summer trip to Israel with a youth group. I was sort of in love, but more I craved experience in ways I didn't fully understand, not realizing how much I wanted to separate and distance myself from my parents, especially my mother—no longer her little girl, no longer a little girl at all.

Most of the ladies admit to necking and some petting. Though I will later learn (please cover your ears if you don't want to be scandalized) that some of the ladies were sleeping with their intendeds before their wedding night. Once you were engaged, I discover, the ban was quasi-lifted though that was never spoken of. Engagement, it turns out, was the gateway to sex.

"Did your mother ever talk to you about sex?" I continue, trying another tack.

"No, never. It was a private thing."

Only then my mother pauses, "Well, I knew my parents were hot stuff."

"Hot stuff?"

She remembers her father coming up from behind her mother and embracing her. "She would scream, 'Murray, Murray!' meaning: not in front of the children." My mother gleaned two things from this: sex is private and that sex is hot stuff.

She learned about sex from reading *Studs Lonigan,* who sounds to me like the protagonist of a Harlequin romance, but the book turns out to be a Depression-era drama about an Irish boy on the South Side of Chicago who goes from being a good kid to a downtrodden alcoholic. When I remind my mother of this after having looked it up, she replies, "Well, it had sexy parts in it. What can I tell you?"

"So you slept with Dad before you married."

"Why are you obsessed with this?"

"Because this whole one-man thing, this saving-yourself business, I just can't fathom it."

By the time the boomers came of age, the sexual landscape had completely changed. There were girls in my high school who were waiting for their wedding night. We, the mighty experienced, looked down on them as if they were pitiable. Some girls wanted to be in love, others were looking to get it over with. I knew a few who were planning to lose their virginity on prom night. Some wanted to lose it before college but didn't manage to make it happen. They hoped no one in their freshmen dorm would detect their inexperience, and if asked point-blank they'd lie and take a sophisticated puff off a cigarette. I remember one girl who was so determined to lose her virginity before going to college that she steadied her sights on a hapless sophomore who thought he was just going out to the movies.

"The Pill changed everything," Bea once said, and she was right about that. She proudly told her kids that when she walked down the aisle, she deserved her white dress.

"Ma," they said. "That's too bad."

"C'mon, Mom. Just tell me," I whine again, shocked at my own childishness. When I sit down to talk with the other ladies, I act like an adult. When they clam up, I respect them. My mother picks at the frayed ends of a dishcloth, "Dad was just wonderful. I've told you before I liked everything about him and he always remained a great date his whole life. It was great going places with him. He always wanted the best seat, the best table. I just loved it. I loved the attention. I loved being chased, and he truthfully was the only one I ever had sex with. That is true."

Okay then.

"Do you think Dad was faithful?"

"Betsy, now you're really going too far."

For as long as I could recall, my mother would make the pronouncement that women who didn't know if their husbands were cheating didn't *want* to know. They couldn't afford to know is more like it. They didn't bury their heads in the sand so much as look the other way. What else could they do, with small children to care for and no means of support?

Apparently there were a lot of affairs in our town, including a much-gossiped-about, high-profile case where a woman hired a hit man to kill her husband's girlfriend. It's as if her violent and dramatic act was fueled, at least in part, by the tamped-down anger of every desperate housewife of Woodbridge. This woman wasn't a hero, but she wasn't a victim either. According to Bette, she went to prison and remarried when she came out, as if that's the moral of the story.

My mother won't budge on the subject of my father's fidelity.

"C'mon, what's the big deal?"

"Why do you want to know so badly?"

"I just want to know."

"Let's just say," my mother says, tossing her dish towel over her shoulder to both conclude our conversation and make an insouciant point, "I don't think he needed to."

Of the Bridge husbands, my father was the biggest gamble. He didn't have a college degree and started out as a truck driver in a cousin's lumberyard when my parents met and married. My mother recognized a hard worker; plus he was ambitious. And maybe more than that: he was decent. He hired the first black truck driver at the lumberyard. It wasn't as dramatic as the Dodgers hiring Jackie Robinson, but my father didn't back down even though it was an unpopular decision.

"It showed character," my mother is proud to add.

"How did you know he would be a good provider?"

"Because he was a hard worker."

I never saw them kiss or hold hands. Sometimes they seemed as chaste as Lucy and Ricky to me, though they didn't sleep in twin beds. Once in a great while they would do a little dance in our long hallway before going out or coming home from a party, a Lindy or a swing. These small bursts of affection, their bodies moving in rhythm together, excited me so much. It was living proof that they loved each other, a certain private energy passing between them.

After everyone had gone to bed on the night before my wedding, in a rare moment of vulnerability, I took my mother into my confidence and confessed that I didn't know if the marriage would last. Was I making a mistake going forward if I had these doubts? She knew that the off-again, on-again relationship with John over many years was the source of much happiness as well as heartbreak. We were sitting on the sectional couch in our den, with one section between us. The moment I confided in her, I regretted it. I was certain she would answer with one of her truisms, either "it is what it is" or my noncommittal favorite, "it will either work out or it won't." I wanted something more from her, something real.

She had knocked herself out making our wedding and I acted put upon the entire time. When she'd call me at the office and ask what color linens I wanted, I behaved as if I were the chairman of the board and she was interrupting me in the middle of a shareholder's meeting. When I called her back and said I wanted white on white tablecloths, she said she preferred color.

I told her do what she wanted; I didn't care. I refused to let her shop with me for my dress, crushing another mother-daughter ritual underfoot. And when she arranged for a stylist to come to our house the morning of the wedding to do everyone's hair and makeup, I refused to let the perfectly nice woman with her "tool belt" of makeup brushes touch my hair, or apply so much as a dab of rouge to my cheeks. It was my wedding day and I was still acting like a petulant child where my mother was concerned.

"What can I tell you, Shayna," my mother said. It was pet name, a Yiddish word for *beautiful*. "I think the marriage will last."

My mother, the most practical person on the planet, cast her vote on the side of love. While we were growing up, whenever my sisters and I would say we wanted to marry someone who was funny, she would say, "Good! Marry a clown." When I wanted to go Vermont with a boyfriend and run a B&B, she said, "I hope you'll enjoy scrubbing toilets for the rest of your life!"

When I asked her why she thought it would work, she said she believed that being married was different from being single. Marriage would change things. It would change us. Normally, I would have argued with her; the divorce rate itself was something like 50 percent. I would have discounted her advice, whatever it was, and written her off with it. What could she possibly know about my chances? About me? About John? She got up from the couch and said she was turning in, and urged me to follow suit.

"We have a big day," she said, not a hint of resentment at my immaturity over the last few months. Whatever I was trying to prove, that I was too cool to have the traditional wedding she planned, too indifferent to care about floral arrangements and place cards, hadn't stopped my mother from making a wedding Emily Post would have applauded. "You'll see," she said, and then kissed me good night on the top of my head.

♠

Back at Jackie's, the ladies settle in for Bridge. A large brown stinkbug grazes the screen inside the windows. It is slow moving, almost drunk in its staggered effort to evade getting squished in Jackie's paper towel. The den, where the ladies play Bridge, could double as an ethnographic gallery. The room is wall-to-wall, floor-to-ceiling masks from around the world decorated with horns, beaks, and raffia beards. Some are as large as canoes; others are as small as coconuts. There are shadow puppets, marionettes, masks with tongues, helmets, some with huge bulging eyes, and some with downcast eyes. Others are terrifying, comic, or ferocious. They could form a small army. Jackie and her husband have built this small museum-quality collection from their travels around the world. What are they doing here in Bethany, a million miles away from New Zealand and Papua New Guinea?

The ladies play at a table made of burl wood with a pretty inlay pattern of curlicues on the corners. Above, an eave with twelve masks, each bearing a different expression: mournful, fearful, sardonic, and so forth, watches over the game—benign gods. Jackie usually wears a three-pronged ring, two of the branches end in garnets, one in a pearl. I've never seen anything like it, and though it's bigger than anything I would wear, I find myself drawn to it and Jackie's ability to pull it off on her small hands always perfectly manicured with a creamy opalescent polish. She also accessorizes with the jewelry she and her husband have bought on their many trips around the world, including a silver cuff with large beads running down the center like balls of mercury that knocks against the Bridge table like a spirit at a séance.

The ladies drop their dollars and the game commences along with the familiar patter. The dealer always bids first, and usually, after they are done arranging their cards, one will ask "Who did this?," meaning who dealt. Only it always sounds more accusatory to me, as in "Who left the mayonnaise on the counter?" I've learned enough about Bridge by now to pull up a chair and observe the game, taking an actual interest in it, though I'm still baffled when the women make certain bids. I'd like to ask what they mean, but it would be wrong to talk and interrupt the bidding. I've started to learn about the most basic Bridge "conventions," which are used to either describe unusual hands or to enable more sophisticated communication between partners. My favorite conventions have names that sound like CIA special operations: The Puppet Stayman, The Jacoby Transfer.

I have also observed various tells among the ladies: Jackie quietly taps her fingernail on the table when she has a lot of points and is eager to bid. The more nervous Rhoda becomes the louder and more emphatically she snaps her tricks along the border of the table, like a schoolgirl snapping gum. Bette gets very quiet when she's anxious, and my mother more voluble. And Bea picks up speed as she collects her tricks, like a schoolboy racing around a playground. An hour into the game Jackie sets a plate of chocolates on the table. The ladies rear back as if they've been bitten by a snake.

When I tire of observing, I settle into Jackie's couch, her cat snuggles in beside me. Jackie says this is highly unusual; the cat doesn't like anyone besides her and Dick. Honestly, I don't have a way with animals, but I'm glad for any advantage it confers. Eventually I rouse myself and take my leave. I say good-bye to the ladies and thank Jackie again for lunch. "Bye, dear," my mother says, again in that formal tone, as if we are passengers on the *QE2* strolling on the deck, getting some air after supper.

Rhoda reminds me that next week's game is at Bea's. She is the secretary of the group. "Don't forget, Bridge is at Bea's," she says, and I think they've actually gotten used to having me around, maybe even like it.

CHAPTER 7

What to Expect

Periods of heavy rainfall hit the skylights with an explosive sound like a round of unexpected gunfire. My mother and I are in her living room today on the huge overstuffed corner couch with giant pink accent pillows. Her glass coffee table is massive, and the side chairs are stuffed and cinched so tightly they look like balloon animals. A chandelier over the dining room table is made up of vertically hanging crystal rods. It alternately looks like a huge spaceship or a tiny earring depending on which end of the telescope you're looking through.

"So, what's on the agenda?" My mother settles into the couch.

My mother is always eager to talk when I come over, as if she were a famous actress and I am Diane Sawyer. We have never really talked like this.

"I want to know about your infertility problems. When did you start trying?"

I've always known my mother had difficulty getting pregnant. On the rare occasion when she'd mention how long it took, it was only to emphasize how fortunate she felt to have us. It's one thing to get something you want, she'd say, another to get something you think you can't have. The way she explains it now: she didn't wait to get pregnant; rather she endured not getting pregnant.

"We never even thought about trying." My mother is emphatic. "It's what you did. Having a family was all part of the package." She looks at me, her famous eyebrow raised. Do I comprehend? I get it: no one was wondering about readiness, about completing a degree or climbing a mountain. If you were married, you were ready.

My mother tried for seven years. All her friends were getting pregnant, some having second and third children during those years.

"It was terrible for me. It was just awful. Everybody was having kids."

There was another woman in town named Marion who was also having trouble conceiving. They weren't particularly close, but her infertility problems also became known through the grapevine. When my mother heard that Marion got pregnant it came as a blow and a wake-up call. The following week my parents started the adoption process, filing papers with the Jewish Adoption Agency.

The truism "if you bring an umbrella it won't rain" worked its backward logic over my mother's womb. Once the adoption papers were filed, it happened. She missed three periods before it occurred to her that she might be pregnant. When she went to the doctor her suspicions were confirmed.

"I went sailing into the lumberyard to tell your father. I couldn't wait until he got home. And I was thrilled to have morning sickness," my mother says. "It confirmed the good news."

My mother loved shopping for maternity clothes and treated herself to the best. "I never felt better than when I was pregnant. End of story." Her contractions began a day before her father's birthday. She called him to say that she was trying to give him a birthday gift.

"He told me not to bother." *Classic.*

Her first child, a girl, arrived the next day, May 12, 1958. It was her father's birthday, and the day after Mother's Day.

Rhoda also had trouble getting pregnant. She and Peter moved twice when he was called back from the reserves during the Korean conflict. In Philadelphia, Rhoda first went to see an expert in the brand-new field of infertility. She discovered she had fibroids and that the only treatment was surgery. In Pittsburgh they consulted another doctor and tried artificial insemination, but they would leave the city childless. It's a small detail, but Rhoda still remembers the marble windowsills of Pittsburgh coated with a fine layer of coal dust. Like chalk off a blackboard, they were easier to clean; her disappointment more difficult to erase.

The young couple would finally land in New Haven, where Rhoda was happily within driving distance of her parents. She sought the help of yet another doctor, who recommended having the fibroids removed. Hopes up, hopes dashed. The doctor told Rhoda that she would need a hysterectomy in five years.

"So we began to actively pursue adoption," Rhoda says, trying to stay upbeat.

"We started with the Jewish Family Service. They told us quite clearly that they average a baby a year. So that was devastating."

Eventually Peter and Rhoda were able to make arrangements through her doctor. She is sure to add that they had an attorney and followed all the protocol.

"And that is how we had our Beth." Then, like many new mothers, Rhoda confesses, "I had never handled a baby in my entire life. I was so frightened. I didn't even know how to hold her. Peter was better at it than I. He took to it right away. I was frightened out of my wits. Really frightened."

Eighteen months later, Peter heard about another newborn that was going to be given up for adoption. Rhoda was floored. She didn't think she could handle another child so soon. Beth was an extremely active little girl, and the thought of two children seemed overwhelming.

Peter said, "We already have one child, what difference does it make?"

Rhoda's voice fills with a blend of disbelief mixed with a tinge of indignation, "I'll never forget that response."

As Rhoda suspected, the responsibility and work of having a newborn and an eighteen-month-old were overwhelming. "I still remember leaving the dishes in the sink and staggering up the stairs to bed, completely worn out."

Rhoda's mother had set the table every night, served a home-cooked meal, and wiped down every last dish. The same for her relatives in New Haven. Her aunt was a fastidious homemaker and gracious hostess. Her way of doing things became famous as "The Sosner Way." Rhoda adored her aunt, was happy to adopt the Sosner Way, which she considered the gold standard, and expected no less from herself. Knowing Rhoda, I can only imagine the defeat she felt going to bed with those dishes in the sink, knowing she would have to face them, and her own shortcomings as a new mother, come morning.

"We never planned anything." Bette insists that none of their three babies were planned. "I know couples plan for their future now, when they're going to have a family, they plan for retirement. We never really planned anything." This is not to say that Arthur and Bette were free spirits, dropping acid and space dancing at Grateful Dead concerts. From the moment they moved into their town house as newlyweds they fully expected to start a family. Following weeks of a cold, Bette went to the doctor and discovered she was pregnant. She stopped at a drugstore on the way home and called Arthur from a pay phone. She picked out beautiful fabrics from the store and had maternity clothes made. Like all the ladies, Bette was on a need-to-know basis with her doctor. He asked her and Arthur to come into the office during her seventh month and showed them pictures. "This is stage one of giving birth, this is stage two, this is how you look and feel in stage four and five." When Bette's water broke, she called her doctor and said, "You know that picture of stage three? I'm in it."

The young couple moved into their first home in November and their oldest daughter was born in December. Two more children, another daughter and a son, would follow in succession. Bette was happily cast in her new role: mother.

A red cardinal pops up from the bushes like a jack-in-the-box and hits the window with a thump like a small cry for help. He's been here for a week already, and Jackie can't figure out what he wants or if he's hurt. I flinch every time he crashes against the glass. When I visit with Jackie now, we no longer sit in the living room. We've moved into the mask-filled den and share the same couch. We're not curling up under a blanket and watching *Gilmore Girls*, but I think Jackie has gotten more comfortable with me and me with her.

I can hear Dick rattling around in the kitchen.

The bird suddenly crashes into the window with more force, and I startle.

"Oh, it's that stupid bird! What does he want?" Jackie loves all animals, but now she sounds annoyed.

Jackie didn't get pregnant for a while, almost as long as my mother, but she doesn't recall getting upset. *Concerned* is the word she uses. She and Dick got checked out and everything was okay. Jackie was twenty-eight when she got pregnant with her first child, a girl born on December 7, and a boy followed soon after. I ask Jackie what she remembers from her pregnancy.

"Well, I didn't have to wear maternity clothes until my sixth month. So I was really only in maternity clothes for three months."

"Oh, were you a tiny little thing?"

"I suppose."

"You didn't show until the end?

"I guess."

"Barely gained any weight?"

"No, I didn't gain much."

"You bitch!"

Jackie looks at me askance.

Too soon?

A few minutes later, two lamps set on automatic timers pop on as if to say time's up.

When Bea told Carl that they should have children, he said, "Why?"

It's not clear if Carl was joking, but Bea provides the punch line regardless: "I should have listened, Betsy."

They waited until Carl finished medical school and finally had a "few pennies to rub together." Because Bea is the most frank of the women, I asked what she used for birth control.

"Diaphragm."

Bea was a sophomore at the University of Louisville when she met Carl at a party. He was an ambitious medical student who was putting himself through school playing piano at clubs and weddings. He asked for her number. When he phoned a few days later and said "Hi, this is Carl Phillips from the other night," Bea asked him if he was the blond. He wasn't. *Awkward!* Then he asked her out for Saturday night, but before Bea could answer he said, "If you don't want to go out it's all right."

Bea wasn't husband hunting. Fort Knox was thirty miles away and supplying a steady stream of soldiers. "I just wanted to dance, and we had a good time. The war was very far away. It's a dreadful thing to say, but we had a good time."

"Any crushes?"

"I imagine I did."

"Necking? That stuff?"

"Oh, sometimes, sure."

Bea can't recall what she and Carl did on their first date. "Isn't that funny?"

"Sparks?"

"I don't know. It wasn't instantaneous, no."

But he called her again. After a time, he'd come over on a Sunday. Bea would make supper while Carl studied. I asked Bea if her mother approved. "At first she wasn't quite sure he was Jewish, with a name like Phillips. Remember, I was a Bernstein. But then she did like him. Carl was very likable. More so than I."

Bea got pregnant right away.

"When I walked into the office, I told the gynecologist that I was pregnant. And he said, 'No you're not.' Then he examined me and said, 'By god, you're pregnant.'"

"How did you know?"

"The same way everybody does, Betsy."

"You missed your period?"

"That's right," Bea says, as if I were the dumbest kid in sex ed.

Bea and Carl had three children: Nancy, their first, followed by two boys. When I asked Bea about the deliveries, she laughs and points her finger at me, her crystal bracelets scattering up and down her thin wrist. "I delivered those babies in twenty minutes."

"What about when Nancy was a newborn, were you scared of taking care of her?"

Bea says she loved getting up at three in the morning to feed the baby. "The phone didn't ring, there was no one around. You're just alone with the baby, and you know what—I liked it."

"Did you feel the maternal instinct kick in?"

Usually Bea is quick on the draw, but she takes a moment before answering. "What is a maternal instinct?"

♠

Bridge is back at the Athenian. The first order of business today is who is making seder. The ladies want to know if my mother and Bette are cooking fish this year; they may be the last two Jewish grandmothers in the tri-state area who still make home-made gefilte fish. I'm scandalized when Bette admits she no longer makes the fish, hasn't made it for a few years. Worse: she buys it at Costco and doctors it with boiled carrots!! She insists no one knows except her mother in heaven.

How this tan and gray mixture the shape of a miniature meteor has been promoted to delicacy status is something I will never understand. All throughout our lives, my mother would first serve the fish to my father. No one would take a bite until he sampled it like El Exigente in the Savarin coffee commercials. All eyes would be on him as he swallowed, his eyes bulging from the sharp horseradish he slathered on the fish. When he pronounced that it was good, the people would dance in the streets, widows waved white handkerchiefs from balconies.

The ladies say I should learn how to make the fish from my mom. *Not happening.* She is now the last of the Bridge Ladies to make it from scratch. In fact, she uses Bette's mother's recipe, which calls for three kinds of freshwater fish: carp, whitefish, and pike. They all need to be special ordered, and according to my mother no one knows how to properly fillet fish any longer. She often curses the men and women who, over the years, have poorly filleted her fish. "I'd like to cut his hands off," she'd say with the same gusto reserved only for hairdressers who "butcher" her. When the ladies repeat that I should cook with my mother and learn the ropes, the subtext is not lost on me: she won't be here forever.

♠

My mother is already wearing her black apron with the red, yellow, and green pepper decorations when I arrive. No sooner am I in the door than she starts muttering to herself about getting it right as she bustles around her kitchen. The ingredients cover the countertops, and two enormous stockpots are on her electric stove, which looks like a rectangle of black ice.

"Really, Mom, after all these years you don't have any confidence about getting it right."

"That's right," she says, and "Okay, make a prayer," and then with some added vim, "Let's rock and roll."

If you say so.

She begins to paw through the packages of fish. This year, miraculously, a young man named Brion (she notes the spelling of his name) at the A&P has done a magnificent job filleting the fish.

"He should live and be well," my mother says, an expression of her deepest gratitude.

She looks up at me from her work of separating the packages of fillets, fish skins, and heads. "I wanted to tip him. Do you think I should have?"

"I think everyone appreciates a tip."

"But is it appropriate?"

It's the word that guides my mother's life. The breath she takes between every thought and action. In this case, I know what she means. Tipping at a supermarket—is it done?

Brion has marked every package with its contents. Apparently, no one has ever done this in the entire history of the world. "I'm going back and tip him."

The fish has to be dry. To that end my mother rolls out fields of paper towel and pats the fish down. Then she starts the great hunt for the recipe; it's either stuck inside a cookbook, her basket of papers—some of which date back to the mid-1960s—or in a folder tucked away somewhere.

"Here it is," she says, proud of the record time with which she has located it inside a FedEx envelope that has been raggedly torn open with the word RECIPES scrawled on one side. The recipe looks like a panel from the Dead Sea Scrolls: stained many times over with fish grease, darkened with age spots like the back of an older person's hand, annotated with figures for doubling the recipe, and a smattering of unidentified *schmutz*. At the top: *From the Kitchen of Sylvia Cohen.* This is Bette's mother, universally acknowledged throughout New Haven and its environs as one of the great all-time cooks.

"Now we take out the eyes," my mother says with too much gusto. And then without warning she raises a knife, Norman Bates–style, and plunges it into the eye of the fish. A wave of nausea moves through me, and I feel like I might faint. I run into the den, plop down on the couch, and pull out my phone while my mother continues her gouging. I know she has moved on to the next step when I hear the whirring of the Cuisinart's blade.

"I'm grinding the fish," she calls out.

"It smells disgusting," I maturely offer, coming back into the kitchen.

"Then go home."

My mother cranks open a window, tacit acknowledgment of the fish stink.

"You take a handful," my mother says, reaching into the fish and matzoh meal mixture, "and pat it like so, into balls."

Ground, the fish looks like brains. "There's no way I'm touching that."

"Why don't you go home, you look exhausted," my mother says, though I have clearly exhausted her patience. I know this was supposed to be some big bonding opportunity and I want to get into the spirit, but it's too artificial. We both know I'm not going to make gefilte fish, it's doubtful I'll even make a seder. A big part of why she goes to all this effort is so that my daughter, half-Jewish and half-Catholic and not raised in either religion, will have an experience of Judaism. She is nervous that Catholicism with its Christmas gifts and Easter bunnies will win out. I'm not sure how she thinks she stands a chance with gefilte fish and plagues, but nevertheless every year she rolls out the Haggadahs and seder plate.

"Now the moment of truth," she says, undeterred in her work. Will the layers of fish balls fit atop the heads, bones, and skins at the bottom of the pot? She layers them like bricks, right up to the top of the pot. She consults the recipe, biting her finger, and says, "Oh yeah," then sprinkles two teaspoons of sugar around the edges, gently urging on the fish, "come on, come on." Then she turns to me and says, without a flicker of irony, "Now, we pray."

We stay in the kitchen until the pot boils, at which point she will reduce the heat. My mother stands over the stove, fiddling with the knobs on the control panel. "This goddamn stove."

I know I should get going, get back to work. But I linger, plop down in "my chair" at the kitchen table, where I sat for every family meal. Eventually she joins me.

"I really can't believe you're still so insecure about making the fish."

"I'm insecure about a lot of things."

"Such as."

"Well, I never feel I'm smart enough."

"Like when?"

"Well, I always felt very insecure meeting people from good schools. Of course in my old age I realize that many of them are horses' asses."

Tru dat.

"And I never appreciated CCNY, which was called the poor man's Harvard. If you must know, I feel like a little gray mouse most of the time. It's only recently that I've started to speak up."

Then she remembers taking a Rorschach test in college. Her friend, a psychology student, administered the test and declared that she was either a genius or an idiot.

"That's quite a range," I say.

Only then my mother confesses that she lied, which "might" have skewed the results.

"Why would you lie on a Rorschach test?"

"Well, a lot of the pictures looked phallic. If a flower looked like a vagina, I wasn't going to say that in front of my friend."

"I guess that would skew results," I say, dumbfounded. Who lies on a Rorschach test?

Then the lid on the pot starts to dance, and steam rises like a volcano.

"Now we're getting somewhere," she says and jumps up. "This is just right."

Then liquid pours over the side and sizzles like hot oil on the stovetop.

"Shit, I knew this was going to happen. This goddamn stove, do you see what I'm talking about?" She says this as fish juice continues to cascade down the sides.

When the crisis abates and my mother sits back down, I ask her whom she thinks I take after.

"Oh, your father," she says with no hesitation. "Don't you think, your work ethic, your humor?"

"Well, what did I get from you?"

"I don't see many qualities."

"What about writing?"

"I never wrote a word. I just wanted to."

"Why didn't you?"

"Fear. I never wanted to expose myself."

"What about your generosity?"

She poo-poos this.

I remind my mother that she pays for her grandchildren's private school tuition, that she lavishes them with shopping trips and Broadway shows in New York. She buys them cars when they graduate! The ladies joke that they wish she were their *bubbe*.

"Maybe, I suppose. It's funny how you have to fish it out of me."

"What about your ethics, your morals. Don't you think you gave us that?"

She isn't sure, or at least not willing to take credit.

My mother always emphasized the mitzvoth, the 613 commandments Jews are supposed to observe, in short: good deeds. When she brings a meal to a sick friend or writes a check to the synagogue, she thinks of these acts in the context of the mitzvoth. But for her these acts of kindness are based only in the belief that it's the right thing to do, not because God commanded. You didn't do good deeds because you would be punished if you failed to, but because in your own heart you knew it was right. It was this she taught us, by example.

I want to leave, but I'm stalling. What do I want? What am I waiting for? Who is this person with her fish show, her crazy apron, and sneakers the color of gravy? My mother tells me to scram; we're done. She wants me to be home when my daughter gets back from school.

"Mom, she's sixteen."

"What difference does that make?"

My mother goes back to the stove, shifts her weight from foot to foot, and adjusts the heat, grumbling to herself the entire time.

"Mom, are you talking to the fish?"

"Really," she says. "Hit the road."

I suddenly feel achingly sad sitting in my mother's bright kitchen, in my designated chair. Everything so familiar: the late-afternoon sun striking her metal cabinets painted canary yellow, the wide pass-through from our kitchen to our den, which often doubled as the bar or buffet when my parents had parties, now piled with magazines and books, the White Pages and my mother's monthly calendar. The white boxes are crowded with notations of doctors' appointments, lectures, plays, lunch and dinner dates, and her standing weekly nail appointment with her Russian manicurist Fania. And every

Monday, as if she wouldn't remember, written in her beautiful script: *Bridge.*

When my father died, my mother made it her policy to accept every invitation extended to her. These keep her afloat, but it's the parties she lives for, the bar mitzvahs, weddings, and graduations, these milestones like a string of lights, a bright constellation in an empty sky.

When I finally get up to leave, we are awkward as always. I give her a peck on the cheek at the door, then she suddenly and uncharacteristically pulls me close and hugs me like a normal person, the way I hug my daughter. The way you might expect mothers and daughters to embrace.

"Whoa," I say, "let's take this slow."

"If I had my druthers I would smother you."

"Why don't you?"

She steps back, gives this question a moment's thought.

"It's not appropriate."

We laugh a little at this, The Duchess of Protocol and me.

"All right, get out of here, I've got to check on the fish."

From my car, I can see my mother tottering down the hall to finish her voodoo over the gefilte fish. I know the downstairs freezer is already filled with matzoh ball soup in massive Tupperware containers, brisket and kugel wrapped in foil. She has all this preparation down to a science. Once, she looked a little hurt when my husband innocently asked if she ever eats fresh food. Months ahead of a Jewish holiday, she'll randomly exclaim, "Well, my brisket's in the freezer." And I tease her about this, too, her mania for freezing holiday dishes, never truly appreciating the amount of work it takes. She's eighty-three and makes every dish for every holiday by herself. When I ask what I can bring, she always says the same thing: a salad and your marvelous dressing (oil and vinegar). I suddenly feel as if I should have paid more attention to the cooking lesson instead of acting like a child.

I remember watching my mother emerge from her bedroom on a night when she and my father were going out, all dressed up in heels and hose, a skirt or dress that cinched her waist, her pearl choker like a ring around the moon. I'd watch her from my perch in the kitchen, walking trancelike as she fastened the back of an earring. I'd like to be small again, just for a little while, and feel close to her. I never really appreciated my mother. I never appreciated myself.

CHAPTER 8

Ruffing It

When I repeat Beginner One, I recruit a friend who also happens to work in the same building as the Bridge Club. When Matty arrives, like me, he is astonished to see this whole subculture and is amazed that it exists just a few floors below the publishing company where he works. I feel a little anxious having lured him here after he expressed only mild interest in Bridge at a dinner party. He seems a little nervous and takes a handful of M&M's while we wait for the teacher. I have no idea if it's going to be Barbara or Jeff (who I learn are married), or someone else. I'm hoping for someone else. I want to start fresh, and I promise myself that this time I will read the book we've been given, that I will study the handouts, and try to come to the supervised sessions to practice.

Ellen blows in as if on a breeze. She is light on her feet, with a flowing scarf and zeros in on us as her new pupils. We introduce ourselves and she tells us another woman will be joining us. She asks if we are a couple, and we quickly disabuse her in that embarrassed way when you are incorrectly paired. *Us, married? No!* She urges us to sit as she disappears to get some coffee. I can tell Matty is nervous. We joke that we'll be able to play in the old-age home. We wish our spouses would learn, but they show no interest. Ellen returns and looks at the clock. Our third has not yet arrived, "Let's give it a few more."

I immediately feel comfortable with her. She has short white hair, a raspy voice, and a cough that sounds like an engine starting. Most important, she doesn't seem world-weary at the prospect of teaching beginners. When she asks why we want to learn Bridge, Matty, noncommittal, says he always thought it would be interesting. When I confess that I am repeating Beginner One, she says that's good, that lots of people do. This makes me feel infinitely better.

Finally, the third arrives somewhat frantic. She immediately launches into a litany of all the ways in which public transportation failed her. She struggles with her coat, her hair gets caught in her necklace. Then she drops her bag and some of the contents spill out. Ellen tells her to take her time, that it's okay. When she finally sits down, still muttering about the train, we introduce ourselves, and she says she is Emily. She looks roughly our age, has red hair that might be natural; her fingernails seem embedded in her fingertips. I don't have a hand fetish per se, but playing bridge does draw the eye, and I can't stop looking at her little shell fingernails.

Matty concentrates as Ellen goes over the basics: how many points to open, how many points to respond. Emily makes a series of quiet baby sucking noises as she listens. I simply like the sound of Ellen's voice. It's musical and warm. She has a New York accent, but I can't quite place the borough. She stops frequently to ask if we follow. As she explains, I finally see that bidding is like working a combination lock. You and your partner take turns bidding in an effort to ascertain the combined worth of your hands (which is expressed in point count and the number of trumps). She mentions the number twenty-six, which is the number Barbara put on the board the first night. Now, I get it: ideally we want to have twenty-six points *between* us. With twenty-six points and eight pieces of trump, we are well positioned to win the number of tricks necessary to fulfill the contract, in this case ten tricks or "game."

Ellen emphasizes that we simply have to memorize these numbers. No way around it. Not only did I fail to memorize my equations when I was in elementary school, I failed a second time, quizzing my daughter with her flash cards.

Emily retrieves a beginner book on Bridge from her bag and starts to consult it as Ellen speaks. It's not clear if she is trying to check Ellen's accuracy or what, but it's distracting and annoying, even disrespectful. Ellen finally asks her to put it away. Emily mumbles something like it's okay and keeps reading it. Matty and I exchange glances. Is she for real?

Ellen tells her again to put it away. We're going to play a hand.

We fumble through a round of bidding with the help of Ellen's instructive prompts and begin to play the hand. When it's Emily's turn to discard she draws her knees up to her chest and twists her torso as if she were Houdini about to escape the confines of a safe. Matty and I can barely look at each other.

After a reasonable amount of time, Ellen says, "Play a card, see what happens."

Emily is still struggling mightily and enters into a staring contest with her cards. I've witnessed this before. It's not good.

"Just play it," Ellen says. "We're learning."

Emily doesn't respond.

"Why don't you try the queen of Hearts?"

Emily glares at Ellen. She has not yet figured out that Ellen knows exactly what is in our hands.

When Matty trumps the queen, Emily gets upset.

"I knew I shouldn't have played that." Her voice is rich with accusation.

Matty has the deeply satisfied look of a person who has discovered the power of trumping. *Take that!*

"I love ruffing," Ellen says with gusto.

"Ruffing" is another term for trumping. This is when you are void in the suit that's been led and can win the trick by playing a card from the trump suit. In order to do this successfully, and not be out-trumped, you must also keep track of the thirteen cards in the trump suit, especially the honors. I can tell that Matty is picking it up. Numbers are his friends. Ellen also sees that Matty has potential. He need only make a mistake once and then is able to correct it the next hand.

When the lesson is over, Ellen gives us handouts with little quizzes. She tells us it takes time, asks if we had fun.

A collective yes! Though we all look exhausted from concentrating so hard, heads swimmy, Bridge brain.

"Good," she says. "That's all that matters."

Then, as Matty gets up, Ellen puts her hand on his shoulder and says, "You have card sense."

Matty, humble, says, "Really?"

"Yes, you definitely do."

What about me? I thought I had card sense. Okay, this game is kicking my ass, but my father had tremendous card sense, and since I resemble him in almost every way, doesn't it follow that I also have card sense? Mingy, I tell myself that Ellen only complimented Matty so that he would keep coming, though I know she's right.

Matty, Emily, and I get into the elevator in a dull silence. Then Emily wonders aloud about her train, and I see that she is one of these people oblivious to how little other people care about the mechanics of her life. When she shuffles off into the night, Matty and I are like, whatever.

The night air feels good.

"What did you think?" I ask.

"I liked it, I think."

♠

In addition to the lessons, we are meant to come to the Bridge Club for at least two sessions of supervised play; these are part of the package. I never made it during my first round of lessons, though we were reminded that we wouldn't improve with lessons alone. When I arrive, people are already parked at tables, some eating lunch from the buffet. Why, at fifty-three years old, is it still so hard to say: Excuse me, is anyone sitting here?

I sit by myself. The room fills and grows noisy. No one joins my table and I start to feel desperate. Just then the Keebler Elf arrives. Happy day! He waves and bounces right over. We both confer on how nervous we are to play, then giggle with our anxiety. Two more men come over and ask if they can join us. Yes! Yes!

The younger man, thirtyish, is wearing a leather jacket and a high school insignia ring with an amber stone. He has a crew cut, a cleft chin, and a day's stubble. In an effort to make chit-chat before the session begins, I ask why he's learning Bridge. He answers, without making eye contact, that he codes and that people have suggested he might like the game. He volunteers that he spends too much time alone playing video games; he is "forcing" himself to try something more social, though from his rigid body language it looks as if he'd prefer to be at home with his joystick. *Why am I always seated next to the Travis Bickles of the world?*

The other man is older, has a big hard stomach, and seems oblivious to all the cookie and pretzel crumbs that gather on its shelf. He has a classic Jewish name from a bygone era like Al, or Lou, or Hen, and I loved him for that alone. He reminds me of the butcher at the Jewish deli in New Haven who gave us free pretzel logs when my mother shopped there, his apron stained with the blood of kosher meat and a box of marbled halvah crumbling on the counter. I don't know what percentage of Bridge players at the Manhattan Bridge Club are Jewish, but let's just say it seems like a lot.

Ellen brings a stack of duplicate boards to each table and tells us to start. Then she recognizes me and says hi and nods encouragingly. She seems glad that I've heeded her advice and come to the session. At any point we are allowed to call her over and get advice on bidding or playing the hand. She floats from table to table, responding to a nearly constant string of questions. Our table is more reserved. I wonder if it's a guy thing, men not being able to ask for directions.

We start slowly, taking our time with bidding. The Elf and I are partners and neither of us have enough points to bid and happily pass. Travis and Pupik arrive at a bid of four Spades. I know this means they have to take ten tricks (which is called "game") and that the trump suit is Spades. Travis Bickle becomes frustrated when it's the Elf's turn to discard. He wiggles from side to side and hums as he tries to figure out what to throw. Travis eggs him on, prompts him with rudimentary questions: Can you follow suit? Can you trump? The Elf touches one card after another, slightly yanking each one, as if to discard it, then taps it back and starts pondering what card to throw all over again.

Then Travis does the unthinkable. He leans over, looks at the Elf's hand, points to a card, and says, "That one."

When the Elf doesn't immediately comply, Travis circles the table with his eyes. He is looking for some kind of acknowledgment from the older man and me that this situation is untenable. I want to stick up for my partner, but I'm afraid of Travis. His leg is jackhammering beneath the table, the floor rumbling like the telltale signs before an earthquake. Then, without warning, Travis reaches back over the Elf, dangles his hand like a mechanical claw over his cards, snatches the card from his hand, and slaps it down on the table. I'm in shock. It's worse than rude. Under any other circumstances, this behavior would likely get a player expelled. But when I look over at the Elf he's shoving a chocolate chip cookie in his mouth whole, happily relieved.

When it's Travis's turn to discard, he tilts his seat back, legs spread wide, and flicks a card into the center of the table as if he were an outlaw, gun cocked, ready for a shoot-out on a dusty main street. In other words, the guy's a douche, but I find him fascinating. He's a classic New York loner, strangely extravagant, and always good theater, so long as he doesn't attack me for throwing the wrong card or making a bad bid. Next to the Elf I probably look like Omar Sharif.

Later, when I blow an easy hand, he asks me if I am an English major.

"Yes," I say. "How did you know?"

He looks away in disgust and says, "Figures."

♠

Over time, I meet all kinds of people at the Manhattan Bridge Club, though one of the things I like most about playing here is the relative anonymity preserved around the Bridge table. In most New York settings, what you do is who you are. And from there a million tiny judgments fall. Not so much at Bridge. The only thing you have to impress other people with is how well you play a hand. In doesn't matter if you are a math teacher or a banker. You could be playing with the secretary of state or the replacement drummer for Mötley Crüe. The size of your portfolio is inconsequential if you fail to pull trump.

I once played with a woman with Louise Brooks–style bangs and Philip Johnson spectacles, round and black as tires. Her partner was dressed completely in leopard prints including her ballet flats, her eyebrows were plucked in the shape of the golden arches. They could have been extras in *Gatsby*. I imagined they would be flamboyant, but they were quiet, efficient players, showed almost no emotion win or lose, flat-liners, all their energy spent concentrating. The social aspects of the game didn't interest them very much. My partner that day could have been Coco Chanel's younger sister, or an Italian screen star. Her accent and age were impossible to pin down. Her clothes were made of crinkled silk, her rings were as big and bright as jelly candies and swam about on her thin fingers, her knuckles like horse knees protruding with age. When she liked her hand, she folded the cards into her palm and "innocently" looked around the room, as if she hadn't a care in the world. When she didn't like them, her lips gathered in a pouch of disgust and she stared into the center of the table.

The most annoying duo I played with was a mother-son team. The mom was corporate in her tailored suit, patent leather pumps, and Hermès scarf. She had an armload of stacked bracelets that could rival Nefertiti and stackable rings, too, bands of diamonds, sapphires, and rubies. The boy looked about fourteen, with Bieber bangs, braces, and a faded Dartmouth T-shirt. I pegged him for a STEM genius, friendless, bored with advanced physics, and slightly aggressive. I figured his mother was looking for activities that could hold his interest. I wasn't fooled by the kid's pimples or braces. He was a killer and he was obnoxious. He openly yawned when I took a long time to bid and laughed every time I made a mistake. And when he won, he fist-pumped as if he'd made a big point at Wimbledon. No wonder he didn't have any friends.

You can feel it: everyone at the Manhattan Bridge Club has a reason for coming. There are widows, divorcées, retired people, people between jobs. It's a game that attracts people in transition, looking for something to fill the time. It's for geniuses on the spectrum, savants, nerds. Accountants take to the game! It's for moms, empty nesters, and the chronically underemployed. It's for people who like the quasi-sociability of the game, or like me have an addictive personality. Something else I've observed: Bridge players are deeply competitive, no matter how much they protest. Ellen is fond of saying that people cheat even when no money is involved!

♠

"You have to play and play and play," Ellen says on the night of our last lesson. I know it's true. It's the only way to remember, for the knowledge to accrue and stick. On the last hand of the night, it's my turn to bid, and I freeze. Ellen asks me what I need to overcall. This is when you bid after one of the opponents has made an opening bid. *Overcall, overcall.* I know what it is, I even know there's a nifty trick for remembering it, but I can't call it up.

"Five-and-dime," she says. "Five of a suit and ten points."

"What is wrong with me?" I say in disgust.

"I wish I were a better teacher," Ellen says, defeated.

"Oh my god it's not you," I say. "I smoked way too much weed in high school."

Ellen laughs at this. But I still feel terrible.

Ellen asks if Matty is going to continue with lessons. He says he'll think about it. Emily is talking to her pocketbook. Me, I'm not sure what to do. I think I should try to find some lessons closer to home. Observing the ladies play on Mondays is good, but I need to play. I need a game.

CHAPTER 9

Welcome to the Club

In the Jewish tradition, part-custom, part-superstition, you don't buy clothes or the crib until the baby is born. I don't get it. Isn't it better to expect that things will go right? To bring a baby home to a pretty room with a crib already assembled? I've asked my mother to explain many times over the years, perplexed why Jews maintain this tradition.

"Jewish people. What can I tell you?"

My mother remembers running around like a "lunatic" furnishing the nursery after my sister was born, mostly fueled by intense anxiety. This longed-for child whose arrival was as miraculous as finding a babe amid the reeds, wasn't thriving. She was projectile vomiting, losing weight, and constantly crying. "It was really hard and really exhausting," my mother says apologetically.

"Finally, it was diagnosed as something called pyloric stenosis, some kind of blockage to the intestines."

I had always been fascinated by my older sister's scar, a horizontal line above her belly button that folds in on itself like pursed lips. No one ever talked about it and she always kept it hidden, never wore two-piece bathing suits, dressed and undressed modestly to keep it from view. When I was in a brief preteen UFO abduction phase, I imagined it might be an alien implant and then eventually I forgot all about it. Now, when I ask my mother exactly what happened, she looks shocked.

"You really don't know?"

"Not really."

"I just can't believe that."

My sister needed surgery, and the doctor reassured my parents that it was as simple as an appendectomy. Still, it was surgery on an infant, and my mother admits that she fled. "It was Dad who went for hours and hours and fed her in the hospital. I'm sure I went once a day, but I'm telling you I can remember running around."

After the surgery, when they brought Nina home from the hospital, it was a Polish cleaning lady who appeared as an oracle to my mother: "This little chicken come September she *vay* ten pounds." And just as she predicted, September came and the baby weighed ten pounds. She was thriving. Disaster averted. My mother had a healthy baby, a devoted husband, and the life she always dreamed of.

Then my mother stops talking. A brass letter opener is on the table, and she turns it over and over. I sort of know what comes next, though over the years I have only been privy to a few details; only under duress has she shared with me a highly selective version of her postpartum depression.

"Mom, can you tell me about it?"

Now she takes the letter opener and brushes it back and forth in her palm, as if buttering toast.

"I couldn't understand what was happening, how it could happen."

How could her dream of seven years come to this? A little baby was just beginning to thrive, a ten-pound chicken just starting to squawk? My mother couldn't have possibly known that a book she'd loved in high school, Charlotte Perkins Gilman's *The Yellow Wallpaper*, would be a cruel prophecy of her own postpartum depression. Only my mother wasn't locked into a yellow room. She got up every day, fed the baby, took her on walks. She functioned, but the world was yellow, the yellow of Van Gogh, the yellow of illness.

The sun slips below the tops of the trees. The kitchen became gloomy, but neither of us moves to turn on the light. I stare at the enormous ceramic bowl on the kitchen table filled with mail: bills, subscriptions, bulletins from the synagogue and senior center and thank-you notes (no one is held in higher esteem in my mother's eyes than the author of a well-crafted thank-you note). It's her pyre, which she lovingly tends to year after year, never throwing anything away. I suppose my sisters and I will weed through it someday. Though it, too, will only tell the partial story of a woman who lived in a house for fifty years and was good and kind, generous and furious, who would sooner implode than say one word about the depression that put her on a long dark wave and nearly killed her.

"I was very, very alone. Having my baby, I was very much alone. It was tedious. It was tiring. Your father did everything, bathing her, feeding her."

I see my father then, working all day, coming home and bathing the baby, still in his clothes from the lumberyard, his hunter green slacks and matching shirt, the white patch with his name stitched in red thread, his sleeves rolled to keep them from getting wet.

For all the years of trying to crack my mother open, I now feel clumsy and sad. I get up and look inside the refrigerator, though I know well its grim contents: sodium-free, fat-free cottage cheese, lactose-free milk, a bag of oranges, a half-filled bottle of white wine from Passover, a bag of hardened Craisins, and in the door a bottle of Diet Coke.

"Oh, you have Diet Coke," I say, delighted, as if finding a stash of pot from my youth.

My mother puts the letter opener back on her pile, looks at her nails, then at me.

I sit down with my flat Coke and try again.

"Did it happen all at once or little by little?"

"I don't know. Maybe it was little by little."

"Was it a blackness, or numbness? Did you have a lot of dark thoughts?"

"I withdrew from things. I didn't want to see anybody, I didn't want to do anything."

"Did you talk to your mother about it?"

"No, not really. She was very worried and upset, I know she was, but she didn't talk about it or ask about it."

"Were you hiding it from her?"

"No, I don't think I was able to hide it. I really don't remember that much about it. I really don't."

"Did Dad try to draw you out?"

"He was very, very supportive and helpful, he really was. I'm sure he was scared, but he always soldiered on."

As I've grown more comfortable talking with the ladies, knowing them better and finding an affinity, the sessions grow more difficult with my mother. She is always eager to talk at first, often knitting her fingers like a grade schooler attentive at her desk. Often, I don't know where to start or what to say.One time I completely forgot that we had an appointment, and when she called me, I kind of brushed it off. I'd have been mortified if I did that with Jackie or Rhoda, Bea or Bette. I find myself putting off our talks. No matter what we say, it always feels as if the most important thing remains unsaid. Whenever I leave her house, I find myself in tears, sometimes just a little, sometimes convulsively crying. This welter of emotions always locates itself there, at the end of her driveway.

Once, after doing some errands, I inexplicably drove to my mother's house instead of my own home and found myself in her driveway, confused for a few moments. Where was I? Did I live here? Was this my home? Was my unconscious that powerful? I should have checked if my mother was home and said hi. But I left feeling pathetic and small. If she asked why I had come, what would I have said, that I came here by mistake, that I want my mommy?

Therapy is like the sound of one hand clapping. The next time I see Anne I tell her about driving to my mother's house on automatic pilot. I'm shocked I've done this and start to cry. She doesn't say anything. I tell her that getting close to my mother is unbelievably painful; instead of being grateful for this opportunity, I am overwhelmed by feelings of sorrow and regret. She doesn't say anything.

I confess that it is my father whom I loved the most, who made me laugh, who indulged me, and whom I respected. A shrink I saw in college was adamant that if I didn't make peace with my mother before she died I would never be my own person, that I would be controlled by these unresolved feelings. My mother herself has invoked the long arm of death and how her expectations and directives will haunt me from the grave. When I was a teenager I just wanted my mother to be real, to be real with me. I sensed she was hiding or faking or blindly following protocol and I constantly tried to chip away at her, challenge her, and call her out. Still, no matter how bad I tried to make her feel, I had no idea someone had gotten there first. *You have always been stupid, you are stupid, and you always will be stupid.*

I want to know what Anne thinks, but she just looks at me. In the past, I'd feel angry and frustrated with shrinks who barely spoke as if trapped in some game of psychological chicken; sometimes I'd remain silent just to show them that two could play their game. Only I'm soothed by Anne's silences. I go into something of a fugue state, staring at the rug between us with such intensity that eventually I can make out every fiber.

I tell Anne about my mother's accident, an event that has loomed large in my personal mythology. It's a story I've told to various shrinks over the years, each time embellishing it a little bit more; eventually, I could no longer tell the facts from my fantasy. This much is true: My mother had been driving and smoking. When she tossed her cigarette out of the window, an ember flew back in, nestled in her coat, and caught fire. A man saw her, helped her out of the car, and somehow got her to roll on the ground. She woke up in Stamford Hospital, her arms grafted with skin from her thighs. She was in the hospital for nine weeks recuperating. That mysterious man saved her life.

Over time I had convinced myself that the fire wasn't an accident. That my mother was on a bridge when it happened, a bridge from which she planned to jump. And I believed one more thing: that she was pregnant with me.

"Where did you get that?" My mother was taken aback when I asked about the accident during one of our talks. "I was newly married. None of you were born. I was happy as could be." Later she will recant, remembering that she had just discovered she wasn't pregnant after getting her hopes up.

Still, where *did* I get that? The two of us dying tragically and dramatically together, mother and unborn child engulfed in flames. I feel so ashamed telling Anne; my fantasy so florid and obvious: wanting so desperately to fuse with my mother as if she were one of the confessional poets whose tragic lives I worshipped. Only my mother is not Anne Sexton and I am not her string bean. However extravagant my imagination, there is nothing poetic, cathartic, or liberating about it. Even after so many years of therapy, I am like a blindfolded child grasping in the dark with outstretched arms: Am I hot? Am I cold?

"Is it time?" My inner clock exactly attuned to fifty minutes.

Anne frowns and glances at the clock in response.

Driving home from therapy, I look at all the young Yalies crossing Prospect Street, so bright and vibrant, and want to mow them down.

♠

The following Monday Bridge is back at my mom's. I bring a home-baked bread wrapped in a white cloth that my father-in-law baked for Easter. On the way over, I pride myself on how thoughtful I am. I look over at the bread sitting on the passenger seat; it's so big I feel like buckling it in. I'm sure the ladies will be impressed with my father-in-law's baking. Plus, the Pogacha is a lot like challah bread; they're going to love it.

I come inside holding the bread like a swaddled infant. When my mother folds back the towel and sees it, she rears back, as if staring into the yellow eyes of Rosemary's baby. "Don't you know it's still Passover! Take that in the kitchen!" She gestures for me to get it out of there, and I spirit away the prohibited bread, feeling both foolish and annoyed.

I have no idea why my mother feels the need to put on this Passover charade for the ladies. She is the first to admit that she isn't observant, more a cultural Jew. I've often teased her about what I call her à la carte approach to religion. I once asked her when she became an atheist. She answered adamantly, "I was born an atheist!" Who would be offended by serving this gorgeous home-baked bread? Maybe Rhoda? As past executive director of the temple, she is the most observant among the ladies. My mother and Rhoda were the only ones to have gone to Hebrew school. In Rhoda's hometown of Salem, better known for covens than minyans, she attended classes in a makeshift Jewish Center where a stocky teacher named Mrs. Kekst threw a stink eye over the young Rhoda for preferring fantasy books to the teachings of Hillel. My mother proudly recalls walking her mother to synagogue on the high holidays, their arms linked at the elbow, European style.

Still, did my mother really need to make me feel like a war criminal for bringing the bread? She can't explain it, won't explain it, sometimes she even throws up her hands and says, "Does everything have to make sense?"

I see my mother has already set the kettle to boil for tea, fresh coffee dripping into a pot. Her dessert, dessert plates, and pretty matching dessert knife are on the counter. I know exactly which dishes and which serving pieces my mother likes to use for every occasion. Every single platter is assigned a purpose from which we never veer. She has made her signature chicken salad with cranberries and celery.

The ladies arrive within minutes of each other. Bea is wearing jeans and a lime-green shirt today with a cream vest with tiny seed pearls sewn in the shape of amoeba. Rhoda sports a creamy white necklace made of many strands and a matching pinky ring that looks like a piece of Godiva chocolate. My mother is wearing a length of black twine with a piece of stone hanging from it that could have been chipped off the Wailing

Wall. Jackie is wearing a piece from her tribal art collection, this one with a cowry shell affixed to the center that may ward off evil. Bette wears a piece I haven't seen before, a wire choker from which dangles a small metal piece, maybe enamel, that looks like a miniature Braque or Picasso, and her pearl earrings, her staple, simple and elegant.

After lunch, I finish clearing as the ladies migrate to the Bridge table. They drop their dollars on the table accompanied by the same stale jokes about paying up and high stakes; the banter is as familiar as sitcom jokes landing like golf balls in a lake. I finish up the dishes to my mother's protestations. From the kitchen I can hear them settling down, then the whinny of cards being shuffled. It's later in the game, between three to four, when I space out. Where do the ladies get their stamina? My mother has put out a bowl of cherries, and each lady daintily takes one or two. I want to tuck myself away in my mother's bedroom, turn on *Ellen*, and take a nap. I'm desperate to check my phone for important calls and urgent messages. My eye goes to the floor; their feet look so tiny.

In the 1950s, women who suffered from postpartum were considered neurotic, and many were treated with electroshock therapy. The illness wasn't recognized or named as such until 1958 and wouldn't be included in the *DSM* until 1994. It's now known that for at least one to two weeks after giving birth, most women experience a mild depression, and that 10 to 20 percent of women experience a more debilitating form of postpartum. In 1958, the year of my sister's birth, Tofranil was the first in a family of new antidepressants to hit the market. My mother knows she was prescribed something when she eventually sought help, but she can't remember what. She stayed in therapy for two years until she had me.

"Isn't two years a lot for postpartum?"

"I don't know. Is it?"

"Were you frightened?"

"More sad than frightened, just very sad. I couldn't pull it together. I withdrew from things. I didn't want to see anybody. I didn't want to do anything. I didn't want to socialize, just down, very down."

"You must have felt robbed," I say.

"Yes, well no. I felt very bad that such a thing could happen."

"Were you ever afraid to be alone with the baby?"

"It was so ironic, finally having this longed-for child; it didn't make sense."

"What about Dad?"

"He was always steady, like I said."

"But what did he think?"

"Well, he didn't particularly appreciate therapy. He was a pick-yourself-up-by-the-bootstraps sort of person."

Again, I think about my father, a young husband coming home from the lumberyard to a new baby and a wife barely able to go through the motions. She was the girl whom he had chased, who had been fun and flirty with a full figure, who was an enthusiastic recipient of his affection and audience to his corny jokes. They made out under the boardwalk, he took her to shows he could barely afford and always bought the best seats. They kissed under the chuppah of a Brooklyn shul where he smashed a glass beneath his foot, they moved into their first crappy apartment with a bathroom down the hall, to a garden apartment (which my mother describes as heaven), to their first home in Stamford, and eventually here, to Woodbridge. It was a train only going up a hill, fueled by my father's hard work and steadfastness.

"Mom, what aren't you telling me?"

She pushes herself away from the table and I know we're done, the way a doctor stops applying paddles to the chest of a heart attack victim. Only then she juts out her jaw and opens her mouth, as if to speak. I can see her thinking, the battle lines of a lifetime drawn across her face: What is the cost of revealing versus the cost of concealing? I can tell she wants to say something. I suddenly feel frightened even as I have yearned for this moment. My eyes start tearing up at the corners. It already feels like more than I can handle, whatever it is she is about to say.

Finally, with gravel in her voice, she says, "Are you using the product?"

"What?"

"The hair product. The cream first, just a dab, the size of a dime."

She recently bought me her hair products, hoping they might do "wonders."

"First the cream and then the serum. Are you doing it right?"

"Are you serious?"

"Then you don't touch it. You have to let it dry completely."

I give up. I have no idea anymore. What do I really want from her?

"You were an easy baby." She has always professed this, and it always made me feel good, though I had done nothing to earn it. I imagine what she really meant was that the crippling depression hadn't returned after I was born; maybe she was an easy mother.

My mother became pregnant again with her third baby, also a girl. She had clearly gotten the hang of it.

"First I couldn't get pregnant and now I'm fertile Myrtle! I couldn't have been happier."

Another girl! People teased my father. After all, what man doesn't want a son?

"He loved having girls, loved it," my mother says, and it strikes me as true: he made fried salami and eggs on Sundays, took us to movies, the circus, Broadway shows. He taught us how to ride bikes and took us skiing, though he didn't ride a bike or ski himself. He tied our rubber ski boots until his hands nearly bled, then cheered as if we were Olympians as we slowly snowplowed down the mountain.

Then my father got a sales job at a lumberyard in New Haven. He traded in his work clothes for a sports jacket and tie in the office. They bought our house in Woodbridge. It had been on the market for a long time, but he recognized that the problems were cosmetic, and they bought it cheaply along with an acre of land and a pond in the backyard. Just as my mother saw potential in him, he saw potential in the house at the top of Milan Road. We were a family of five moving from Stamford into a three-bedroom ranch in a suburb known for its excellent school district and active Jewish community. It was everything my mother dreamed of. Now, all she needed was a Bridge game.

CHAPTER 10

1964

This is the part of the story you don't want to read. It was a November night when the worst thing happened. It started as a cold and developed into pneumonia. Overwhelming pneumonia, they called it. Those were the days of house calls, only this time the doctor didn't come. He said she didn't need to go to the hospital, and my parents dutifully listened; doctors were beyond reproach in 1964. An ambulance took my baby sister away in the night. She was two years old.

The next morning, my mother gathered my older sister and me together on our green couch and told us that Barbara had died. Nina was six. I was four. Was I even listening or climbing, the way I loved to over the spine of the couch, dangling there as if it were a cliff? Two days later, as if nothing unusual had happened, my mother sent us to Sunday school, business as usual. Only our uncle picked us up from the synagogue. Why was he here all the way from New York? Nina remembers coming home to a party, or what she mistook for a party.

"She was very confused," my mother says. "She couldn't understand why we would be having a party." Why our new home of only a few months would be mysteriously filled with grown-ups in the middle of the day, old Stamford friends, family from Brooklyn, lively the way these gatherings get: people smoking, drinking, and even laughing. My mother is surprised that I have no recollection of this.

She and I are at my house in a little room lined with books, and furnished with an old walnut table and a blue couch. The table is also covered with piles of books. Many more are stashed under the table. My mother usually comes in here when she babysits for us and inexplicably gravitates toward *Infinite Jest* by David Foster Wallace. She'll read some pages, doze. I always tell her she can borrow it and she always declines. She has more reading than she knows what to do with. Outside the window, the last russet leaves of fall dangle from the branches. I've always admired them, not the season's prettiest leaves, the ones that hang on the longest.

"I want to talk about Barbara," I say.

What is death to a young child? What did it even mean that Barbara had died? The next day every picture of her was swept away. Someone, my mother I guess, folded her little clothes and gave them away. My father must have disassembled her crib, or had she already been in a big-girl bed? Young children don't really get it. To them, death is more like going to sleep; they believe that people who die will come back, as if they just popped out to buy milk. I think I was even more confused than that: was she ever there?

Nina, older by just two years, would carry a heavier load. In every way she was like any first grader, with plaid jumpers and Danskin separates, and penny loafers. She had recently gotten glasses I envied: a fashionable cat-eye frame with tiny diamond chips where the corners flared. She believed that she had given our sister the cold that turned into the pneumonia that took her life. She would eventually break down and tell her terrible secret to a trusted teacher who immediately called my mother into school. It's hard to imagine what my mother was feeling driving there, facing the teacher, and more, facing her daughter, who had shined a light on all her carefully tamped-down pain.

It's called magical thinking when a child believes she has caused the death of another. What did my sister look like when our mother arrived? Frightened, guilty? Would she get my mother in trouble, be sent to the principal's office? When she arrived, my mother reassured her over and over that it was impossible for her to have made Barbara sick. That none of us could have done that. It was nobody's fault.

"Did I believe I killed her?" Nina says now. "No. But it happened."

Like all the Bridge daughters, my sister's childhood memories center on how the ladies dressed. "The ladies teased their hair and dressed up for Bridge. I loved watching them. It was all so grown-up. What I really loved about it was we got Entenmann's. It was the only time we had it in the house."

Nina remembers that my mother started playing Bridge with the night ladies. They were my mother's first Bridge club in New Haven, and their monthly appearance when it was our turn to host was like a raft of ducks reliably returning to a lake, plump and noisy. She got recruited by my nursery school teacher, and when it was our turn to host I was excited to see her in our home, as if a celebrity were dropping by. I knew the ritual by heart, my mother reaching up into the corner cabinets for the good coffee cups and saucers, laying out the spoons and napkins on the counter, the cake or Danish or *babka* set on a platter with a pretty serving knife. And on the card table was a matched set of cards, matching score pad, and a pencil skinny as a swizzle stick.

The house grew quiet when they played a hand, interrupted by chatter when they'd shuffle the cards and deal a new hand. Sometimes they called it "washing the cards," and I couldn't help but think of a soapy sink where the cards were submerged, my mother's hands in pink latex gloves washing each one and affixing it to a clothesline with a pin. Eventually she got invited to the Monday day game. This, she says, was like cracking the code. These ladies were the New Haven equivalent of Jewish blue bloods—they were born and raised in New Haven, went to Hillhouse High, went away to college, came home and married New Haven boys with college educations and good prospects. It was heady for a girl with a socialist's heart and a Brooklyn accent.

Entree into the Monday club was a more gradual process. Shirley, one of the night ladies, was BFF's with Bette. Bette and Jackie had started the club. Various women came and went until Bea joined, and eventually my mother. At first, my mother was invited to substitute when a regular lady couldn't play. After a time, she was promoted to regular alternate. None of the ladies can remember when she became a regular, only that she did, like an initiate at a sorority getting pinned. (Rhoda also started as an alternate. Now, with about twenty-six years of play under her belt, she is the newest "regular" member.) My mother was very happy to be promoted to a regular in the Monday Bridge club, only now she had to turn out a meal. "I was very nervous about preparing lunch. I went out and bought the *New York Times Cookbook*. And for me to have spent that kind of money on a cookbook shows you how nervous I was." She can no longer remember what she prepared, and when I press she says, "I don't know; what difference does it make? I made lunch."

The Monday ladies were like ghosts. Once in a great while, we caught a glimpse of them just as we were coming home from school. They seemed more formal and primmer than the night ladies, and we always addressed them as we would any adult using the honorific: Mrs. The Bridge Ladies have circled this topic more than once. Rhoda is most adamant; she believes it's a sign of respect to use Mr. and Mrs., Grandma and Grandpa, Uncle and Aunt. She doesn't appreciate it when young people call her Rhoda and she doesn't want her grandchildren calling her by her first name. She was taught to respect adults and teachers, and addressing them as such was a sign of respect.

My mother can't stand hearing this. "Respect isn't automatic. It's earned," she nearly growls when the topic comes up. I know that she is thinking about her father first and foremost, but Rhoda doesn't know this. Rhoda more than respected her father, she worshipped him. Bette often sounds like an anthropologist, asserting that what we call people is all learned and culturally prescribed.

Bea once mentioned running into the funeral director who orchestrates most of the Jewish burials in town. He addressed her as Mrs. Phillips.

"I said call me Bea. He said his mother would slap him silly."

I asked Jackie what she thinks. She says it doesn't matter to her. I ask what her grandchildren call her and Dick.

"Oh." She brightens. "They call me Geo and they call Dick Puff."

It was at the night games where my mother met the one truly great friend of her life, the closest thing to a soul mate. Gloria also had three daughters, and we exactly matched up in age. Her youngest, coincidentally, was called Barbara. Nina thinks it must have been part of what drew my mother to Gloria: this little girl, this double. I refute this theory. Our mother had so completely disappeared our sister, not a single picture to be found, I was convinced that it must have been more painful to see this little girl, same age, same name, that she would be a constant reminder of her loss.

"But she isn't. Mom loves her and feels a special connection to her. Always has."

I ask my sister how she knows this, and she says she just does. She has other recollections that I have no memory of, such as coming home from Hebrew school, the early evening already dark, the house dark, finding my mother sitting alone in the den.

"The parent driving the car pool would ask if anyone was home because the house was so dark. I'd say it was okay. I knew she was home."

"Then what happened?"

"I'd come in and she'd startle, jump up, and say, 'Oh, I have to make dinner.'"

She also remembers my mother being so angry with us that she would sequester herself in her bedroom or drive off in a rage. "It was really scary. You don't remember that?"

I remember my mother in glimpses: when she took deep drags on a cigarette, as if she were communing with the universe. When we missed the bus and she drove us to school in her housecoat, her eyes angrily trained on the road. Or looking up words with the intensity of a witch searching for a spell. How do any of us know our mothers? By example? By osmosis? Every child a small sponge? By her smell, the way she looks in the mirror? Applies lipstick. How did I know my mother? All throughout those years growing up, she never spoke of Barbara. She had erected a firewall, and we knew never to ask. And we never did. How do you console someone who doesn't want to be consoled?

♠

"We were new in town." My mother says this over and over, an alibi, a mantra. We had moved to Woodbridge, and Barbara died three months later. She believed that people didn't know. As much as she adored her Stamford friends, she guiltily admits that she was relieved not to be near them.

"I didn't want to be pitied," my mother says. "I didn't want her death to define us."

For the first time I get it. Her secret would be her salvation. People wouldn't avoid her in the grocery aisle or knowingly nod a pitying condolence. She could mourn in private, be left alone with her grief. My mother would be like any other mother filling lunch boxes with sandwiches and pieces of fruit. She would pull up to the bank window in our car and the teller would send the cash through in a tube with a Dum Dum lollipop for us, no eyes downturned with sympathy. She would do the marketing, assemble meat loafs, and chauffeur us to our slate of after-school activities and Hebrew school without ever saying a word about her loss. And when she played Bridge she followed suit, making small talk about vacations and summer camp.

When Bette told me about the death of her sister during one of our first meetings, I asked her if she knew about Barbara.

"Everyone knew," Bette tells me. "Of course, we did."

"But how?" I ask, suddenly feeling exposed and naïve. Wasn't Woodbridge our fresh start, our clean slate, and a sanctuary from public scrutiny?

"Betsy, everyone knew about your sister. Surely your mother knew that, in a town like New Haven."

I suspect Bette's right, but I don't say anything.

"I really think she knows that people were aware." She is being incredibly gentle with me. She would never want to upset me or betray my mother.

"What about Bridge? My mother never brought it up, no one ever brought it up all these years?"

"Never," Bette says, "not once."

I want to bury my face in Bette's couch. It's too sad to contemplate. My mother putting on this face because any other would have been too hideous, would have scared people, scared herself. She needed to move forward, and she did. Playing cards, I like to think, helped.

"It was one of the mistakes I made. I tried not to mourn in front of you, and I didn't want you guys to mourn. It was just to keep going." My mother picks at a blue thread in the couch. The back of her hand is maroon with bruises that no longer heal, the tissue paper skin of age. She thinks better than to pull the thread, not knowing where it will end, and pats it down instead.

Grief counselors and bereavement groups all came too late for my parents. Though I doubt my mother would have participated. When my father was in hospice, she had no interest in sitting in on a support group, frowned on it. She greeted the priest and even the rabbi, when they made their rounds, with tight smiles, dismissing them and their prayers. When one of the angelic nurses caring for my dad came up behind my mother, and put her hands on her shoulders, my mother's entire body tensed, and she glared at the nurse with a clear message: Do not touch me. Do not soothe me. *Shove your empathy.*

An aunt had told me that my mother didn't go to the cemetery, and from that single misleading piece of information I concluded that she never mourned, had hardened herself to life.

"Of course I went to the cemetery." My mother is appalled that my aunt would have said such a thing or that I would have believed something so ludicrous all this time. How could I have possibly known what to believe? No one ever told us. Only now, sitting so close to my mother on my shabby blue couch, close enough to smell her makeup, I can't ask her. We can't make eye contact. There is a vast lake between us, black and still. A hawk circles slowly on a wide current of air, wings as big as branches. My mother returns to the blue thread sticking out of the couch like an inchworm, working it between her thumb and forefinger.

"When your father came home from the hospital empty-handed . . . ," my mother starts.

Only I'm stopped right there. Burglars leave banks empty-handed. Gamblers leave casinos empty-handed. How does a father come home from a hospital empty-handed? My mind is so literal sometimes that I see my father coming home, holding a blanket where a baby should be, and turning his hands over as if to say: see, empty.

"Mom, didn't you go to the hospital?"

"I had to stay home with you guys."

My mother keeps reminding me that we were new in town, had only been there a few months. We didn't even know our neighbors. There was no one nearby to call.

"He went. And when he came home he said, 'I wish it could have been me.' And I said, 'Oh, no, no, no.' There were two little kids to be taken care of. How could I possibly do that on my own?"

"Did you really mean that?"

"I did. Definitely."

My parents were new to our synagogue and the round chapel with its stained-glass depictions of the Jewish holidays. My mother was thirty-four years old when she buried a daughter, when she stood in the place where so many have come to mourn. Did she steady herself on the row of seats before her? Did my father put his freckled hand over hers? Did she stiffen and pull away? And what of the apricot light falling in shafts through the stained glass with dust motes, like fireflies, suspended there? Did she say the kaddish, mumbling over the Hebrew, as most Jews do, or did she remain silent, her back the target of a hundred eyes: *There but for the grace of God go I?*

"Did you have a sense of what kind of a child she was?" I ask, barely able to hold back my tears.

"Oh yes. When I dropped you kids off or picked you up from school, she would call out from her car seat 'my cool, my cool.' And she was very, very fast. When Dad came home at night, she would reach him first before you two big girls. I never knew how she did that. I felt at two that she ran the house. Now that can't be true. But I had this sense that she was going to be fantastic. I did."

This is the most my mother has ever told me. It's just a few sentences, but it feels like the world. Then she looks down at her manicured nails, the lacquer flawlessly applied, the color changing week to week like a mood ring. I always knew Barbara brought her great sorrow; I didn't know about the joy from this lively little girl, less turtle more hare.

I no longer want to know anything else. I am willing to end it right here, this lifetime of unanswered questions, of magical thinking. We are close enough to hug in this little reading room, but we won't. Close enough to apologize for all the things we never did as mother and daughter. We won't. Where would we start? The room full of books is silent. Stories trapped in type, unable to take wing, sentences marching across the page that cannot explain being born or dying. *Infinite Jest*, indeed. I was far too young to understand that I had lost my sister. The far greater loss, I realize now, was my mother.

CHAPTER 11

The Finesse

"Have a look." My mother sends me the newsletter from the Orange Senior Center, which is in the next town over. She's affixed a Post-it to the flyer with the message in her pretty script with graceful loops. When I call the center and ask about the beginner class I'm told I need a partner. When I relay this to my mother she volunteers without hesitation. I remind her that it's a beginner class and that she's been playing for more than fifty years. She insists that there is always more to learn. Yes, I'm sure there is, but this is a *beginner* class. My mother says she doesn't mind.

On the drive to the lesson, I ask her what she will say if the teacher asks why she's come for lessons.

"Do you think he will?" My mother is startled by this possible eventuality.

"It's usually how teachers start classes."

She bites her finger to pantomime thinking. "I'll lie."

We enter the senior center through a large cafeteria with a bingo game in process. My mother clutches my arm and hurries us out, as if we've barged in on a famous chess or tennis match. The place has that cafeteria smell of institutional food, and the seniors look defeated by life and the checkerboard squares before them. We wend our way down a long hall. The walls are papered with flyers about free lunches, movie nights, and lectures. The classroom is depressing, cement block walls, dusty chalkboards, a hodgepodge of tables and chairs. A few women, mostly in their fifties and sixties, and an older couple are milling about. The teacher is late, and everyone is looking at the clock.

The woman in the couple makes it her business to go to the office and inquire after our missing teacher. She has curly white hair and large, black Swifty Lazar–style eyeglass frames. She is slim and dressed in all black. I can tell she is the kind of person who marches into the projection room when the sound goes off in a movie, or reports a carton of milk spilled in the grocery aisle.

When she returns, she tells the group that the teacher got the time wrong and is going to be a half hour late. Then she introduces herself and her husband, Barbara and Bernard Barkin. She has a fabulous New York accent.

"Born and raised in Manhattan," she says, as if she were part of the Seneca Nation. I like Barbara right away. She has a great laugh, more, a great attitude. She and her husband have moved here after living in Westchester and Greenwich for sixty-two years. She explains that Bernard had an aortic dissection (usually fatal); they moved from their three-story home when it became too much to handle. Their kids had relocated here some time ago and urged them to move closer, and that is how Barbara and Bernard find themselves on a Thursday afternoon in a senior center in Orange, Connecticut. She's upbeat, allows that the move and sale of many of their things was traumatic, but people here are so friendly. *Get to know us.*

Barbara proudly informs us that her mother was a master Bridge player. She urged both her daughters to play. Barbara's sister listened. Today, she's a terrific player, plays four days a week in Florida. Barbara wasn't interested. Her mother warned her that she'll be sorry when she's older. Barbara freely admits her mother was right.

Finally our teacher arrives, looking somewhat bewildered and apologetic. He introduces himself, but I can't quite make out his name. Al Cone or Cole. I nickname him Al Capone, though I think he's an old Jewish guy who I'm fairly certain never mowed anyone down with a Thompson submachine gun. He appears to be in his mid to late eighties. His hair is a victim of hat head and he hasn't shaved, which makes him look slightly depressed. And his glasses have a light brown tint, the kind that darken in the sun and, once inside, take time to clear. He doesn't wear a wedding band, and his fingers are slightly bent at the top knuckle. I wonder if he's single and if he might be a possible man friend for my mother. It becomes clear pretty quickly that he has at least three things going for him (a) he really knows his Bridge, which is hugely impressive, (b) he has a sly sense of humor (which elevates a person in romantic consideration at any age), and (c) he's standing.

Barbara and I sit across from each other as partners. My mother sits to my left and the table is filled out by a lady named Ruth. She is wearing a fleece the color of oatmeal and matching wide-wale corduroys. Over the course of the lesson, we will learn that Ruth is a bookkeeper, is single "by choice," and older than she looks. She wasn't carded until she was thirty!

Barbara's husband, Bernard, is a terrific player, but he stays off to the side with his Sudoku book. He's wearing gray sweatpants, a sweater, and sneakers with Velcro straps, standard-issue senior wear. I will learn that he and Barbara do everything together; they say of themselves that they are joined at their hips. It's not clear to me if it's out of undying affection or if in the aftermath of Bernard's illness she is afraid to leave him alone. Bernard comes over to the table from time to time and kisses Barbara's neck the way you blow raspberries on a baby's belly. He is more affectionate with her during two hours of Bridge than I have witnessed over a lifetime in my parents' marriage.

I know my mother finds this inappropriate. In fact, I purposefully avoid looking at her because I know I will crack up to see the disapproval scrawled on her face. She doesn't believe her face betrays any emotion, but it's not even subtle. Bernard picks up on her uptight disposition and starts to call her Rozzy Baby. This is like calling Queen Elizabeth Queenie or Lizzie. Then he asks a bunch of personal questions: Is her husband still alive? How did he die? How long ago was it? Then with absolutely no information, Bernard remarks that he must have been a wonderful man. Mother is taken aback. The sentiment is nice, but he doesn't have a clue about my father.

"Yes, he was," my mother curtly responds, hoping to cut off the conversation, which is way too personal and again totally inappropriate by my mother's standards.

"Did you have a good marriage?"

My mother looks at Bernard, cocks her head. He's gone too far.

"I'll bet you had a good marriage." Rozzy Baby isn't pleased, but again, she answers curtly, "Yes, we did."

Bernard has gotten to my mother in record time. I'm impressed. Then he goes over to Barbara, kisses her on the neck.

"Bernard! Enough!" Over the months getting to know and play Bridge with the Barkins, it will become clear that this is their shtick. Bernard says outrageous things and Barbara hushes him. Only Bernard will always come back for another round. I see the mischief in Bernard's face and I sense the kindred spirit of a sad clown.

Al Capone doesn't provide a formal lesson so much as shuffle between the two Bridge tables and dole out advice. We all have enough experience to wing it to some extent. Barbara has brought two books and a bidding guide, which she consults regularly (once a teacher always a teacher). My mother starts to call Al over almost every time she has to lead. I find this baffling, as she has been playing for more than fifty years. The opening lead in Bridge is critical. It's the first card thrown by the defenders and it impacts the play of the hand. The rule of thumb is to lead either the top of an honor sequence from the same suit (king–queen–jack) or without that, the fourth card from your longest and strongest suit. I've memorized this rule, but I have no idea what's behind the thinking. In fact, that pretty much describes where I am with Bridge. The rules are starting to gel, as Jeff promised, but I don't exactly understand the logic behind them.

There is another important component to choosing a lead: it is a signal to your partner of what you'd like him to lead back. The first time I learned about this kind of signaling it seemed like the stuff of Morse code and decoder rings. For beginning players, it's the first taste of understanding how you and your partner work in tandem. By feeding each other hints about suits we are strong in, our partnership can launch a more robust defense. It's fun to win your contract in Bridge. It's also really fun to set your opponent.

At one point when I'm confused about what card to play, I wave Al over. He looks at my cards and the cards laid out in the dummy, assesses the situation, and suggests I try the "finesse."

I'd learned about the finesse at the Manhattan Bridge Club, but I was more taken with the elegance of the term than actually understanding the mechanics of how it works. Barbara, still a great teacher, explains how the finesse is a technique where you attempt to take a trick with a lower card *whilst* a higher card is still at large. Doing this successfully depends on where the higher card is sitting, either with your right hand or left hand opponent, and thus only works 50 percent of the time.

I point to the seven of Hearts in my hand. Al nods and I play it. My mother, opponent to my left, follows suit and plays low with a four of Hearts (second man plays low—this is another rule of thumb), I take the queen from the dummy (Al nods again that this is right). And the fourth, Ruth, throws the king of Hearts, and wins the trick. Delighted, she bounces around in her seat like a child tasting pudding for the first time.

I'm pissed that I've lost the trick and I look to Al for an explanation. "There's a saying in Bridge," he says, " 'Give unto Caesar what's due Caesar,' " then he goes back to the other table, where the women are shouting for him.

♠

In the car on the way home, we estimate the Barkins' age and we wonder whether this move to our hamlet was a good idea. Staying put, downsizing, and moving into assisted living is a constant source of conversation. Bea and Rhoda moved into their condos when their husbands were still alive and it turned out to be the perfect step for when they became widows. For Bette, Jackie, and my mother, who all live in the same homes they lived in for more than fifty years, there is a lot to consider and manage. When I tell my mother I can convert our garage into a beautiful studio apartment for her, no stairs involved, her own entrance, she graciously replies, "Over my dead body."

As we get closer to her house, I accuse her of flirting with Al Capone, calling him over for bidding advice as if she were a schoolgirl. She roundly protests.

"Do you think he's single?"

"Who, Al?"

"Yes, Al. Maybe he's available."

"For me?"

"Is there anyone else in the car?"

"Don't be ridiculous."

At this Mother looks out the window, thoroughly irritated with me.

For my entire childhood, she drove us down these same roads to Hebrew school, pottery lessons, and doctors' appointments. All that time, all those miles of carpooling, I sensed resentment and resignation on her part, or maybe the car had been filling up with my own teenage fumes. It's hard to pinpoint exactly when I became so difficult or why. Only now, when we talk about not getting along, my mother says it wasn't that bad. At least she doesn't remember it that way. Surely I am exaggerating is her implication.

"Mom," I say, "do you have amnesia."

"Maybe I do, I just don't remember it being that bad."

"I think you like to whitewash things."

"If you say so."

We pull into her driveway. She's slow getting out of the car. I can see the effort in her back and shoulders as she pulls herself out. I feel the effort in my own back and ask if she needs help.

"No, no, I can do it. Just give me a second."

Once out, I tell her I had fun.

"Good," she says, and goes inside.

CHAPTER 12

The Revelation of Self

"There is no man worth dying for," Bea says as soon as I sit down to join her for breakfast. I sometimes feel with Bea that I've entered the film somewhere in the middle.

"It's what I tell all the girls doing community service who help out at the Soup Kitchen. You know, instead of doing prison time." Bea says she'd hate to see a good kid wind up in the brink over some loser. When she started volunteering at the Soup Kitchen, she never asked the people doing community service what crime they had committed, only after a time she got more comfortable, more familiar.

"I've heard it all," she says. "Last week, a gal told me the cops found drugs in the trunk of her car, but they weren't hers. Yeah, right." I love this tough talk of Bea's. I can picture her with a detective's badge interrogating some perp on the set of *Law & Order: Criminal Intent*. Bea talks a good game.

When I asked if I could join her and volunteer at the Soup

Kitchen, see her in action, she was delighted. She has been serving on the line twice a week for nearly ten years, since her husband died. She has proudly told me that they serve more than three hundred meals a day, and more toward the end of the month when the checks run out. When she mentions the Soup Kitchen at Bridge, which she often does, no one ever takes it up, asks her what it's like, or commends her service. "Betsy"—she's not dropping it—"do you think there is any man worth going to prison for?"

"Probably not," I wager.

"Probably?"

"Okay, definitely not," I agree.

"Damn straight."

After we finish eating, she pulls a pillbox out of her purse. She shakes it and a little white pill goes rolling across the table. She's fast on the draw and snaps it up before it rolls off. "My birth control pills," she says, winking. Then she takes out her lipstick and a small round mirror that fits in the palm of her hand.

"See this?" she says, and hands it to me.

On the back is a black-and-white photo of Bea and her mother. I've asked Bea a few times if they were close. "Personalities don't always mesh" is all she'll tell me. Still, she carries this novelty mirror from the Catskills with her more than eighty years later. When I hand it back, Bea says, "That was taken a hundred and five years ago," and then, as an afterthought, "I was a beautiful child."

When we approach the Soup Kitchen, a few guys in low-slung jeans, doo-rags, dreadlocks, aprons, and work boots as big as loaves of bread are outside smoking. As we approach, they all call out to her like three little birds on a wire: Hey Miss Bea, Hey Miss Bea, Hey Miss Bea. She greets each man by name and introduces me as a helper. Inside, it's the same. She takes me into the kitchen and introduces me to the cook and dishwashers. She knows everyone by name and what they're up to. Bea is knitted in here. Before she takes her place on the serving line, she fills the birdbath in the pretty courtyard between the church and the community room. Seconds later the bath is crowded with birds shoving each other out of the way for a drink. Bea looks back, delighted.

She puts on her apron and her plastic gloves and takes her place on the line where she serves dessert. There's usually a choice of donated cakes, doughnuts, and cookies on a large silver tray, but you better decide quickly. Bea will not have the line held up on account of you being fussy. Nor will you get away with sneaking back in line for a second piece of cake. If you think you will put one over on Bea on account of her age, think again. I may be wrong, but she seems like the center of the whole operation.

Usually a divinity student from Yale comes to lead the assembled in prayer before the meal. The day I was there a young woman led the room in prayers and then she moved from table to table, talking with the clients. Bea explained that most of the pastors leave after they say the prayer. She is impressed with this young woman taking the time to stay.

"So what if she has an earring in her nose," and by this Bea didn't mean a demure diamond stud in one of her nostrils but a thick septum ring with balls at the end.

"I think she does a good job, she can have whatever *chazerai* in her nose for all I care."

The people who come to the Soup Kitchen have obviously hit hard times. It's the mothers with small children who get to Bea. She always gives a small child two desserts and calls them "sweetie" or "cutie" and encourages them to take their time and choose whatever they like. Some of the men look threatening to me, either because of their size or body language. Only then they say, "Hey Miss Bea" and give her a big smile. I wish the Bridge Ladies could see her. Most people on the line thank Bea by saying, *Bless you*, and *God bless you*, and *Have a blessed day*.

"I bet you've never been so blessed in your life, have you, Betsy?" Bea says as we leave.

Heading back to our car, Bea takes my arm as we cross the street, our aprons rolled beneath our arms, the sign of a good day's work.

♠

The light in Rhoda's condo is snuffed out under a ceiling of gray sky. It's been raining on and off for days. The ladies always show up in exactly the proper outerwear, some in rain bonnets, rain boots, others toting umbrellas with Monet lilies from the Met, NPR giveaways. When I arrive and my mother sees that I don't have a coat, she predictably quizzes, "No coat?"

I don't believe I have ever, in her judgment, left the house properly dressed. She is a coat stickler. No, she is the Inspector General of Outer Wear, the Commissar of Coats. Not only do I have to wear one, but I should also have a coat for every kind of weather. For a girl who only had one coat, my mother now has a closet full because in her view: all jackets are not created equal. No longer able to get me to comply, Inspector General has turned her hawk-eye on my daughter. It makes her "crazy" the way I "let her out of the house" without a coat. When I buy my daughter what I think of as a three-season coat, my mother investigates the fabric and says with absolute authority, "Two. At best."

Instead of pushing all my buttons, this conversation almost amuses me, as if we are in an off-Broadway play reciting tired dialogue. Only then she escalates the inquisition. "Did it come with a lining?"

"Yes."

"Did you buy it?"

"Yes," I say.

"Don't lie to me."

"I'm not."

"I see that you are."

"Okay, I'll go get it."

"Will you really? Do you want me to get it? You *have* to get the lining. When will you have time to get it? You never have any time."

The worst thing about this insane conversation is that I have similar ones with my daughter. I bug her nearly every morning as she leaves for school. *Are you going to be warm enough? Do you want your boots? Don't you want any breakfast?* Like a lot of my friends, I swore I would be nothing like my mother. Only there it is, all the warnings and criticisms tumbling forth from my mouth in what must be an invisible strain of maternal DNA.

Still, women of my generation are fairly well convinced that we are doing a better job raising our kids, are more connected and attuned than our parents were with us. After all, we use the same technology and we share the same music, went to the same colleges, and experimented with the same drugs. My daughter and I share clothes. The idea of ever borrowing anything from my mother's grown-up wardrobe was out of the question. The woman wore girdles and bras with cups the shape of funnels.

We're even a little ambivalent about being adults ourselves. Dude dads wear Arctic Monkey T-shirts and Converse sneakers to work. I know a mom who surfs!

My daughter and I watched *Girls* together and binge-watched the entire series of *The Office* when she was in tenth grade. Sometimes I'd plead for one more episode, but she'd beg off claiming she had homework! I was so proud when she borrowed my Doc Martens for a concert! I didn't even mind that she hadn't asked me.

When she said she wanted to get a nose ring, I said go for it. My mother was horrified to learn that I encouraged her. Didn't I know that nose rings lead to heroin addiction, poverty, and death? I wasn't sure if my mother was more appalled with her or with me. The fact is I've always loved blue hair, mohawks, and tattoos, no doubt because my mother finds them so offensive. I never had the moxie to stand out like that, but I gave her enough tsuris in my army pants and collection of T-shirts with band names that either stymied or frightened her: The Clash, The Sex Pistols, and the Grateful Dead. Why on earth would you wear a shirt with a skull on it? What was this ghastly uniform I had adopted? Wearing it to the country club and freaking out my mother was my idea of civil disobedience circa 1975. When my daughter finds a long-retired Jerry Garcia T-shirt from my former collection, she's thrilled. It's the coolest thing ever.

♠

Rhoda serves sardines. I wonder if I can hide them under the salad. I know I can't spirit them away to the bathroom and flush them down the toilet the way I used to when my mother served cod. I gather myself and politely decline when they come my way.

"Are you sure?"

"Yes, thank you so much. I'm fine."

Everyone starts eating when Rhoda lays her hands flat on the table, stands up, and clears her throat for an announcement.

She easily commands the table. She is the only seasoned leader among them, having been executive director at the synagogue for sixteen years. Though Rhoda claims to have nearly fallen over when they offered her the position, but she was a leader waiting to happen: a confident only child, a graduate of Russell Sage, a proud women's college whose motto was "To Be, To Know, To Do."

It was the highest administrative position in the congregation; she supervised a staff of five and was in charge of everything from baby naming ceremonies to building maintenance. Plus it came with a salary.

She tells me about walking into a boardroom of all men for the first time.

"Like Peggy in *Mad Men*?" I ask, but Rhoda looks at me blankly. (Ladies, watch cable, it won't bite you!)

"The first conference I went to, I took notes the whole time and barely breathed. One of the other executives came up to me and said 'Rhoda, relax!'" She traveled alone to conferences. "I got on a plane all by myself and navigated new cities; that was really something."

A six-month trial basis turned into sixteen years. Her mother had moved to the area and helped out with the kids. Rhoda wouldn't have said she had it all, or leaned in, but her life was multidimensional, always challenging. Peter was completely supportive. Sometimes he would join her at conferences. When the spouses started an association, they elected Peter president; he was pretty much the only guy and he loved it. Peter was crazy like that, up for anything, a total goof. One Passover, he taped the *Afikomen* to his stomach.

Today, Rhoda is excited to let everyone know that Fran Kay, her longtime friend from high school and maid of honor, has produced a revival of *Pippin* on Broadway. Rhoda and her gentleman friend, George, saw it over the weekend, and she reports back that it's marvelous, sure to win Fran another Tony.

Fran Kay came to town during Rhoda's high school years. There was something intoxicating about her; when Rhoda speaks of her you can still hear the infatuation in her voice.

"Francis Kay was a beautiful girl with high cheekbones and long gorgeous black hair. Gorgeous." According to Rhoda, she could choose an outfit that anyone else would have passed over and turn it into something stunning. She always had a boyfriend, with one in the wings. "When she wasn't on the phone with one of her beaus, she was on the phone confiding in me."

Rhoda followed Fran all the way to the Poconos where she had a job at a Jewish summer camp called With-a-Wind. She convinced her parents to let her work there, and took the bus by herself. Rhoda would have followed Fran to the ends of the earth, which With-a-Wind pretty much was.

Here, at the Bridge table, you can sense Rhoda's pride. With all that charisma, Rhoda isn't surprised that Fran's made it big on Broadway. *Pippin* wasn't her first hit either. Rhoda reminds the ladies that Fran, with her husband, produced *Chicago* along with other countless successful shows and have won six Tony Awards. And, at eighty-six, she has another show headed for Broadway. The reaction at the table is underwhelming. Maybe they've already heard about Fran, maybe a hundred times. Still, the woman is the real deal; her list of successes is staggering.

Sometimes I think a meteor could strike earth and destroy everything in its wake with the sole exception of these five ladies, this luncheon of silvery fish, two decks of cards, and scoring pad nearby. I wish one of the ladies would jump on the table and start tap-dancing, share a piece of unseemly gossip, or open up about her life.

One afternoon on Bette's pretty screened-in porch, I asked her what the girls talked about when they were young.

"Why can't I remember anything?" she asks. "We must have talked about something."

"Did you gossip?" I ask, hoping to prompt her for something juicy.

"Kids!" she finally says, pleased to have produced an answer.

"We talked a lot about the kids. My Amy and Jackie's Lisa were born on the same day. We all had kids around the same age." It all starts to come back to her like slides flashing through a projector: pregnancies, doctors, schools, teachers, and preparing trays of hors d'oeuvres for parties.

"We talked a lot about entertaining, we'd plan parties for weeks, we'd prepare like crazy, clean our best silver, plan menus, and swap recipes. Parties were a big deal, whoo."

Bette was warmed up then: beach clubs, summer camps. Some shared ski houses, took Christmas vacations together. The more Bette thinks about it she admits that, yes, the Bridge club did form a kind of support group.

"Well, as you kids got older and things became more diffi- cult, we talked about that, too." Bette tells me that the Bridge Ladies came to each other's rescue when the 1970s ushered in a terrifying time and an atmosphere of disrespect from their kids they would have never dared level at their own parents. It's when all their values were swept aside in a tidal wave of premarital sex, illegal drugs, and music that freaked them out. Even the Beatles were too way-out! Our mothers thought pot caused brain dam- age and acid schizophrenia. I thought they were square; talking to them now I realize they were rightfully terrified. There hasn't been a radical change or cultural shift between my generation and my daughter's. Her world doesn't look all that different from mine. When my daughter found a joint and a couple of buds in a plastic bag in my night table, she waved it in front of me. "Mom, seriously?"

Rhoda replenishes beverages and conversation cycles through the weather, weekend activities, medical reports, movie reviews, and book reports. Most of the ladies watch *The Good Wife* on Sunday night. Everyone loves Alicia Florrick, the main character in the show. She speaks to their gen. The stand-by-your-man wives, the look-the-other-way wives. Women of their generation largely stayed married out of financial necessity coupled with the fear of social stigma. If any of the Bridge Ladies cheated on their husbands or were cheated on by them, they will go to their graves with it.

I've learned that bragging is permissible, but only up to a point. College acceptances, getting engaged, having babies, getting jobs are all on the preapproved list. To listen to the ladies, none of their adult children has ever stumbled, gotten divorced, lost a job, or lost their way.

Bette has been granted special dispensation in the bragging department. She became a grandmother at eighty, "the oldest living grandmother on earth," she says. One Monday, when Bridge was at her house, the ladies filed into her office and watched a video on her computer of the boys standing in their crib and acted as if they should receive Heisman Trophies. Today she announces with glee and relief, "the twins are walking!" Everyone whoops. Sometimes I feel that for Bette the glass is half empty, but with the arrival of those boys her cup runneth over. "I have this feeling the boys are a part of me, they have crawled into my soul."

The ladies discuss obituaries of both local friends, public figures, and movie stars, especially if they are Jewish, like Bess Myerson, the first Jewish Miss America, and Lauren "Betty" Bacall, who downplayed her Jewishness as her Hollywood star was rising and later acquiesced when Humphrey Bogart wanted their children baptized. The ladies would make a killing on a Jewish-themed game of Jeopardy. *Alex, I'll take Jewish Beauties for $100.*

Last spring they were all glued to their televisions, watching the manhunt following the Boston Marathon bombings. They couldn't understand how a young man with friends and good at school could turn into a killer. The world makes no sense. They are pained for the people who have lost lives and limbs. This is the world today: a pendulum swinging from bad to worse, from random acts of negligence to premeditated acts of terror. Or maybe things *are* worse. Bette once commented that she stopped believing in God after 9/11, which shocked me after all she and her generation had already lived through. I suggest other factors that may make things seem worse today: the twenty-four-hour news cycle, a media that turns events like the Boston Marathon bombing into made-for-TV movies, and all of the social media and its reach. No, the ladies were adamant: things are worse now. They are united in their chorus that the world was never this dangerous. Their indignation is keen. Didn't they live through worse? I wonder if aging makes you more fearful, more vulnerable. Or are new problems scarier? How do the bad old days become the good old days? Is the devil you know, as my mother says, better than the devil you don't?

Rhoda's made blondies. They are cut in perfect squares and arranged like a checkerboard on a china plate. Dessert plates have been set out, and Rhoda is poised to refill teacups and coffee. Everyone compliments the dessert. Rhoda loves to cook and bake; she mentions that George loves her cooking. I can't imagine my mother cooking for another man; she hung up her spatula when my father died.

Rhoda has lucked out with George. She didn't expect it, wasn't looking for it.

"I never thought about dating. I was busy. I have a lot of friends, my subscriptions," she told me during one of our talks.

"How did you meet? JDate? A bar?"

Rhoda knows I'm joking but she still protests, "No! A friend set us up."

"Did you go out to dinner?"

"She invited us to her house for dinner."

We were on Rhoda's couch, and she was transferring shells from one dish to another. I'm not sure, but I think she had some seasonal decorating scheme in mind.

"Were you terrified?"

"No. Why would I be terrified?"

"I don't know, not having dated for so long, possibly getting rejected, taking off your clothes, stuff like that."

Rhoda levels her eyes at my impertinence.

"Not even a little nervous?"

"I guess I was a little nervous."

"What did you wear?" I'm sort of kidding, but Rhoda answers right away. I gather she had put some thought into it: black silk pants and a pale pink sweater.

"What was your first impression?"

Then Rhoda remembers something: she had arrived at her friend's house first, was just about to get out of her car, when she saw George pull up and park. She stayed inside her car then, and watched as he carried a cake box to the house, and continued to watch as he was greeted by the hosts and welcomed inside. She took a moment before getting out of her car, walking up to her friend's house, and ringing the bell. It's was an Alice Munro moment; a short story capturing a woman who quietly hesitates on the cusp of something, the past and future merging. Did she think of Peter just then, the only man she had ever known, did she ask his permission to move on, or was she only gathering herself for an evening out, nothing lost, nothing gained, or so she told herself?

"What did you think?"

"I thought he was very nice-looking."

"How did the evening go?"

"It went very well."

"Did you wonder if you would hear from him?"

"I hoped I would."

The ladies ooh and aah over the blondies.

"Sorry, Betsy, they have nuts." Rhoda remembers my nut allergy, though at a previous lunch she commented on how so many more people have allergies than ever before, nuts, lactose, gluten, you name it. She sounded dubious, as if I were making it up. In fact, the ladies are generally dubious of a whole host of conditions and maladies that seemingly didn't exist, or at least were not as widespread, in their day such as autism, PTSD, ADD, and dyslexia. Only today, Rhoda brings out a box of ginger cookies she bought especially for me. "I read every single ingredient on the package! No nuts!"

She likes me, she really likes me.

Rhoda wraps the leftover blondies in plastic wrap as carefully as a mummy and sets them to the side. The ladies root around in their pocketbooks and drop their dollars on the table. Early on there are some flare-ups over wrong bids. Bridge brings out the best and worst in a person: how competitive you are, how generous, how petty, and how kind. A person's sense of decorum or lack thereof is immediately on display. How patient you are or how easily annoyed. How much of a show-off, or how cool. Your essential self comes out when you are challenged, when your partner makes a costly mistake, when you go down, or are victorious. A friend's mother and longtime Bridge player called it "the revelation of self." This game, I think, is intimate. You can't be anything but yourself.

After an hour or so, I watch a few hands, sit back with my pad, and sketch the ladies' accessories. How do they choose what to wear, their bureaus crowded with a lifetime of rings, pins, bracelets, and necklaces? How do hands no longer flexible work a clasp? Thread an earring? How do they still care? *If these beads could talk.*

When my mother wins the first contract, meaning she will play the hand, she mutters the entire time, counting her trump in a stage whisper. After she wins a trick, she looks at the four cards again and starts to make noises about how she won't be able to make it. The more she complains, the more likely she will win. And when she does, in keeping with this grand charade, she exclaims, "Phew! Thought we weren't going to make it," as if she has just hauled up a dozen children from an abandoned mine.

The women are deep into the afternoon of play. Just as I can no longer concentrate on the game and am about to leave, I feel my phone vibrate in my back pocket. I had forgotten to leave it in the car, and whoever is texting is persistent, two, three, four times in a row. This could only be my daughter.

Growing concerned, I excuse myself. "Sorry, Raffi's been texting me."

In the hallway, I read the four texts, the first one asking me to bring a book to school that she'd forgotten, each subsequent text growing more indignant that I hadn't answered:

Hello?

Where r u

Hello

In fairness, when she doesn't answer my texts right away I completely overreact and immediately go into worry mode.

When I return to the table, my mother asks if everything is okay.

"Everything's fine. I just worry when she texts me so many times."

"Maybe she should learn patience," Rhoda says, cutting but not inaccurate.

I wonder how history will judge us, the helicopter parents accused of hovering over our kids well into their twenties? Or how bitterly our kids will complain to their own shrinks about how we overshared, micromanaged, and at the same time were never really there for them, either always working or too busy fulfilling ourselves. When I once boasted at a holiday dinner that I attended all of my daughter's soccer games, she countered, "But you were always on your BlackBerry."

They are on their last hand of the day. I've zoned out and am staring at the pretty dish of brightly colored glass candies with ruffled edges like the collars of Dutch masters on Rhoda's coffee table. Next to the dish is a miniature trio: a frog made of green beads with red eyes that pop like raspberries, an elephant made of green glass, and a crystal seal balancing a ball. Perhaps they come to life at night and play a few jazz standards while Rhoda sleeps. Perhaps the Bridge Ladies come to life when I leave as well, confiding in each other and opening up. It's true they all have loosened up considerably from where we started. They greet me at the door with less trepidation, more enthusiasm. And they all tell me that our talks have brought back memories that come unbidden. When I ask what they remember, it's always out of grasp, like a dream that lingers near. Why am I so desperate to imagine hidden depths and secret lives? Perhaps the reason they don't divulge very much is they don't actually feel the *need* to open up. In fact, it goes against their nature. They seem content with the way things are. Bridge may be a tonic for them the way opening up with friends is for me.

Perhaps in my desperation for something to happen, I have missed what is actually happening.

CHAPTER 13

Zig-Zag

Goats Head Soup was the album cover on which I first witnessed a joint being rolled, the careful separation of leaves from the sticks and seeds, which caromed down the flat surface of the album like silver balls in a pinball machine. Bea's daughter, Nancy, came to stay with us for two or three days when my parents went away. I was fifteen, Nina was seventeen, and Nancy was probably a college senior home for break. She wore bell-bottom hip huggers with a wide leather belt and had long brown hair. I thought she was a rock star. She had a loud voice, a hearty laugh, and like a hippie version of the Cat in the Hat, she made herself right at home, plopping down on the Rice-A-Roni-colored shag carpet in our den, and told us that we were going to have fun. She spread the pot out on the album cover and picked out the twigs the way Eli Whitney's cotton gin separated the seeds from the fiber. (Whitney went to Yale, and every schoolchild in New Haven has gone on a field trip to the museum dedicated to his invention.)

Nancy was a groovy Mary Poppins with her own bag of goodies. When she took out a slim orange packet, I mistook it for gum. On closer inspection, I saw that it said Zig-Zag, and there was a man who looked like a prophet on the cover. These were rolling papers. She expertly licked the edge of one, like the glue on an envelope, and attached it to another. Then she filled it with the freshly cleaned pot and rolled it with élan. Then she put the entire thing in her mouth and pulled it out quickly to seal the seam. Voilà!

Mick Jagger's face was swathed in some kind of chiffon bonnet, and at first I mistook him for a woman. I had heard of the band. One of my friend's older sisters had *Sticky Fingers* and we went crazy over the fly with the real zipper embedded into the album cover. At a sleepover in her newly created basement rec room, we danced like maniacs to "Brown Sugar."

A few of Nancy's friends came over, and the music got louder. She feverishly worked to assemble a tray of Chex Mix. Happy conspirator, I proudly showed her where my mother kept the baking trays, expediting the preparation of "munchies." It was a combination of wheat, corn, and rice Chex mixed with peanuts and pretzels and doused with either honey or maple syrup and baked. The operative word: *baked*. I had already started sneaking cigarettes, and the arrival of Nancy Phillips was like a gateway to everything I wanted in on. She was the first cool person I had met up close. If she had told me to jump off a bridge, I would have leapt.

The 1960s came to New Haven (in the 1970s), and there was no turning back. At thirteen, I was just beginning to recognize that the pungent smell behind a movie theater or in a parking lot was weed. It was still fairly exotic. I had no idea where to get any or how the older siblings of my friends always seemed to have a nickel bag on hand, or a dime. By the time I was in high school, I was getting high at the bus stop and in the basement and in my car, and my friends and I had many dinners at our parents' homes stoned out of our minds, devouring the food and laughing hysterically at almost anything, including, for example, the farting sound Tupperware used to make.

"Everybody was smoking pot, everybody," Nancy tells me when I reconnect with her and confess how those few days influenced me. The Phillips kids were known for their good looks, they were swimmers, had lean swimmers' bodies, and they liked to party. "But we never got busted." Bea found some pot growing in the backyard, and once she found hash in her son's room. "She thought it was a rock and was about to throw it out. My brother screamed at her, 'Don't you dare.' And she didn't." All Bea has to say when it comes to raising three teenagers in the 1970s: "It was the times. Those were tough times."

"We loved rock and roll," Nancy says, filling in the picture. "*Loved* it. Even my dad, who was a trained musician, loved Hendricks and Led Zeppelin. He didn't get it all, but he'd say, 'listen to that guitar.' He could appreciate it." When Nancy tells me there was no prejudice in her house, I'm immediately reminded of Bea's home in Bedford, where the help ate their meals with the family. Nancy is proud of the liberal example her parents set; their only expectation was that the children marry within the faith. When Bea graduated from high school, Bea's mother left small-town Bedford for Louisville, for the larger Jewish population. No doubt about it, they were husband hunting.

When I reach Nancy at her home in Florida, we admit we are equally astonished by the sheer longevity of our mothers' club. I start by asking how much feminism influenced her, and she doesn't hesitate. "I distinctly remember telling my parents that I would go behind their backs and date non-Jewish boys. I stood up for myself. Women were supposed to be independent. If I don't get married, I don't get married. It wasn't a goal."

Nancy knew from day one that she would rather be alone than be in a crummy relationship. She tells me all this laced with laughter. "That's what we got from feminism, right?" Nancy wanted to work, make money, and have her own apartment. "I know I was supposed to get married, but women got to be independent. Betty Friedan was a total influence."

When I ask Nancy if she is close with Bea, she says, "We are now." Nancy is as frank as Bea is guarded. "Did I tell her I hated her? Sure. Don't all daughters?"

♠

Jackie's father-in-law owned the New Haven Arena, a venue for every concert, circus, entertainment, and sports attraction that came to town. Jackie's daughter Lisa grew up ringside to every event. She remembers attending her first concert and bumping into this very tall, blonde person backstage, only later realizing when the group took the stage that it was Mary of Peter, Paul and Mary. She was twelve when she saw the infamous concert where Jim Morrison, the first rock star to get arrested in the middle of a show, got hauled off the stage for calling the New Haven police pigs and throwing a mic stand into the audience. She was safe inside the press box with her grandfather, who quickly shuttled her home.

When Lisa and her friends got older they wanted out of the press box and onto the floor. Lisa admits it was always a little fraught, bringing friends. Discerning real friends from convenient ones brought its own teenage agony, like when Bette Cohen sidled up to Ginger Bailey for Shubert tickets. Still, she saw Chuck Berry open for Jefferson Airplane, Traffic, Leon Russell, and Van Morrison. Dylan played there, the Rolling Stones, the Kinks, Joan Baez, the Supremes, and Elton John's farewell tour in 1972. Jackie never went to a single concert, didn't care for the music. When I mention all the greats who played there, she couldn't be more dismissive. "No, no, no, never heard of them."

"Discipline was out of the question," Bette says. From the time Amy was three years old, or so the family mythology goes, she took control. I challenge the veracity of a three-year-old having that much power, but Bette insists it's the case. "We belonged to the Surf Club in East Haven and I thought it was a good place to go every day to occupy her, but Amy said, 'no, no, no,' and then she started banging her head on the floor until she knocked herself unconscious."

We are in Bette's kitchen and she points to the very spot where her toddler knocked herself out. "I was on the phone with my mother-in-law and all of a sudden her eyes rolled up, and I start screaming, and my mother-in-law hangs up and calls the neighbor across the street." By the time the neighbor came, Amy had roused. "Can you believe it?"

When Amy and Bette's two younger children were still small, Bette heard that the Jewish Center in downtown New Haven had formed a Theater Guild. She wasn't exactly April Wheeler in *Revolutionary Road*, the suburban housewife desperate to reignite her failed acting career, but she busted out of Woodbridge to see if she still had it, but not before making dinner. And Arthur, ever accommodating, was always very good about being home in the evening with the kids because the rehearsals were at night.

Bette landed the lead in the first play she tried out for, *The Monkey's Paw*, and every subsequent drama the group mounted. When they put on musicals (Bette couldn't sing), she'd do makeup, props, work backstage, and stage-manage.

"I just loved being there. There's a certain kind of ambience that, to this day, when I walk into a theater, it's like hearing a song that reminds you of something great in your life and being transported right back there."

When I ask Bette if she remembers anyone in particular from that time, she zeroes in right away. "Yeah, there was one guy, studying directing at the Yale drama school who came to direct a play. He was very talented, very good-looking, and I think in my dream world I was in love with him, even though I had three kids and a husband at home. But he became very, very important in my life."

"Was it reciprocated?"

"No. It was a complete fantasy. I'm sure he liked me and thought I had some talent, but that was all. We didn't have a social thing at all. It was just a fantasy of mine."

I look up *The Monkey's Paw* when I get home and discover that it's based on a 1902 British story by W. W. Jacobs about a couple being granted three wishes. Only each wish comes with a hideous twist, punishment for tempting fate. When they wish to see their son who has died in a horrible accident, he comes back to them as he has died, mangled and rotting. Bette had her own three wishes: a part in a play, a dashing young director, and a life in the theater. But she would never tempt fate. The Theater Guild would eventually come apart and then cease to be altogether. Bette tells me she saved every program. "They're somewhere in the basement."

I ask to see them. She laughs at that. "I'm sure my kids will throw them all out when I die."

In high school, Amy had a boyfriend with a motorcycle. *Was there nothing this girl couldn't do?* Bette would try to keep her home, she had school and exams for god's sake, but there was no telling her what to do. To hear Bette tell it she was completely outmatched by Amy. When she was a senior, Amy staged her greatest insurrection yet. She ran away from home for three days. Unlike most spoiled suburban kids who run away for an hour or two until the smell of lamb chops on the broiler draws them inside, Amy vanished. I'm impressed. I can't help it. Amy's daring and selfish act embodies the kind of rebellious spirit I felt but could never act on. Bette asks me how I would feel if my daughter disappeared for three days, and I get the picture, though somehow I am still on the side of Amy's insurrection. They called every friend and sought help from the police. Eventually they found her at a friend's house. To this day Bette doesn't understand how the parents didn't call. I know Amy as an adult. She has her own law practice and is a college law professor as well. Like Bette, she is slim and beautiful, and she, too, speaks with crisp enunciation. Everything she says sounds important and authoritative. Bette and Arthur and Amy usually join our family for Rosh Hashanah. Amy is always stunning and usually has her dashing boyfriend with her.

Bette tells me that boys were "knocking down her door," many potential husbands over the years, but she didn't give them "the time of day." Neither of Bette's daughters married nor had children. She still feels some piece of their life is missing, and hers by extension. To me, Amy seems complete. Bette had lived to please her mother and did, producing a slate of straight-A report cards, performing in every play where the world could see Sylvia Cohen's talented and beautiful girl. She married a Jewish man and gave her mother three grandchildren. Is that too much to ask? Bette insists that she just wants her daughters to be happy, but by whose standards?

♠

When Rhoda's daughter Beth announced that she was going to marry her high school boyfriend, there should have been an EMS on hand. Forget that he wasn't Jewish! Of all the shocking things kids were doing to rebel: dropping out of college, dropping acid, and dropping out, Beth had done the least expected thing by wanting to get married. In fact, most kids opted for living together—in and of itself a difficult pill for our parents to swallow. One of my friends' mothers put it this way, "Why would a man buy the cow if he can get the milk for free?" You might also ask why a woman would buy a car before she had a chance to look under the hood.

Rhoda and her husband insisted that Beth finish a yearlong business course before she married, hoping that the time might put an end to the idea of this Romeo-and-Juliet-style love. It didn't, and a wedding was planned at the young man's home after she graduated. It was a wrenching time, and Rhoda debated whether to attend the wedding. Her own mother was boycotting the affair. Rhoda and Peter brought their anguish to a rabbi for some guidance. Surely the deck was stacked. What rabbi could possibly condone this interfaith marriage? Only he asked them just one question: Do you want to retain a relationship with your daughter? Because if you do, you must go to the wedding.

"So we did." Rhoda sounds as if she is still struggling with the decision.

They didn't stay for the party, but they did go to the wedding.

The marriage lasted four years. Beth would get on the roller coaster of her life and not let go for many difficult years. Eventually she would marry again, and have two sons. There's a Yiddish word, *nakhes*, which describes the particular mix of pleasure and pride that only a child can give to its parents. There isn't a word for its opposite: when a child disappoints you. No one talks about that.

Years later, Beth admitted to her mother that she knew it was a mistake. Beth also agrees to talk with me, though I hear some apprehension in her voice when I call. But she laughs with recognition when I start by saying that her mother is a self-described Victorian. "That's definitely my mother."

Then she asks if I know that she and her brother are adopted. It's not exactly clear to me how Beth factors that into her difficult history with Rhoda. What she does say is that her mother, the only child, was the "perfect child, perfect grades, perfect attitudes, behaviors."

"That's a lot of perfection," I say.

"I was a rebellious child. I was very difficult. I got married out of rebellion. Everything I did was the opposite of what she was."

Rhoda was clear that she was against open adoption. "They were our children. Period. When a woman gives up a child it's for a damn good reason. She made a decision." But she also believed in telling her children as soon as possible. She was ahead of her time on that score. She couldn't fathom waiting until her children were adolescents.

"We chose you," she would say. "You're our chosen child."

Within just a few minutes, Beth and I are sharing personal details about our lives: maternal conflicts, low points in our own lives, dealing with it. And there it is again, a willingness to open up that is anathema to the Bridge Ladies. To them, our lives must look like a massive oil spill off the Carolinas.

I ask Beth how her relationship with her mother is now. "She is the dearest thing to me. I appreciate the tough love. I appreciate her so greatly."

I know that Rhoda has not exactly relaxed her standards. When she looks out at the body of water that is her view, I sense that it helps her navigate a world that continues to trample most of her values. There would be many more days when Beth would test her mother and Rhoda would return to the same fork in the road: *Do you want to have a relationship with your daughter?*

♠

I was three when JFK was assassinated, five when the antiwar movement gained national attention, when horrific images of Vietnam were on the cover of *Life* magazine and on the TV. I was eight when Robert Kennedy and Martin Luther King Jr. were assassinated two months apart. Nine when Neil Armstrong set foot on the moon and when mud-sliding hippies took over a farm in Woodstock for three days of rock and roll. Every boy in my class wanted an astronaut suit; I wanted a suede vest with long fringe. On my ninth birthday the Manson Family killing spree started with the murder of Sharon Tate.

In 1971, *All in the Family* captured the generational divide, splitting the world into Archies and meatheads. It defined the generation gap. I knew which side I was on. Like Nancy, I wanted my own apartment, my own car, and my own career. It's not that I thought I could do anything, be anyone, my imagination wasn't that bold, but I knew I wouldn't be making meat loaf, carpooling, or playing Bridge. *No fucking way.*

That said, my own rebellion lacked boys on motorcycles and police sweeps through the woods of our rural town. It was weight gain, tinted glasses, black T-shirts, and diaries. It was a combination of polarizing anger and debilitating sadness. Again and again, I'd paint myself into a corner I couldn't escape. Teenagers sometimes ask each other grand questions: If you could live anywhere in the world, where would it be? What would you do if you had a million dollars? Or in my case, how would you kill yourself? I had waded into the swamp of adolescence, first to my waist, then up to my neck. How do you tell normal adolescent mood swings from manic depression? How does a bank of clouds obscure the sky, slowly or all at once? Did I really sleep with a raft of selfish, stupid boys? And turn on nearly every friend I ever had?

When I ask my mother about my teenage years now, she explains I was becoming difficult to live with. When I ask her to elaborate she says I was "rude, nasty, whatever." And then she tells the same and only story she has repeated my entire life to explain what happened. "You were a perfect, bubbly, bright little girl, and the very day you turned thirteen you became surly, uncommunicative, and withdrawn."

She always said this in a spirited way as if she could pin all that misery to the day in August when I turned thirteen. Then she'd hurl one of her famous curses my way: I wish on you a daughter just like yourself. Yes, of course it was all said in fun. Only one question always remained: What *did* happen when I turned thirteen? And fifteen? And twenty-five? Why, when I needed my mother most, was she the last person on the planet I would turn to for help?

♠

"Are you bipolar?" My daughter was ten when she asked me. We were in her bed reading together before she went to sleep. It was something I knew I had to tell her one day, but I didn't expect it to come this soon, and in the moment she had taken me by surprise. I felt instantly awash in shame. By way of explanation, she said that her friend's mother has googled me. Google! *Fucking Google.* For the first time I regret having written a memoir about my illness. She was a toddler when I wrote it.

At the time, a handful of friends suggested that it was irresponsible of me; what would my daughter think when she was old enough to read it? Insulted by the question, I was cavalier in my response: Aren't men allowed to write about their illnesses, their affairs, their acts of aggression and unkindness? Why are women held to a higher standard? Why is our mothering called into question when we reveal something unpleasant? All of my indignation fell away when my daughter looked up at me. I had told the world my story, only now I faced the only person for whom the truth mattered. It was a straightforward question, but it felt as if a hole had opened up in the mattress and that I was about to fall through.

"Yes," I said, choking back tears. *Hold it together.* No matter that I hadn't had a single "episode" since she was born, the stigma was as huge as the biggest sunflower against a southern wall, the dark velvet center large enough to swallow a small girl. I told her that medications don't work for everyone, but I was fortunate because they worked for me. I asked whether she has any questions and stopped there, remembering to keep it simple. She hasn't asked to see my medical chart.

By then it seemed like she was barely listening, even bored, looking instead at her wall of pictures pulled from fan magazines: Zac Efron, Hilary Duff, and Raven from *That's So Raven.* Then she turned on her side, put her hand on her hip, and said unequivocally, "I don't have it."

I desperately wanted to believe that I had broken the chain of secrets and untruths, that I was *not* my mother, only I now suspected that it didn't ultimately matter what I thought or what I knew or what I told myself. I was convinced that had my mother told me the truth about her life, had leveled with me about her father, her depression, if she could have talked about Barbara, we would have had the opportunity to help each other, or at least know each other. But isn't it also possible that I would have judged her, that she would have been even more diminished in my eyes?

My daughter's response had startled me, even though intellectually I knew this statement of differentiation was the healthiest response of all. She has her own will, desire, psychology, and agency. Only I feel fused to her, my little girl. I feel each and every disappointment of hers in my bones and every victory. When she ran in the baton race at her school, I felt the baton in my own hand, my legs pumping and lungs straining to reach the girl ahead for the handoff.

Years later, when I relay this to Anne, she uncharacteristically speaks. First, her foot slowly circles like a marionette coming to life. "It does matter," she says, "it matters that you told her the truth."

CHAPTER 14

Get the Kiddies off the Street

Barbara Barkin says I'll never get better unless I play. Then she calls one night and says she has a partner for me. She is as excited as if she were fixing me up on a date.

"He's a very nice man. He just retired, something in finance, and is looking for a Bridge partner for the Tuesday game in Orange. His wife still works!"

I back off, saying I'm not ready. Barbara will not take no for an answer. I need this, she's sure of it. She gives me his number.

"Call, call," she says. "Call tonight. He's expecting your call. Then call me." If my mother pulled this, I would have killed her. But coming from Barbara, I go with it.

Tuesday Bridge at the Orange Senior Center is held in the lounge. It starts at one but Barbara instructs me to arrive at twelve forty-five, when they collect the money and set up. The buy in is a dollar and the winnings are divided three ways among the top three winning partners. All over the room, seniors are reaching into handbags or fishing out wallets to pay up. There are about fifteen card tables, and the room is noisy with people socializing. I can't tell if partners have regular tables; it looks a little like musical chairs, with people trying to find a place to play before they're all taken.

I spot my partner right away. He's crisp in khakis and polo shirt, with a pair of tortoise readers perched on his nose as he scans the *Wall Street Journal*. He's probably midsixties, still handsome in that unfair way that men age. I walk over and introduce myself.

"Jonathan," he says, reaching to shake my hand, super firm handshake. I immediately launch into the fact that I'm a beginner. Just then I spot Barbara and Bernard socializing. I'm happy to see them knitting in. They gave up their home and a wide circle of friends when they came to New Haven. After my dad became wheelchair bound, my mother used to say that between his brain and her body, they made up one person. Maybe Bernard and Barbara are one person now. Bernard has said if Barbara goes first, he'll "take the hemlock."

"It's true," Barbara confirmed, "but I'll survive."

And this also seemed true. It's what women do.

Nearly everyone else in the room, as far as I can tell, is in their eighth decade, some older, just a few younger. They say nothing prepares you for having children but the thing no one really prepares you for is aging, looking like a mushroom cap, your hands gnarled. Or your body shrunken down and in. Some of the women look like men. Some of the men look like women. Is this what it comes to? Will you never pluck your eyebrows again, your chin? I can't help but wonder if this is where it will end for me, pushing my body forward with the help of a walker, neon tennis balls fixed to the front legs. Will my game ever improve? Will I have my marbles? Will I even be lucky enough to have a game of cards and camaraderie? I recognize, too, that the folks here are the lucky ones. I can't help but think of the seniors who are homebound, or stuck in a facility watching *Days of Our Lives*.

When I asked the ladies when they started feeling old, they all said seventy. "It's when things break down," Bette said. "Eighty is awful." Bette Davis was right, "Old age ain't no place for sissies."

♠

Bridge is especially interesting to researchers who study the aging brain because it combines two elements that are thought to decrease the risk of developing dementia. For one, the game keeps you mentally sharp combined with the added social component. Isolation for older people can be disastrous.

"A healthy human mind can go blank and quickly become disoriented," according to a *New York Times* article, "At the Bridge Table, Clues to a Lucid Old Age." My mother doesn't believe that playing Bridge wards off dementia. "If you have dementia, you don't play."

Bridge players do fear the day when they might slip. "We're all afraid to lose memory; we're all at risk for that," said a woman at the retirement home where studies are being conducted on nonagenarian Bridge players dubbed "the super memory club." Every older Bridge player I've talked to comments on how difficult it is when one player can't keep up, makes mistakes, is clearly on a downward slide.

Bernard Barkin is still a sharp and a terrific player though he has trouble holding the cards. His stroke has left his fingers bent. He's slower at picking up cards and arranging them into suits, always apologizing to those he plays with. Barbara always shuffles and deals for him. It's truly no big deal, but you can see on his face that it's a blow, a reminder that he is no longer the vigorous man nicknamed Buck coaching basketball or covering his side of the tennis court with power and grace. When my father could no longer handle the cards, he used a card holder, but that didn't last long. For others it's a decent solution; for him it was humiliating, like wearing a bib.

The Bridge Ladies are exceptional in this way: all of them sharp, quick, and independent. It's hard to image a day when one might no longer be welcome, what they would do should they come to that crossroads. Another member of the super memory club also noted a sad correlation: when people stop playing, they don't live much longer.

♠

The room is incubator warm. I feel sweat gathering at the underwire of my bra, the back of my neck, and my forehead. I tell the couple we are playing with that I'm a novice. When I played with the Bridge Ladies, I knew they would forgive any mistake. This is big girl Bridge. No training wheels. No questions allowed. The seniors are here to win, rack up points, take home the jackpot. It's intimidating as hell. My mother tells me that they're glad to play with a newbie; it means more points for them. Not especially comforting.

My chest has tightened with the onset of a panic attack. Why did I let Barbara push me into it? I already know before we start that I'm totally out of my depths. I don't even know the protocol for which person shuffles, cuts the cards, and deals. It didn't seem important to me so I never paid attention, but Bridge players are fanatical when it comes to table etiquette. Put the cards in the wrong place at your peril. The rules seemed uptight in the extreme. Later, as I get more experienced, I will find myself hewing to all of the rules, enforcing them. There is an unspoken elegance like the changing of the guard as the cards are shuffled, cut, and dealt in a specific rotation. I recognize, too, that the protocol has a purpose. Bridge etiquette conveys both the decorum of the game and principles of fairness.

It's my turn to deal the first hand and I'm even afraid of messing up the deal and giving everyone the wrong number of cards. I tell myself to calm down. I know how to deal for god's sake. And even if I do mess up, it happens. I pick up my cards and organize them by suit. Dealer bids first. My lessons have gone out the window. I'm flooded with anxiety. I was more relaxed when I lost my virginity!

Our opponents tell me I'll be fine. They are a married couple. She is petite, lovely, and curiously decked out in a turquoise bear claw bolo, turquoise rings, and a matching belt perhaps from a recent spending binge on Pueblo.com.

"It's just a game," she says. Make no mistake: people who say it's just a game are out for blood. I've seen it over and over. It's the kind of thing you say to psych someone out, to establish dominance. Nothing is just a game, especially Bridge. The man flicks his ear and tells us he's hard of hearing. His wife continues to speak in very soft tones. *Gaslight!* His Velcro strap sneakers are so large you can't distinguish the right foot from the left. Jonathan asks if I play the "Weak Two." He might as well have asked if I swing or like leather. What the hell is the "Weak Two?" Later I will learn that the Weak Two and bids like it are called conventions and they generally convey hands with exceptional distribution, in this case six of the same suit and between five and ten high-point cards.

The bell rings. *Shit.*

I open my cards: I have fourteen points and five Spades. I have to bid. I freeze. I feel my back wet with perspiration, my shirt clinging. Everyone waits for my bid. My shorts have crawled up my crack. They are still waiting. I make a first bid of "one Spade." Okay, nothing bad happens.

Only when it is Jonathan's turn, he says, "two Hearts," and I freeze again. I've learned that his response means he has eleven-plus points and five Hearts only I can't access this information. I don't know if I should make another bid or pass. Instead, I hear the "Bohemian Rhapsody" in my head, and it's crowding out all rational thought.

Scaramouch, scaramouch will you do the fandango.

"Can I ask a question?" I am met with stern glares. That would be a no. When I blow the hand, I want to go home. Only I'm not five years old. I have to stick it out. I tell myself I'm learning. But nearly every card I play is wrong. I watch my partner's disbelief as the opposing team takes the tricks that should have been ours. I've been taking lessons for nearly a year. If it weren't for the ladies, I would have probably quit by now. Maybe I should play bingo! Maybe I need Bridge special ed. At the very least, my chair should be marked with a handicap sign.

After we play four hands, the bell rings to signal time. Partners sitting in the East/West position rotate to a new table. Jonathan and I are North/South and stay put. The room looks like a senior square dance until everyone finds their new table. Jonathan reviews the last hand with me. I can see his mouth moving. I can tell by his tone that he is trying to be gentle. But I can't hear a word he says. The next couple comes and I am grateful to pull some hands too weak to bid and thus pass.

This team has been partners and friends for more than fifty years. The taller woman wears slacks and a shirt with a faint floral pattern. Her partner is petite and wears a dress and a broach that looks like a marigold. They both have white hair as light as meringue. When I tell them that I'm a beginner, they just look at me: who cares. They are quick to bid, quick to discard, quick to collect tricks, and quick to win and tally their points. I've noticed that Jonathan likes to pull a card from his hand and tap it on the table multiple times before he discards, the way a tennis player bounces a ball before a serve. I can't tell if he's buying time to think or showing off.

I lose the one hand I get to play (having won the auction) because I fail to "pull trump at the outset of the hand." Pulling trump is generally the first order of business: drawing out the opponent's trumps so no one can trump your winners in other suits. It's also one of the very first things you learn, and Bridge players refer to it as "getting the kiddies off the street." When I started playing, I wanted to hold on to my trumps, thinking I would need them later in the game. It took a long time before I realized that you need to get the trump out early so no one can trump you later. It seemed counterintuitive to me. When the tiny woman plays a trump and Jonathan overtrumps it, her friend says, "Don't send in a kid to do a man's job." I hadn't heard this expression before, but after a time I become more familiar with Bridge vernacular. The first time I heard myself say "Give unto Caesar what belongs to Caesar," I realized I'd crossed a line. In between hands, the two women exchange Bridge patter in the form of encouragement: "Good job," and "That was a rough one," and "Barely squeezed that out."

The rotation is such that we never play with Barbara and Buck, but Barbara rushes over at the end of the afternoon. She is eager to know how I did, if I enjoyed myself. Will I play again? Only just then, Bernard calls her over.

"Wait a minute, Bernard," she calls back.

"Barbara," he calls again, more urgently.

"Shhhh," she says, slapping the air with her hand.

"Now, Barbara!" This time there is panic in his voice, and she rushes over. I see her take his face in her hands and look into his eyes. She says something and he nods. Then she hurries back to retrieve her bag and apologizes for the disruption, says she'll call and we'll talk. Then she quickly joins Bernard at the door, reaches around his back, and together they make their way out of the center.

Watching them I long to rush home and hold John's face in my hands. We had become distant in a longer-than-usual stretch of marital ennui. Nothing was wrong; nothing was right. I hoped we would still be together in our eighties, that there would be things to talk about. If we made it, would we draw close, fall back in love the way we did at the beginning? Is this the reward of a long marriage? No one expects to be the couple in the restaurant sitting in silence, having run out of things to say, or unable to muster the energy to say them. Whenever we spotted one of these grim couples, we'd feel sorry for them, convinced that would never happen to us, the arrogance of youth on our side.

CHAPTER 15

The Hands of a Clock

"I didn't have to give up Bridge," Bette says. "That was the best part." We are sitting in her enclosed porch, her favorite room in the house, the sun diffused through the dark mesh screen. Three years after her youngest went to college, Bette went back to work part-time as a camp consultant. She had heard about a franchise business out of Boston, and while she didn't have any experience per se, it sounded like something she would be good at. It turned out to be the perfect fit, her first year alone more than doubling her projected earnings. Plus, she could make her own hours. The same was true for Jackie, who went to work at Triple A, also in an advisory capacity. An experienced traveler herself, she liked plotting trips for the clients, walking them through the particulars of their journey. Bea went to work for two and half days a week in Carl's office handling the paperwork. She liked the other gals in the office and enjoyed having lunch with them. She, too, kept Monday free. Work was great, but Bridge was sacred.

"I was liberated." Bette laughs when I ask her about the "empty nest." Arthur set up an office for her, and Bette went about writing away for brochures, visiting camps, and interviewing the kids and their parents, determining their interests. In no time she was known and highly regarded throughout the area as the "Camp Lady." She wouldn't have called it multitasking, but Bette like most women had mastered the art of juggling responsibilities and fulfilling the needs of others. And then there was the paycheck. "I put a lot of time into it because I enjoyed it. I really did like it, and I made a lot of money. It turned out to be really lucrative for me."

Bette got special dispensation from the head office to check out camps with Arthur instead of traveling with a pack of other consultants. "At that point I was the top salesperson, and they didn't want to let me go." Arthur loved navigating. Together they would explore the boondocks of Maine, New Hampshire, and upstate New York. He would drop Bette off at a camp then scout for a place to set up a picnic lunch. Later, they'd find a nice little place for dinner. "It made all the difference, going with Arthur. I loved going with him." Things were good.

Then: not so good. Bette was diagnosed with uterine cancer. Scary as it was, it didn't compare with her first bout with cancer. Bette was in her midforties when she discovered she had breast cancer. The kids were still young and all she could think about was what would happen to them if she died. It was terrifying and the lack of information was staggering. Bette was of the generation of women who went into surgery and woke up with anything from a partial to double mastectomy. Her surgeon instructed her to return in six weeks for a follow-up and then he summarily dismissed her. "When my surgeon said good-bye that was the end of my relationship with him. It was frightening. There was no support."

In 1976, journalist Betty Rollins broke the national silence surrounding breast cancer in her book *First, You Cry*, at a time when no one used the word *cancer* and no one said the word *breast*. "For all I know," she writes, "I was surrounded by one-breasted women, but we didn't talk to each other because we were all in hiding."

It was a convergence of three events that brought Bette's days as the Camp Lady to an end: the uterine cancer (which she would also beat), internecine wars among the camp franchises, and the advent of the computer age. Initially, Bette composed all of her correspondence on a manual typewriter. When she eventually upgraded to an electric, she thought she had joined the twentieth century. "Hoo-wee, am I advanced." Once computers entered the workplace, Bette withdrew. "I thought oh my god what is this all about. I didn't understand computers, and I didn't want to understand computers. And I knew that the future of the job would be with computers." Same for Jackie; she also opted out when databases came to dominate the travel industry.

It was Rhoda who had left her nest before her kids left home and bridged the technology gap. She supervised the networking of the synagogue during her tenure as executive director. She researched, installed, and had implemented the first software system, basically taking B'nai Jacob from biblical times into the twentieth century.

The ladies still reach for the Yellow Pages before they google. When anything goes wrong with their computers, they are rendered helpless and are further convinced that computers are more trouble than they are worth. I'm my mother's tech support. I can usually remedy any problem within seconds, and she marvels at my skill and thanks me profusely for having saved her from "hours" talking to someone at the Apple Help Line.

"Heaven help the person who fields your call," I say.

"They're terrifically patient," she says. "The other day one spent over an hour on the phone with me."

I imagine the poor techie somewhere hanging from a rafter with a computer cord around his neck.

♠

By 1970, my mother's biological clock had long stopped ticking. She had also started a part-time teaching job at a local Hebrew day school that she was thrilled with. The school was just a few miles from our house and it was just a few mornings a week. Then the unthinkable happened: she got pregnant. She was thirty-nine, Sarah by biblical standards. She and my father took my older sister and me into their room, and we gathered on their bed for a "family meeting." Nina was twelve and I was ten. This was a new concept, and I wasn't sure I liked it, though I also remember the sensation of the bed as a raft. Our parents asked what we would most like to have: another TV for sure, a swimming pool, a foosball table. Were we warm?

A baby girl arrived in February, just a few days after my mother's birthday. She hadn't been born with the blue-tinged skin of an Indian god, or the shimmering veil of a caul, yet it seemed she had arrived from a magical place with magical powers. Our flowers bloomed and our rivers ran. New life had brought life with it. This little girl would quickly become everyone's pet. We were better with her; we got along better, our family brighter. She brought out the best in us. She brought out the best in my mother.

Once Nina and I left for college, Gail became an only child with all the privileges of that vaunted position. My mother was easier, lighter, more relaxed. She left little notes in her lunch box, valentines, and silly gifts. Gail made it easy, too. She was pretty and smart and funny with blond ringlets and blue eyes. She was a good student; she didn't shoplift, never smoked pot or gave blow jobs in our basement, or engage in any other high-risk teenage behaviors.

The first time I talk to Gail about the Bridge Ladies we are in our grown nephew's long abandoned room, the bookcases filled with paperback series of fantasy and science fiction. The rest of the family is downstairs getting ready for our annual Hanukah gathering.

When I ask her if she thought the ladies were square, antithetical to feminism, she shakes her head no. "I didn't judge them. They just seemed like glamorous adults." She remembers Bea always wearing scarves and thinking that was tremendously sophisticated and Bette impeccably dressed in slacks and ribbed turtlenecks.

"A bone or off-white turtleneck. She could rock the hell out of that," Gail said.

"I really did think smoking was glamorous. I loved those embroidered cigarette cases. I loved looking at the special things to eat and nicer plates. I remember getting up on the counter, pushing myself up and being on my knees and handing the good plates down to Mom, and feeling like I was taking the Torah out of the Ark."

I want to know when she found out about Barbara.

She doesn't have to search her memory or think about it. She tells me that our mother had gone out on a weeknight, which was highly irregular, and she wanted to know where she had gone.

"I asked Dad where she was and he said Bridge, but I knew it wasn't a Bridge night."

She asked him again, and this time he answered that she was at the movies.

She knew our mother would never go to the movies alone. Gail didn't let it go at that, either.

"He said, 'Well, it doesn't matter,' and by then I was like, where is she? And it was then he sat me down and explained that she had gone to synagogue for *yahrzeit*."

"How old were you?"

"Seven."

My father told her that there was a baby who died before she was born. He told her that it really upsets our mother to talk about it and that she goes to say this prayer on the anniversary of her death.

"And I said, 'Well why don't we go with her?' And he said, 'I don't think she wants us to go with her.'"

Then he went to their bedroom and opened the top drawer of his green dresser. Inside was a framed picture of Barbara, maybe a year old, in a white dress with a dark bib and frilly collar. "He showed it to me and then said, 'Don't tell Mom that I told you.'"

Did you ask Mom?

"No. I never said anything about it."

♠

Bette, during a walk with my mother, once mentioned that her own mother was able to get over the death of her daughter after Bette was born. Did my mother feel that way about having Gail? Was she able to stop mourning Barbara?

"I'll never get over Barbara," my mother answered, and Bette never brought it up again.

I always thought Gail was protected from the tragedy that embraced our family. I realized too late that no one was unscathed. It didn't matter that she came later, after Barbara died. She was a part of us, my parents, my poor mother and father, and all of us had gotten lost in all the silence, secrets, and shame. When she was little Nina thought she was responsible for Barbara's death. Gail thinks she replaced her. What if she had smashed those fancy plates when she took them from the Ark, what if all the commandments we lived by were shattered and some truth was allowed to filter in.

Recently, in a rare and unexpected moment driving past our synagogue, taking my mother home, she told me that she loves Thanksgiving but that it's always tinged in sadness. At first I can't think why and look at her for a reason.

"Barbara died in November," she says.

The utterance of her name on my mother's lips is startling. I want to reach out, reach over to her, but I stay on my side.

They say you're supposed to tell the people you love that you love them every day. My mother and I never say those words. Sometimes, when she stalls for a moment before getting out of the car, I think she's going to say it, but it never comes. And I'm relieved. Saying it at this point feels scarier than not saying it. I always watch as she punches in the code to her garage, turns to wave, and disappears inside the house. I see the light in the front hall pop on.

"Mom," I've often asked, "why don't you leave lights on?"

"Why should I leave lights burning?"

"So you can see."

"I can see plenty."

I've always imagined that my mother doesn't say I love you as a hedge against further tragedy, the same way the Israelites marked their front doors to keep their firstborns from being slaughtered in the Passover story. With their doors marked, their houses would be passed over. Our house had not been passed over. The Jewish practices surrounding death are specifically designed to help a person gradually move through the stages of grief. Instead, she went it alone: driving herself to *yahrzeit* on a cold, dark November night.

♠

"Nancy Pelosi called," Bea announces. Bridge is at Jackie's.

"I won a trip to Bermuda," says Jackie, amused at such nonsense.

"People still call the house looking for Peter," Rhoda says. This seems particularly cruel, as if a call from a solicitor isn't bad enough. And what are you supposed to say: "Sorry, he's dead."

Everyone nods with recognition. They are all targeted for contributions by every possible organization. Their phones constantly ring with solicitors, telemarketers, pollsters, and scammers.

Once, when my mother answered the phone, a young, female voice on the other end said, "Grandma?"

She wasn't sure which granddaughter it was and took a guess. "Freddie?"

"Hi, Grandma, it's me, Freddie."

"Hi, honey, is everything okay?"

The caller said she was in Mexico on spring break from college and lost her wallet. Could my mother wire some money right away? Freddie was still in high school.

"I hung up on her then and there," my mother says. "I wasn't born yesterday."

"They think we're idiots," Bea adds.

When they sit down to play, a dispute over what to lead turns fiery. My mother had led trump, which is generally not done, Bea jumped down her throat. My mother looked both chastened and pissed.

"Why would you do that?" Bea wants an explanation.

"I was sleeping."

The next hand, Rhoda makes a mistake, putting an ace on a trick her partner has already trumped. My mother and I exchange glances. We both saw it right away, a costly mistake in a hand of Bridge. It's a small thing, but the recognition between us feels conspiratorial.

Rhoda scolds herself, "Dumb, dumb, dumb, dummy." It sounds like duck, duck, duck, goose.

"It happens," Bea says, forgiving when you least expect it.

When they go down, Bea doesn't make a big deal of it, but I can tell she's annoyed. "Betsy," she says. "It's the beautiful hands that can screw you." The ladies settle down. Twice in a row, none of them have enough points to bid and the dealer has to go again. This constitutes some excitement as they show each other how few points they have.

♠

Before we leave, Rhoda brings out her calendar to set the next week's game. It's my mother's turn to host, but she realizes she will be out of town. Impulsively, I volunteer. The ladies glance at each other: why not. It's been a year of free lunches and seems like the least I can do for the ladies. Later, my mother calls me and launches into a barrage of reasons why I shouldn't trouble myself, only then she also admits that she'd like the ladies to see my house, show it off. The mixed messages mount. She offers to make lunch or cater lunch. I resist all offers of help; isn't the point that *I* make the lunch? She knows better than to offer to polish a single serving piece, though I know it's probably killing her. Thanks to Anne, I've been able to hang on to some semblance of adult behavior around my mother. The Richter scale is nowhere near registering anything like the earthquakes that erupted under our feet when I first moved back. It's more like a game of tug-of-war, only it's not clear how you define winning in this scenario: holding tight or letting go.

I never shop at Whole Foods. I resent the prices, and the varieties of kale make me anxious. But I find myself in the produce section, convinced the meal will turn out better if I shop here. I put ingredients in my basket and take them out. I'm not much of a cook, and while I've been standoffish with my mother, I have been in a tailspin all week trying to think of what I could make, rather what I could pull off. I am staring at a bin of brightly colored miniature peppers small enough to string a necklace with. I'm drawn to them and tiny yellow squash in the next bin. At the end of the row is a single ostrich egg you'd need two hands to hold. Its shell is veined and mottled like aging skin. What recipe could possibly call for this prehistoric egg? I'm tempted to buy it just for the sake of absurdity. Maybe I'll sit on it until it hatches, and give birth so some slick creature, its neck curved like a clef, its feathers like the quills on a porcupine. *Are you my mother?*

I've been here for nearly a half hour and I'm still in the produce section. I have cold feet about the meal I've planned. This is all taking too much time. I check my phone. E-mails are piling up. *Stick with the plan.* I head over to the fish section. The tuna and salmon gleam. Shrimp is piled high into a pyramid. I could get a cashmere sweater for the cost of the swordfish. The man behind the counter is improbably cheery. When I ask for the swordfish, he flatters me. "Great choice." When I choose one in the shape of Vermont and another Massachussetts, he again validates my choice. Overkill, I think, walking away with the fish wrapped in paper, heavy as a full diaper.

Last minute, Rhoda can't make it. I'm disappointed. The

Jewish touches were mainly to impress her. I even considered running out and buying napkin rings but got hold of myself. Rhoda and I have made a connection I hadn't expected. The Rhodas of my life have always put me on edge, women who are unbending in their opinions. Early on when Rhoda announced she was Victorian in her ways, she was unapologetic. I know that had I been her daughter we would have been at each other's throats. Or perhaps she would have sent me away to Miss Porter's School for girls, where I might have become a world leader or an equestrienne. Her absence means I will have to fill in for her. Look at it another way: I was about to become a Bridge Lady.

Monday morning, I start getting ready the minute I wake up, like a parody of a 1950s housewife anxiously preparing a meal for her husband's boss. Of course, I've made many dinner parties over the years and set the table exactly the way my mother has taught me: cutlery flanking the dinner plate just so, glasses placed above the knife in descending order. Emily Post via Roz Lerner has filtered down and taught me well. Though it wasn't just by rote. As a child, I loved helping her set the table, opening the mahogany box that housed her silver, lined with purple satin and velvet dividers, the forks, spoons, and knives, all facing in the same direction, snug in their slots. That gleaming world contained all the pageantry and order that my small being desired. In another life I might have been a soldier in the Queen's Guard.

I bought Bea her favorite Coke ("the real thing, not that diet dreck"), brewed coffee for Jackie, boiled water for Bette's tea. I had set out the cards and score pad the way the ladies do, prewashed the grapes and set them on the counter. In the nervous minutes waiting for their arrival, I glimpsed my reflection in the kitchen window: Betsy Lerner, former Dead Head, poet, and pothead standing over the sink, staring down a stick of butter and contemplating whether to slice it into pats.

As I bustled about getting lunch together, I kept thinking about myself growing up as a teenager, the ladies standing for everything I wanted to get away from. Wasn't I the girl getting high in our high school parking lot with a boy I had an impossible crush on, the girl writing poems and wearing all black, or the girl who won a local Frisbee contest in the distance division. I can still feel the snap of my wrist as the disc released and caught a lucky current of wind that took it a little farther than it should have gone. Only now, setting a graceful table, making a meal, was I not my mother's daughter? Wasn't I doing all this for her?

Conversation starts with a rousing discussion of direct deposit and online banking, specifically paying bills online, which are met with universal distrust. The ladies want to know what Tweeting is, are not favorably disposed, and still don't grasp it after I explain the basics. I take out my smartphone to show them the app, and they rear back. (I make a mental note: stay current with technology.) But the meal goes swimmingly: The ladies loved the swordfish. Bea drained her Coke. Jackie was delighted with the strawberries, and Bette asked for the couscous recipe.

I'm insanely nervous as we head over to play. Until now, I've only played Bridge at the Manhattan Bridge Club in a supervised setting where you're allowed to talk and ask questions. I am drenched in perspiration before the first hand is dealt.

I am partnered with Bea, who is as quick as a snake. Bette and Jackie both take their time bidding and playing the hand. I feel less afraid of making a mistake in front of them. And here's the thing about Bridge: when you make a mistake in the bidding, it becomes immediately obvious to everyone when the "dummy comes down." How it works:

One of the partnerships "wins" the auction with the highest bid.

The partner who first introduced the trump suit (or no trump) will play the hand (and is called the declarer).

The declarer's partner literally lays his cards on the table in four rows, each suit from highest card to lowest (as in Solitaire). This is the dummy. The declarer then plays both his own hand and the dummy's. (The dummy sits out.)

When the cards are laid out, everyone sees exactly how many points and how many trumps are in the dummy's hand and if the bidding was accurate.

It's the Moment of Truth and it is like taking off your clothes for the first time in front of a new lover: What have you got? Hopefully, you have what you advertised in your bids: a promise of so many points and so many trumps.

In big-girl games, there is no talking or commenting on the dummy, but here in Woodbridge, on Mondays, there is no end of debate or comment on the dummy. If it has lots of points and supporting trumps, the ladies admire it, saying things like "Oh that's beautiful" and "Thank you partner." If it's a disappointment, they challenge the player: "How could you make that bid?" Or "Is there a reason you didn't mention your hearts?" A wrong bid can leave your partner in a precarious situation by not having enough strength to take the number of tricks you've committed to winning.

Right away, I start messing up the bidding. Bea is my partner, and when I lay down the dummy she reprimands me. "Betsy, you have to bid no trump with so many points," or "Betsy, you can't raise with so few points," and so on as I bid each and every hand incorrectly. I've learned the rules for increasing bids, but I have performance anxiety to the point where I really can't think straight. Bea isn't being mean, but she sounds accusatory and a little shrill. I want to go home. I am home!

Only then Bea says, "Okay, let's see what we can do."

She settles as quickly as she flares. She knows her way around the four sides of a Bridge table. If the hand can be salvaged, Bea can do it.

When Bette is my partner, she looks at me with big encouraging eyes. All along, she has been the Bridge Lady who most wants me to learn and always suggests I sit in on a hand or two when they play. I always decline, completely intimidated. I bid a little better with Bette as my partner, either that or I've calmed down a bit, and we actually win three hands. It could also be that the hands are less complicated. No two hands are exactly alike. Sometimes it's clear what to bid or whether to pass. Other times, there's more gray area, such as with an unbalanced hand or when you and your partner can't find a fit. When Bette tallies the score at the end of the afternoon, unbelievably, I am the big winner. The booty is all of three dollars, which I will take up to my office and pin on my bulletin board, as proudly as a storekeeper framing the dollar from his first sale.

"See," Bette says, "you know more than you think you do."

Forgetting that I was serving three women who weigh an average of a ninety-five pounds, I have lots of leftovers, which I pack up in Tupperware. They thank me profusely and promise to return the containers the following Monday and do.

As they are leaving, Jackie looks back. "Your mother would be very proud."

♠

During the first nervous week of my being a new mom, my in-laws came every day. My father had just had his first stroke and my mother couldn't leave him. My in-laws would arrive late in the afternoon when the baby would predictably squall for an hour or two and nothing could soothe her. My well-meaning mother-in-law kept making suggestions to calm her, none of which worked and only provoked greater anxiety in me: change her formula, chamomile tea, leave her in her crib, hold her, bounce her. I felt clumsy and uncertain of how to care for this new creature.

I had been terrified that I wouldn't take to motherhood. I was most paranoid about not being able to hear the baby cry in the night. What if I slept too deeply, or didn't have that sixth sense, the so-called maternal instinct? While I was pregnant I bought a set of baby monitors and set them up, testing myself to see what noises I could pick up, my ear pressed up to the monitor like a World War II spy hunched over his shortwave radio. Insecurity flooded all other feelings. I was afraid to bathe her in three inches of warm water! Her umbilical cord grossed me out! There was only one thing I wanted, and much to my surprise, it was my mother.

In the middle of week two, my mother showed up at our door, completely put together, hair blown out, nails boldly polished fire truck red. I was never happier to see her, though I also felt confused and overwhelmed. Who was the mother now? She or I? Now that she was here, what did I want?

Before any proper hello, she went directly upstairs and stopped at the entrance of the baby's room, at the crib. She was sleeping, her butt bunched up. I'd been observing from the day we brought her home how she turned around in her crib like the hands of a clock. I have never seen my mother cry, and she didn't cry then. Instead, she was quiet for a good long time, the room hushed like a church.

Then she said, with her eyes still on the baby, "Look what you've done."

I could hear the depth of her pleasure in her voice, but I hadn't really "done" anything. I didn't have to work for this. What I had finally done was something my mother unequivocally approved of. She has always said that I wouldn't appreciate motherhood until I became a mother. I'd always rejected the idea that you can't understand something until you have done it yourself. Do I have to be a quarterback to feel the joy of catching a football that torpedoes down the field? Do I have to be a birch tree in a grove to feel myself keening in the wind? I truly believed that empathy and imagination could transport me into any experience.

I also didn't think it should have taken having a baby to finally please her. But in those few minutes standing over my daughter's crib, her tiny body at two o'clock, I realized it was all semantics. The amazing truth is that the thing she most wanted for me would be the best thing in my life.

CHAPTER 16

Jew in a Box

I am leaving the JCC when the call comes. It's Rhoda, and I
know right away something is wrong. She and my mother had
been filling in at another Bridge game and my mother had a fall.
Rhoda assures me she's okay but that I should meet her at Saint
Raphael's, where an ambulance has taken her. An ambulance?
I call my mother, who on her best day can barely excavate her
phone from the depths of her pocketbook, and miraculously she
answers. In characteristic self-denial, she tells me she is fine, just
a cut on her forehead they need to stitch. I tell her I'll be right
there. "Take your time," she says, acting as if I have time to do
some grocery shopping or get a manicure.

When I meet her at the emergency room, she is chatting
up the young Jewish resident as if he were a possible suitor for
her granddaughter. As he's examining her, she's worrying out
loud that she might not be able to host Rosh Hashanah just a
few weeks away. She's already frozen her soup and brisket. This

comes as a huge relief to me; if my mother is obsessing about the Jewish holiday she will be okay. Her face is covered with a paper sheet. But when I draw close I can see that the cut in her forehead is a deep gash, and no matter how much the doctor and a nurse try to staunch the flow, it keeps bleeding. Closer, I see that her nose is broken and her eyes are ringed in deep purple. *Mommy Raccoon.* Her curly hair is matted with blood. And her handbag, like a deflated metallic balloon, is slumped on the visitor's chair. I take her hand. She brushes off this small gesture. This isn't our way. Not even here. Not even now.

It's possible she's in shock, but she introduces me to the doctor as if we were at a bar mitzvah, providing salient facts from my life, namely that my husband is the director of Yale University Press and I am a literary agent. The doctor is only barely listening. It's not as if he's stitching up Christy Turlington. Worse, he is condescending, calling her young lady in a tone reserved for young children and pets. Only today it doesn't bother her. Instead she wants to know where he's from, where he did his undergraduate degree. Then she asks him how many years he has been working at Yale. Oh, he tells us, he's a resident, a first-year resident.

When his pager goes off and he steps out, I beg my mother to let me find a plastic surgeon, this kid is barely out of diapers. But she counters there's no point. *"Now* they're going to make me look beautiful?" she says, with classic Yiddish inflection. Translation: Gimme a break. Then she jokes that maybe she'll get the nose job she always wanted. How long can my eighty-three-year-old mother keep up the Borscht Belt shtick with half her forehead sliced open?

Just then a woman from the cubicle across the way starts screaming a stream of expletives. "Why won't anybody fucking help me? Do you know how many fucking hours I've been waiting?" I have a partial view of her through a crack in the curtains. Her blond hair has been cheaply colored so many times it's got a green patina and is flat as a sheet of tin. She could be thirty, could be fifty. The physician's assistant finally tends to her. She starts wailing as if she's been shot, then coughs up all the leftover phlegm from the bubonic plague.

The doctor returns and affixes safety goggles and a contraption like a miner's flashlight that emits a light beam in a narrow blue tube. He wants to get started, but he can't make a single stitch until they staunch the flow of blood. I overhear him tell the nurse that the gash may be all the way to her skull and sit down for a minute, feeling weak. My mother is still talking up a storm, asking the doctor all kinds of questions. I am ashamed to admit this but I have taken an immediate dislike to him, mostly because he is the kind of professional Jewish man that my mother had always wanted me to marry. I don't like his tone, his look, or his purple Crocs.

When the doctor's pager goes off again, he cuts out for the second time. The nurse says she'll be right back, too.

Across the way, the woman is begging the physician's assistant, her voice amplified and full of gargle. "I already got cough medicine. I need something stronger." Then she starts crying and pleading. It's Oscar worthy.

"What do you think is wrong with her?" my mother whispers.

"She's a junkie."

"How do you know that?"

"I know."

"I don't think you can jump to that conclusion."

"Whatever." I don't feel like defending my extensive street cred with my mother at this moment.

"You don't know that."

"Mom, she's begging for drugs. It's obvious."

I take a closer peak at my mother's forehead under the covering. It's too awful to think of her going down, face-first into whatever split her forehead like the Red Sea. The nurse returns with a tower of cotton bandages and starts applying them to her forehead. Her work is methodical, applying a fresh one as the saturated bandage comes off, working with both hands. I feel calmed by her steady work and tell my mother I'm going to step outside to call my sisters. She really doesn't want me to bother them, but I know my older sister would kill me if I didn't let her know. If she were the brains of this operation, we would have already located a plastic surgeon and left the first-year resident quivering in his scrubs. Nina is the daughter-in-chief and the person you want in any emergency, especially a medical one, but I'm the one who's here.

A few people are smoking outside in a huddle. A security guard goes in and out of the building and, like a child newly fascinated by the effect of his step, triggers the automatic doors to open again and again. Nina wants to know exactly how it happened and I explain what I know: the hall to the bathroom in the hostess's house is brick, and on either side are recessed planters. Her heel got caught in one of the planters, and she fell facedown into the brick. The hostess's husband is a retired dentist and was able to stop the bleeding temporarily. Though my mother could tell she hadn't broken any bones, she thought it best to go to the hospital in an ambulance. She says she had no idea the cut was that deep, that her nose was broken. "Look," she'll later say and more than once, "I'm lucky I didn't break a hip. I could have lost an eye!"

"Didn't the hostess offer to go with her?" Nina is shocked and outraged that my mother went alone to the hospital. My mother defended the hostess, explaining that she was extremely unsteady on her feet, and that she didn't want to inconvenience Rhoda and the other women.

"Inconvenience?"

As I head back into the hospital the alleged junkie comes out, fishing inside her jacket for what turns out to be a pack of Newports.

"I hope you're feeling better," I say, watching her light up, knowing full well she's fleeced St. Raphael's for opiates.

"Me! What about your mom? She's tough."

I nod in agreement.

"She's got a gash in her head and a broken nose and all she can talk about is her holiday. Brisket! Soup!"

The woman takes a drag that burns down half the cigarette then lets it dangle from the corner of her mouth as she starts rooting around in her pocket.

"God bless her," she says. "You mother is the salt of the earth. They don't make 'em like that anymore. Tough lady. Tough old bird."

Then she pulls something out of her pocket and hands it to me.

I start to decline, but she insists and presses it into my hand.

"God bless," she says, coughing and smoking all at once before disappearing into the New Haven night. When she flicks her cigarette on the ground, it spits orange sparks for a second before dying.

Going back inside, I look down at my hand. It's a tattered red poppy on a wire, a forgotten token from Memorial Day.

When I return to my mother's room, the nurse has finally stopped the bleeding. She is the real hero here, but the doctor takes all the credit, now that he can do the stitching, three layers deep. When he finishes he looks at me and asks how he did. I don't answer.

"No really, give me a grade."

"B minus."

"Aw, really?"

He takes off his plastic gloves with a snap and offers to write my mother a prescription for Percocet, which she refuses.

"Take it, Mom, you might be in a lot of pain later."

She refuses again. Aspirin will be enough. Then she wants some privacy to pull herself together and asks me to hand her purse to her. I tell her I'll pull the car around.

"That's okay," she says. "I can walk."

♠

It was a few weeks later and Bridge is at Bette's. My mother is almost completely healed. Her broken nose no longer looks like a piece from Mr. Potato Head, and what's left of her bruises she attempts to camouflage with too much makeup. The ladies express concern, but she sloughs it off. A wrecking ball could land on her head and she'd insist she was fine. Bette implores the girls to eat, and they pass around the basket of rolls, salad, and dressing as if in a game of Wonder Ball.

Bette brings a casserole out from the kitchen. It's another one of her mother's recipes, only it's not come out as firmly as she hoped and she castigates herself while the ladies coo over the buttery smell. She works the spatula like a cranky plow through a field, doling out pieces. Everyone served, Bette kicks off the conversation by decrying the state of the obituaries, which are starting to resemble high school yearbooks, mentioning everything but the kind of pizza toppings preferred by the deceased. An acquaintance has died and she is disgusted by the write-up. "Who cares if she played mahjong?" Apparently, if you croak in New Haven, no detail is too small to be included in your obit.

Rhoda defends the obit, saying it's what the family wanted.

"What sickens me," my mother says, "is that they mention the name of the cat. I ask you, is that appropriate?"

Jackie demurely manages to stick up for the cat. "I think it's okay to mention pets."

Jackie is the only real pet lover among the women. She once divulged that her cat likes to drink directly from the spigot. My mother will never in a million years understand how you could allow a pet on your countertop; you'd think the cat was taking small sips from a demitasse to hear my mother's disbelief. Months later when Jackie's cat dies, she and Dick waste no time adopting another from a shelter.

Again, my mother is astonished. "At their age! What do they need it for?"

I point out that a cat needs very little care.

She's not buying it.

"Mom," I say, "they love cats. Why should they stop having pets just because they're older."

"Whatever."

Whenever my mother adopts the dismissive language of my generation it's a bad sign. I want to get her to admit that she's being too judgmental, that for Jackie and Dick getting a new cat has nothing to do with age. But she wasn't having any of it and ended the conversation with her standard sign off: "They should live and be well." Only it has the unmistakable ring of condescension from a person who clearly knows better.

Bette brings in dessert. A pretty tray of pastel-colored coconut candies in the shape of tiny Jell-O molds. Bette explains that they're from Vermont, which in this context suddenly sounds exotic. Everyone agrees they are too rich to eat more than one before taking seconds.

Conversation returns to an ongoing story in the news: whether or not the Metropolitan Opera will stage *The Death of Klinghoffer,* a controversial new opera. Ever since the production was announced, the Met has been besieged with protests and cries of anti-Semitism. The ladies have been following the story for months and are disturbed by the pivotal scene in the opera, based on a true story, wherein an elderly Jewish man in a wheelchair is thrown overboard and killed by Palestinian terrorists. They all believe in free speech, but you don't scream fire in a movie theater is how my mother justifies her opinion that the opera should be shelved. Jackie alone is of the opinion that the opera should go on. Without seeing it, she will not be convinced that the message is propagandist. On the contrary, she thinks it might do some good. I'm with her on this, but when the Met cancels the international simulcasts it becomes clear that powerful voices have shut it down. It's not clear to me whether censorship or safety was more responsible for the decision, but the ladies are relieved.

In Berlin, an exhibit at the Jewish Museum has been dubbed "Jew in a Box," where a Jewish person sits in a Plexiglas box and the public is invited to ask the person questions about Jewish life, customs, and identity. The exhibit was meant to promote an open dialogue between Jews and Germans. Instead, it caused a public outcry. Some in the Jewish community believed the box itself was reminiscent of the boxcars that transported Jews to the concentration camps. When the ladies read about it in the news, they agreed it sounded awful. They also admitted that when they meet a German in his seventies or eighties, they wonder where he was during the war. It was only Bea with her twin gifts of being straightforward and friendly who once posed the question to a German woman with whom she found herself playing Bridge at the Senior Center. "I asked her where she had been during the war. She said she was from a small town, that she was a small child. I left it at that."

The ladies act shocked at Bea's temerity; Bea remains unfazed.

Whenever I've asked the ladies what they knew about the Holocaust when they were growing up, they claim very little. They were too young and the atrocities were not prominently reported in the newspapers; the true horrors of the Holocaust would be revealed more fully over time.

In high school, Jackie dated Edward Lewis Wallant, a boy who went on to write *The Pawnbroker*, a novel about a Holocaust survivor who loses his family and ends up a bitter and broken man working in an East Harlem pawnshop. I ask Jackie if she had any idea that these things were on his mind, if they talked about the Holocaust.

"Not at all. I really thought he would be a painter."

"Did you stay in touch?"

"He died," Jackie said.

"Recently?"

"No, a long time ago."

"You mean as a young man?"

"Yes, he was in his thirties and had an aneurism or something like that. That's why I remember him."

We're quiet then, as if observing a moment of silence.

Then Jackie adds, "He died right after the book was published."

Though none of the ladies experienced anti-Semitism directly, they are aware of it as an ever-present threat, whether in anti-Israel politics, when a small comment could be misconstrued, or when something like the debate over this opera is waged in their own backyard. Becoming the potential object of persecution is always on their radar. Their bags aren't packed with unleavened bread in the event they have to flee the country, but they are highly aware of a terrifying rise of anti-Semitism, especially in Europe. These news stories never escape their notice.

As children in Hebrew school, we were given white pins with bold Hebrew letters in red that said *"Zachor!"* Remember! They were always trying to instill in us something the ladies had in their bones: fear.

My first teenage rebellion against religion took the form of refusing to return to Camp Laurelwood, where all the good New Haven Jewish boys and girls went every summer and where I had gone since I was ten. My father was in line to be camp president and my refusal to go stung him both personally and publicly. But I prevailed and coerced my parents into letting me attend Cornwall Workshop, an artsy camp in Litchfield County, nestled along the Housatonic River. My worldview opened before me: I met kids from Manhattan! From divorced families! I got my first crush on a non-Jewish boy with a thick ponytail of black shiny hair! Even more sacrilegious: the drama counselors said Neil Simon was a hack! We were here to make art! Art!

On afternoons when the theater barn was too hot to rehearse in, we'd sometimes take inner tubes down the river, floating the mile or so toward the covered bridge in Cornwall, where we'd get an ice pop. We'd be together in our little flotilla but alone, too, draped over our inner tubes fat as doughnuts, our feet and hands dangling a path through the silty water. The leaf pattern from the trees above continuously changed as we floated downriver, the sun filtering through an infinite grid like mirrors inside a cylinder. It was my thirteenth summer. Everything I craved, everything my parents feared, was here.

My parents, like many Jews of their generation, sought the comfort of a known world. Coming from Brooklyn and without a college degree, my father was able to establish himself relatively quickly within the business community by becoming a trusted member of the Jewish community. I once asked him why he went to synagogue if what he really wanted was to play golf, especially on those perfect days of Indian summer when the tips of the leaves were starting to turn. I couldn't believe his answer: "It's good for business."

I was shocked at the time; now I'm shocked at how naïve I was.

I once asked Dick if my father's take was accurate, if you had to align yourself within the Jewish community to succeed in New Haven? Absolutely, Dick said. His family was among the first wave of Russian immigrants to settle in New Haven in the late 1880s and they did extremely well.

When Dick's grandfather settled in New Haven, it was a one-temple town with 1,000 Jews. By the 1930s, the Jewish population had swelled to 25,000 people, with eighteen separate synagogues. Dick took a sociology class at Yale and remembers the professor referring to New Haven Jewish life as a "ghetto system" whereby German, Polish, Russian, and Ashkenazi Jews largely stuck together in separate neighborhoods. "And he called Woodbridge the Golden Ghetto," Dick says, referring to the suburb where my mother and Bette still live. "I'm not saying it's right, but it's how he said it."

At the same time, the quota system was firmly in place when Dick went to Yale, but he claims he didn't notice it. Dick had come from a Yale family. He wanted to go, assumed he would get in. So secure was he that he didn't apply to any other schools. When his father went to Yale, the Jewish students weren't allowed to attend proms or other social events. They were restricted from dorms, sports, and Yale's famous secret societies. It was only as part of the Yale University Band that Dick's father was allowed to attend the prom. More unbelievable, Jackie had an uncle who graduated in 1899, likely the first Jew to do so.

Only he changed his name from Bernard Goodman to Burnett Goodwin and became an Episcopalian.

"Didn't it bother you? The quota system? All the restrictions against Jews?" I continue to prod Dick. "Didn't the anti-Semitism get to you?"

He says it never crossed his mind. "If I wasn't welcome, I just stayed away. It was a similar experience in the military if you must know."

Dick also tells me that there were companies that wouldn't hire Jews, and as a young engineer he stayed clear of them. "I guess I was arrogant enough to feel that they were the loser."

I can't get over Dick's attitude. Wasn't he supposed to internalize some of that anti-Semitism as self-loathing? Hadn't he read his Philip Roth? Seen a Woody Allen movie from time to time?

♠

As the ladies make their way over to the dining room table, my mother mentions that a good friend had died earlier in the week. At the service, her grandchildren told stories about her warmth and generosity, and her one triumphant win at Yahtzee, how she proudly hung the score on her fridge. Sitting next to my mother at the memorial, I found it was impossible not to imagine the day when she would be gone, my own daughter choking out words of remembrance. I've stood on the sidelines and marveled at the relationship between the two of them. Mall rats to the core, they spend endless hours in the dressing rooms of various department stores, the scene of so many of my teenage meltdowns. My mother hasn't missed a beat, still continues to espouse her belief in flattering cuts, slimming designs, and bright colors. None of this my daughter minds. She loves her grandma unconditionally. So what if she's opinionated? So what if she's intrusive? She's a grandma!

My mother visited with her friend right up until the end, though I could see it rattled her more than most. Her final weeks and days were cruel testament to the body's stubborn will to live no matter how incapacitated. Once when I was visiting with Rhoda she had just come back from seeing a friend in hospice. It was a grim chore; her friend mostly gone, just a body, but Rhoda continued to visit as long as the woman held on. A small container of ice cream had been left on the tray, though her friend had stopped eating for days. Rhoda brought a spoonful up to her friend's mouth. She only just touched it with her lips. "What if I hadn't been there? She wouldn't have had that ice cream." Rhoda and I both know the truth: her friend was already gone.

Rhoda's eyes filled with tears just then, she tilted her head back, took a moment, and stared at the ceiling. I stayed quiet, not sure how to comfort her. When I put my hand on her back, she sat up at my touch, composure returning to this proud, strong woman. Then she said she hoped God would be more merciful when it was her time. "Just take me," she said, lifting her arms to the skies the way people sometimes pray for rain.

I dread the day when one of the Bridge Ladies dies, these women whom I barely knew a year ago, who I didn't think worth knowing except as the ladies who played cards with my mother for a million years. I also worry that the club will fall apart. My mother laughs at this. "The club won't fall apart," she says. "We'd find someone to fill in."

It seems cold to me, but Bette confirms this to be the case. Some years ago, when a former member suddenly died, they found someone to fill in and played the following week. "Of course we all went to the funeral, and we were all sad, but it didn't stop us at all."

When my father died after a series of strokes, our family was relieved to the extent that his suffering was over. I think my mother was pleased with the funeral, especially with the way my sisters and I comported ourselves. (She has two edicts for funeral protocol: keep remarks as brief as possible and no sleeveless dresses. You'd think our synagogue was a mosque, given her insistence on sleeves.) Of all the images I take from that sad day, I mostly remember gnats flying around a huge arrangement of edible fruit, a sculpture mostly made of pineapple and melon on wooden skewers sticking out in all directions from a half globe of Styrofoam. They swarmed around the bouquet as if it were a dead dog in Cairo. "Have you ever seen anything more stupid?" my mother said when she dumped the half-eaten sculpture into the trash.

Rhoda's husband, Peter, also suffered a series of strokes. When I ask Rhoda to tell me about it, she delivers a series of facts: he had a stroke on a commuter train, he was taken to Bellevue, and no one called Rhoda.

"Until I got somebody to talk to me, I thought I would lose my mind."

Peter would make a full recovery, but over the next seven years he would continue to have ministrokes, each one more debilitating, until he finally started to show signs of dementia. He still recognized Rhoda and could communicate, but his behavior became erratic and sometimes violent.

"I was despondent, despairing. It was a terrible time, terrible. I wondered what in the world I could do. I just couldn't bring him home, there was no way I could have managed him. What's worse, no one from that damn place said to me 'You know what's happening here.' No one ever said anything, which I don't understand to this day."

Peter spent the last year and a half of his life in a nursing home in a section for Alzheimer's and dementia patients. I ask Rhoda how she coped, and she didn't hesitate. "I coped by living as closely to my normal way as I could. I kept up with my theater subscriptions, my concerts, and activities at B'nai Jacob. And I had many good friends, and without them I could not have survived." There was a support group at the nursing home, but Rhoda wasn't interested. "I had my own friends, and I had my own tale of woe, and that was enough for me."

I ask Rhoda if she was able to grieve.

"Yes, oh yes. Absolutely. There's no question about it. I'm still grieving. Fifty-nine years is pretty long to have a relationship with someone." She tells me that she thinks about Peter when he was healthy. Maybe even as the robust young man who ditched his date and exclaimed that Rhoda was going to be his bride literally at first sight. But I can see the shadow image: her husband in his wheelchair or being lifted in and out of the pool by a hoist. My father, too, had been transported in one of these cranes with a sling tied from end to end that made me think of a stork carrying a new baby. Rhoda's voice cracks, "That was my athletic husband."

♠

My mother isn't one for going to the cemetery, but on the day of her friend's funeral, she's brought some rocks from our yard to place on my father's grave.

"I don't know why, I just felt like it."

My father's grave is a simple stone with just our last name carved into it. No "beloved husband," "devoted father." I like the simplicity of it. He was a man with plain tastes, didn't own a single thing more than he needed. He didn't even have a middle name, joked that his parents were too poor to afford one. I know my mother won't talk to him, as people do, grave-side. She wouldn't know what to say: confess her worries, kvell over the grandchildren, or admit to how angry she still is that he got sick and abandoned her. What's the point? She knows he can't hear it. The stones will have to speak for her.

The last time I visited my father's grave, I was agitated; a work situation was spinning out of control. These were the times I missed him most, as my business mentor. I know how he would have advised me, but I felt like visiting. Once there, the idea seemed forced and I felt self-conscious. Plus the day suddenly turned ugly with a sky the color of cement. I got up to leave after a few minutes and looked around at all the graves of the men my father knew. They are all buried here, the men who attended B'nai Jacob, who financed the building of the JCC, and gave bonds to Israel. All the men my father did business with, golfed with, and played cards with in the men's room of our country club. They're all here: Katz, Kasowitz, and Shapiro. It sounds like a law firm. I give a nod to all of them, this place where the *alter kockers* have come to rest. All their headstones crowded with rocks.

Suddenly I was seized with the need to find Barbara's grave. We had gone once as a family when my father died. My older sister had found out where she was buried from the undertaker and arranged for us to go after the burial. There wasn't a head-stone, just a plaque in the ground. Whatever catharsis she hoped for us, for my mother, wasn't forthcoming. She barely got out of the car before she got back in, her body shrunken, hunched over. I don't remember the drive back to my mother's house, only that when we returned it was already filled with people.

There were rows and rows of plaques in long lines like a fallow field. I walked up and down, reading the names, growing increasingly distressed when I couldn't find her. I surveyed the entire cemetery, certain that I had walked down every row. She was gone again. Disappeared. *This is so fucking typical.* Determined to find her, I started to search again, even more methodically this time. Then I saw it, her plaque beside a tree, moss beginning to take the edges. I touched it as if I could touch her. I left three rocks, one from each of us, her sisters. Then one more, for my mother.

CHAPTER 17

Bette in Flames

It's been months since the Bridge Ladies have gotten together. Their vacation schedules were all over the place, didn't mesh. Winter weather. Worse, Arthur got a bad case of shingles that landed him in the hospital. From there he went back and forth from the hospital to rehab, having been weakened by each hospital stay. Bette was out of commission as a result. She had too much to deal with even to return most phone calls. For the most part, she fills my mother in on Arthur's progress or lack thereof, and my mother relays what little news there is to the Bridge Ladies and a larger circle of their friends. I know my mother does not want to be illness central, the designated bearer of bad news, but she is a devoted friend. I ask her nearly every day about Arthur's health, and she says the same thing: What can I say? Or: a little better. When I see her and ask after him, she tilts her hand back and forth like a flipper, by which she means: so-so. I leave Bette some messages just to say that

I'm thinking of her. I fear they sound hollow, but I hope they are better than nothing.

When I finally reach her, I ask how she's coping and she tries to sound as upbeat as possible, but the strain is there.

"Not great," she says, and then with her characteristic semi-ironic laugh she adds, "and by that I mean terrible."

We laugh a little, better than crying as my mother would say. I ask Bette if I can bring her some carrot cake I've made for a party and she protests mightily. I insist.

"Just a sliver."

Bette is a sliver, and I fear that she isn't eating enough. I worry that all the anxiety and uncertainty surrounding Arthur's medical condition, combined with dealing with the hospital, rehab, and insurance companies is sapping all of her strength.

When Arthur is home for a spell, Bette insists she'd like to talk. Our visits take her mind off things. I hesitate at the front door. The exterior facade of their home is a green-gray brick with the cement, as a design element, oozing out between the bricks like cake frosting. I touch it, half expecting it to be soft. Just as I'm about to ring the bell, Bette opens the door. She looks smaller, her face drained of color. I tell her I can come back. No, no, no.

We are back in her formal living room where we had our first conversation. She apologizes for keeping the phone nearby but she is waiting to hear about a doctor's appointment. The phone rings twice before we even get started. Bette excuses herself to take the calls: both times telemarketers, as if they weren't annoying enough, let alone when you're expecting an important call.

Bette's agitation is palpable and again I offer to come back at another time. Again, she insists I stay, and I realize she needs to talk. She is the classic woman from her generation, who let the men do everything: make a living, pay bills, take care of the taxes, manage the finances, do the lawn work, clean the gutters, gas up the car. Her sphere was entirely domestic, housekeeping and child rearing. She never imagined the day when her husband's duties would fall into her lap, even now as the bills begin to pile up inside their envelopes with the glassine windows. Conversely, it was Bette's own mother who handled the family finances.

"My mother had a budget and she would put the money aside in little envelopes for electricity, gas, this is for the heat, this for food. I thought that was the way to do it, but when we got married Arthur said, 'No, whatever you want, write a check for it.' I didn't have to have the little envelopes."

Bette was coddled and protected by her mother, and later by Arthur. At the hospital, from his bed, Arthur walks her through every step of how to deal with accountants, lawyers, and lawn men. Still, she feels inadequate to the task and shocked that she has never learned even the basics. Arthur didn't just make the trains run on time, he was a buffer to every emotion or crisis or simple annoyance that threatened Bette's equilibrium.

"Last week when I went to see him in rehab," she says, "I had just received some upsetting news. I was very worried but I counseled myself not to tell Arthur. I didn't want to burden him. Only the moment I walked into his room, I threw myself on him and started crying. I couldn't help myself."

"What did he do?"

"He comforted me, like he always does."

The phone rings and Bette sees it's from a friend.

"I won't take this."

"Are you sure?"

"Where were we?" she asks with resolve.

"You said you threw yourself down on Arthur."

Bette laughs at herself as if to say: pathetic.

"Tell me about your marriage," I feel emboldened to ask.

"If we had five arguments during the sixty years we were married that was a lot. I think a lot of it was Arthur. He was very accepting and very non-confrontational. We were always very happy with each other, very content, very compatible. I always felt safe. We were different personalities, but he sort of adjusted to me. Whatever I wanted was fine, wherever I wanted to go, whatever movie I wanted to see it was fine. When I look around at all the men I know, I got the pick of the litter."

Each of the ladies uses the word *safe* at some point during our talks, describing their husbands and marriages. It's not a word that particularly interested me, especially when I was young. I was drawn to tragic relationships: Anna Karenina and Count Vronsky, Cathy and Heathcliff. I was a freshman at NYU when Sid stabbed and killed Nancy in the Chelsea Hotel; I became obsessed with the case and would skulk past the storied hotel for as long as the story was in the news.

The phone rings again. This time I can tell from Bette's tone and body language that it's the doctor. As she disappears into the kitchen, I give her a small wave and let myself out.

♠

Rhoda is late, first five minutes, then ten, and then fifteen. It's Bea's turn to host, and instead of going to the Athenian Diner she has selected a Thai restaurant in one of the many nondescript strip malls in the area. There is much speculation. Has Rhoda gone to the wrong one? There is another strip mall close by with another Thai restaurant. A campaign to locate her has begun. My mother embarks on her regular archaeological dig to recover a small spiral address book of important numbers from her bag, its pages rounded and thin with use. Success! Bea whips out her flip phone. My mother calls out the numbers. This whole operation puts me in a bad mood. Rhoda comes the longest distance; she'll get here.

I don't know if it's true for the other ladies or of aging in general, but my mother's worry meter is off the charts. If there is a flake of snow in the sky she won't go out. She reviews travel plans over and over, departures, arrivals, directions, as if she were in Winston Churchill's war room. She wants to know where my now teenage daughter is every minute of the day. Does she have rehearsal? What time does she get home? Will I be home? Am I making dinner? *No, I'll be out pole dancing so she'll have to fend for herself.* And if I so much as sniffle in her presence, she will interrogate me about my health and watch it hawk-like for days. *Have you seen a doctor? This is going on, what, two-three days? I don't like the sound of that!*

Moments before we let loose the dogsleds, Rhoda enters the restaurant. Traffic on 95; that's all. After all that tumult settles, the table goes weirdly quiet. I want to say something about how great it is to see everyone, especially Bette, who won't have time to play but wanted to come for lunch. She has to get back to Arthur.

I've learned by now that their reticence is largely generational. For them, the word *share* meant splitting a sandwich, not automatically opening up about your life. I also get it that long-term relationships can grow threadbare (as can all relationships, for that matter). Still, I want the ladies to love each other more, to have more fun and be happier to see each other. Even after all this time, knowing their penchant for reserve over ebullience, I'm still surprised at how cautious and circumspect everyone is. Once I asked Bette why the lunches weren't livelier. She thought about it for a while and finally said, "We've become dull to each other and dull to ourselves."

Before I played, the game looked boring and repetitive. Now, I get it: Bridge is incredibly fun. It's absorbing, crowds out all other thoughts. You don't need to be anyone's best friend; teamwork naturally develops between partners. Plus, winning a hand of Bridge is like shooting the rapids and outwitting a fox at the same time. Maybe it's the game that keeps them together more than the bonds of friendship. Maybe Bridge itself is the glue that has kept the ladies together for over fifty years. Sometimes you have to call a spade a spade.

At lunch, it comes out that Bette doesn't know how to put gas in her car. Arthur always filled her tank. When she confesses this I am more than astonished, I am slightly appalled. It would be like not knowing how to withdraw money from an ATM. I'm not sure if this makes Bette a princess or an invalid. Maybe a little bit of both, only now she is certainly handicapped as a result. Her daughter Amy, who has been coming most weekends to help out, decides it's time for her mother to learn how to fill her tank. She had already shown Bette how to pump gas a few times, but over the weekend Amy insisted that it was Bette's turn to actually do it. Amy went inside the convenience store and Bette took out her credit card. She explains that everything was going fine up to that point. She's got the door open to the gas tank, swiped her card, entered her zip code, and selected the kind of gas she wanted. She lifted the nozzle and put it into the tank, or so she thinks. Somehow, and she will never know how, the gas started gushing back at her, completely dousing her in gasoline.

"It was like a volcano," Bette says, lifting her arms as if she's being doused all over again. In response all she could do was scream, completely frozen and unable to act. Amy and the attendant came running out. Somehow, Amy was able to stop the gushing, only not before she too was covered in gasoline.

"And she was wearing a new outfit," Bette nearly cried.

Mother and daughter were taking the first afternoon off in weeks from keeping Arthur company at rehab. They had tickets to a play and were determined not to miss it. They raced home and changed clothes. For the entire play, they could tell that people were sniffing and whispering about the smell of gasoline emanating from their direction. Bette and Amy sniffed and whispered as well, to throw their fellow theatergoers off the trail. Bette laughs at their pathetic attempt at subterfuge. Then, also in characteristically droll manner, she concluded by saying, "You know, there was part of me that wished I had a match to end it all right then and there."

♠

Back at Bea's for Bridge, she is eager to show off her newly installed chair lift. It goes from her basement to the landing, spanning the length of ten or so steep steps. She loves it, uses it to haul groceries and laundry. If she needs it to haul herself, bad knees, bursitis, or arthritis, she isn't saying. The women are good at hiding their infirmities. It may be pride, but I sense something else as well, akin to how an animal in the wild will attempt to camouflage an injury lest she be more vulnerable, easily sighted as prey. I hear the ladies comment on other people, noting that one is using a cane, another one a walker. One friend no longer drives. Another has gone into assisted living, another has moved across the country to be closer to their kids. Each marks a step in the wrong direction, an admission of decreased capacity.

Bea volunteers Jackie to try the lift. At first, she is game and scoots herself back into the chair. As Bea starts the lift, it lurches the way a Ferris wheel jolts to pick up passengers or release them. Jackie looks around for something to hold on to, but the arm had been left up. Only a third of the way there and she is visibly terrified; it looks as if she could easily slip off. Bea tells her to hang on, there's nothing to it. When it reaches the landing, there is a slightly tricky maneuver to get off that involves swiveling the chair. We watch from down below, helpless as Jackie negotiates the distance from chair to landing. There is an audible sigh of relief when she makes it. No other volunteers, the rest of us trudge up the stairs for what looks like a long afternoon of Bridge.

Just as the ladies take their seats a surprise snowfall blankets the road outside Bea's condo and elicits groans. This is our state with her freakish weather: late snows and Indian summers. A ring of worry emanates from the table, but the snow disappears as quickly as it fell. The ladies make so many mistakes the first game that they decide it's off the record. This would never fly at the Manhattan Bridge Club or the Orange Senior Center, but this is a breakfast nook in a condo on Forest Road on the border of New Haven and West Haven. No one risks expulsion for dropping the wrong card and blowing the game. A few hands later, Rhoda makes a big mistake when she opens the bidding with four Spades; you need five cards in a major suit to open. Even I know this. This is Bridge 101. Bea is sharp with Rhoda, accusatory. "How could you open a four-card major? Not for forty years have I seen that!"

Sparks flew from the table. Rhoda was flustered, though irritated and possibly embarrassed as well. Bea can sound sharp, only she's usually right; where disputes are concerned she is the acknowledged authority.

"Okay, let's move on," she says. "Let's see what we can do."

Bea focuses on whether she can take enough tricks to win the hand. In the end, she does, but it's a nail-biter.

"You made it, Bea," Rhoda says with the implication that she was overreacting.

"Just," Bea returns.

♠

Arthur's health becomes increasingly precarious. "He's old," Bette tells me. "He's old and the doctors don't really care. Or if they do there is nothing they can do." Her voice is a mixture of despair and disgust.

I remember so well how my father tried every newfangled treatment he could find to walk again, one more outlandish than the next, including a protocol where his healthy arm and leg were bound to his body in an attempt to force his limp ones to work, the way a good eye is patched to coerce the other to focus. No one quite knows how it happened, but some aides apparently dropped my father at the facility and he had to be rushed by ambulance to the local hospital and then flown home on a stretcher. That's when my mother called it quits on these experimental treatments, each one depleting or worsening his condition. Though I also noticed that when my father stopped trying, his depression settled in for good. His eyes looked magnified behind his glasses, which perched crookedly on his face. It was a death knell, but he would live like this for a few more years, receding into himself, giving himself over to a never ending parade of home health care aides, who bathed him and helped him use the toilet, and counted out his pills in a seven-day dispenser.

I had never seen my parents as vulnerable until then. I think my mother felt robbed most of all. Caretaking didn't come naturally to her, and she seemed to resent my father, his illness, and the whole crappy situation. She vowed never to put him into a nursing home and she would fulfill that promise. Every morning she would set out a bowl of salt-free Cheerios, two prunes, a small glass of juice, and his pills. She had him on a sodium-free diet; it hardly seemed worth living. My mother would take her seat across from him and bite into a quartered orange, sucking all the meat out of it.

One aide after another marched through their lives. Some had to be dismissed right away because they clearly could not lift my father. Others stayed longer until they committed some egregious offense. One heavy-set man with dyed hair the color of orange soda strung a clothesline between two trees on the front lawn and hung a quilt on it. This made my mother apoplectic. She ran out the front door in her bathrobe and pulled the quilt down like a sailor his mainsail heading into a storm. Then she demanded he remove the line. *Okay, lady, take it easy.*

The same aide sang or whistled constantly as he worked, as if he were one of the seven dwarfs. My mother couldn't stand it, but how do you tell someone to stop singing without sounding like Mussolini? My mother didn't fire him until she received a call from the cops one night. He had taken my father's handicap van out for a spin and was picked up outside an after-hours club in New Haven.

After that, I feared that I would come home to find my parents back-to-back and bound in duct tape, the valuables gone. One lady disappeared with my father and the van for twelve hours. We were frantic. They returned without any explanation apart from saying they got lost. I noticed the crumpled red-and-white-striped detritus of a Kentucky Fried Chicken meal in the backseat.

Mercifully, my father's last aide was a gentle man who figured out how to slalom between my mother's moods and quickly learned her precise way of doing things: loading the dishwasher just so, folding the rags. (Yes, folding rags!) And unlike me, snatching permanent press clothing from the dryer before they wrinkle (a technique my mother has elevated to an art form). More amazing, he could anticipate my father's needs without being intrusive and not take his abrasiveness personally. When I'd come over with my then young daughter he would play Connect Four with her, letting her win, tapping his chip on the table to warn her about making costly mistakes. We would try to get my father to play, but after slipping a chip or two into the plastic slots he'd lose interest.

Whenever I read an article about the unexpected benefits of aging, I groan. It's not fun, you don't become wiser, and worse, the world is hurtling away from you. Old age is nothing if not managing losses: physical ability, appearance, memory, spouses, friends, economic independence, and finally freedom. True, some people hold on to their faculties and abilities longer. Often you will hear the Yiddish term *kaynahorah* reflexively muttered after a statement like "She's ninety but she still drives. *Kayna-horah.*" It's a Yiddish expression, meant to keep the evil eye away. For my father, there were no reasons to rejoice in the last years of his life, no stretches of time where he got his sense of humor back, when he could finish a crossword puzzle, or play a mean hand of gin. At the end of his life my father went from the hospital to hospice. There, too, he had to endure more pain, holding on for days, mostly unconscious. It was unbearable. We were told he could live for a few days or a few months. We thought hospice would make things easier. During those difficult days, when talking about the question of when you should pull the plug, my mother said, her voice thick with anger, "There is no plug."

♠

Bette has completely stopped coming to Bridge. The ladies always ask my mother how she's doing, what's happening.

There isn't much to tell, and my mother doesn't like to say much. There is a tacit understanding among the women. All of them have been through it, having lost their husbands of fifty-plus years, except for Jackie. Dick still plays tennis. He still travels the world. Still adds masks to his collection. *Kaynahorah!* Everyone feels for Bette but there is nothing they can do. I offer to spell Bette so she can get her hair done, her nails. I offer to play cards with Arthur, kibbutz the way we do when I run into him at the JCC. Bette declines all offers of help. She says Arthur doesn't want visitors, doesn't want to see anyone.

All of the men go first. Men who went to work every day, smoked cigars and wore fedoras, men who might have strayed but didn't leave their wives, trade them in for younger models. Played ball with their sons and walked their daughters down the aisle at their weddings. These were men who poured tumblers of scotch and read the paper when they got home. Men who golfed on the weekend, played tennis, pinochle, poker, and couples Bridge with their wives. They didn't read *GQ* or *Esquire*, didn't need to. They knew how to tie a tie, do a push-up, and wax the Cadillac. They took Polaroid pictures at birthday parties and paid the bills. That their wives didn't have to work was a point of pride, as was putting their children through college, affording a second home in a gated community in Boca or Palm Beach with automatic sprinklers and manicured putting greens. They left nest eggs and continued to take care of their wives from the grave.

When Bette comes home every night from the hospital there are at least a dozen messages on her phone; she is too exhausted to answer any. Sometimes my mother or another friend has left a meal on her porch. She doesn't have an appetite. Her refrigerator and freezer are filled with food she hasn't touched.

. . .

On the morning my father died I had arrived early at hospice. I didn't have a premonition. I just liked being there alone with him in the early hours, the empty parking lot scored in rows of herringbone. Inside it was so quiet you could hear the wheezing of the breathing machines. I would pick up a Starbucks on the way and just sit quietly in his room before the nurses made their first rounds of the day. That morning, my father was sleeping on his side. Usually he was on his back. I slipped off my shoes, climbed into the bed, and curled around his back the way he did with me when I was little and needed help getting to sleep.

I started to quietly sing all the songs we loved: "Downtown," "Winchester Cathedral," and my favorite "If the Rain's Got to Fall," slipping into our best cockney accents: *Sunday's the day when it's got to be fine, 'cause that's when I'm meeting my girl.* I was my father's girl. We resembled each other physically, were business-minded and social chameleons; we earned money and lent it, we battled the bulge, and we liked to make people laugh. He couldn't say no to me, peeled off a twenty and then another when I was going out with my friends.

When I turned fifteen and sixteen, my father couldn't understand my clothes, my friends, my music, or what was happening to me when depression enveloped itself around my teenage life. He once told a therapist that his other daughters were fine, implying there was something wrong with me. Why couldn't I get with the program? Why did I reek of pot? What had happened to his straight-A girl who used to sail down our front hallway into his arms when he came home from work? Why had I become sullen, uncommunicative; why could he no longer make me laugh?

The Bridge Ladies would say I was spoiled. That my father was a pushover, that there wasn't anything he wouldn't do for his daughters. In many ways, this was true. Often he would openly defy my mother and approve of things she had vetoed: going to a movie on a school night, buying a treat, or staying up late. Of course what they didn't see, at least with respect to me, was how all that indulgence, all of his generosity, was contingent on my doing what he wanted. Many fights, the worst of them, ended with him saying: *After all I've done for you.*

What could you say to that? It was an excruciating double bind: I fiercely disagreed with him and deeply craved his approval. Eventually our differences came to define our relationship: he was disgusted when I moved into an East Village tenement with a friend ("If this is how you want to live"). When he read my first published poem, he threw the small magazine on the floor ("If that's what you want to write"). And he acted as if I were throwing my life and my money away when I pursued an MFA in poetry instead of an MBA. (Okay, he called that one.) My mother had often equated him with King Solomon for his keen and fair decision-making skills, and she deferred to them. We all know how that story ends: the baby is spared. Why did I always feel cut in half?

♠

You could hear the nurses dispatched from the nursing station by the squeak of their white wedgies making early-morning rounds, beginning the administration of morphine like earthbound angels. I knew if my mother had seen me beside my father, she would have turned away or told me to get up. We are not a family of easy affection, physical displays. I knew there would be no support groups for my mother, she wouldn't join the grieving people in the mauve-colored solarium at the hospice, pamphlets scattered on the coffee tables for people of every faith looking for solace. She had hidden her grief for her entire life. Why would she start now?

Holding my father like that was almost unbearable. I longed for one more movie, one more gin game, one more walk around the neighborhood on a brisk fall day when we would sell wooden brooms and lightbulbs for the Lions Club with me proudly holding the cigar box we used to collect the checks and cash, keeping the bills in their own tidy sections like the Monopoly bank.

When the nurse came I was afraid she would chase me out, but she said she would come back. Still I got out of bed a minute later, feeling embarrassed. When she returned she gave him more morphine and said it was close. Soon after his skin roiled purple, as if boiling beneath the surface. It was like a great wave gathering force in the middle distance of a dark ocean. I ran to get the nurse then called my mother and sisters from the pay phone. Then I flew out of there to get my younger sister. I knew he would be gone when I returned, but I was too afraid to stay. I couldn't watch him die.

When we got back, a cloth like a shower curtain was pulled around his bed. My mother and Nina were collapsed in the chairs beside his bed. Nina had gotten there in time to say goodbye, but it was my mother who had been with him when he died. I never could bring myself to ask what she said, if anything. If she thanked him for the fun they had, the nights under the boardwalk, the Broadway shows. If she told him how sorry she was about her depression, how it robbed them of joy when the baby finally came, or how grateful she was for his constancy, his soldiering on in the face of losing Barbara. If she said what she never says: that she loved him.

I stepped inside the curtain. His skin was porcelain, as if all the blood had drained from his body. He looked like a marble saint lain out on a tomb in the shadows of an Italian church. I openly wailed, could not control it. Then my mother, my sisters, and I were squired into a small room to make arrangements. There was a half-eaten leftover sheet cake from the day before, garish with neon pink and green icing. We dared each other to eat it and started laughing hysterically, the way you do when life is most absurd and cruel. My sisters and I hugged. My mother was untouchable.

CHAPTER 18

When the Student Is Ready, the Teacher Appears

I return to the Manhattan Bridge Club. Its down-at-the heels, vaguely grimy aspect remains reassuring to me with its rickety tables and bald carpet. This is a regular Tuesday-morning session conducted on a drop-in basis. A brief lesson is followed by two hours of supervised play. As the group gathers, it's clear that most of the attendees know each other. Chitchat is exchanged about summer vacations. One woman says she is going to Wyoming for the umpteenth time. She loves it! A couple chimes in that they went there in the 1970s and search their collective brain for the name of the hotel they stayed in. The husband snaps his finger next to his temple in an effort to call forth the name. She starts vocalizing, "The West something, The Western. That's not it." This kind of conversation usually elicits suicidal ideation on my part, but I sort of smile as I follow the thread.

"It will come to me, it will come to me." The woman closes her eyes and tenses her entire body as if she were moving her bowels.

When older people can't remember something they get really upset. Is this the beginning? Are they losing it? They don't recall that people of all ages forget where they left their keys, forget to pay their bills, can't recall the capitol of Wyoming. Mind-bendingly, the couple is still trying to recover the name of the hotel. Next to them, I overhear a side conversation between a woman wearing wooden beads the size of testicles and a man in a straw cap. She is grilling him on where he works and what he does. I can't tell if she is hitting on him or just being friendly. The male-to-female ratio is roughly about ten to one. Then, two more women enter. One is quite beautiful, a languid Modigliani with half-closed eyelids. The other is chipper and annoying as she scuttles off to the ladies room and mouths to her friend to watch her bag as if it contained uranium.

The teacher finally arrives nearly fifteen minutes late. He is wearing black slacks, a black shirt with white pinstripes as thin as floss, and black slip-on shoes. I imagine that he has just gotten off work as a dealer at a casino or as a rumba instructor at a dancing school. He is tall with an athletic build but also graceful and precise in his movements. It's hard to pin down his age, maybe midthirties. When he greets us he apologizes for being late but doesn't dwell on it, then he introduces himself, Jess Jurkovic. He welcomes us, reminding us that we are here for the Tuesday lesson and supervised play, just in case anyone has boarded the wrong train. Three students have set up bidding boxes at one of the tables and left a seat free for him, which he assumes like a king on his throne. It's where thousands of games have been played, the borders scored and scuffed with use, the scene of many victories and defeats. He sets up an open hand, meaning all cards visible for each of the four hands, and he asks us how the dealer would bid (dealer always bids or passes first). I am astonished at how deep and sonorous his voice is, fit for late-night radio, and how he imparts his enthusiasm and wisdom for the game in equal parts superiority and affection.

Everyone crowds around the table and starts counting the points in each hand, assessing the distribution of cards according to suit, throwing out suggestions. He fields each one and tosses it back. After we offer all the wrong answers, he revels in showing us the best way to bid the hand, sitting up a bit straighter in his chair and eager to hold forth.

I start looking at the other people gathered and notice inconsequential things: a label sticking out of a shirt, orange nail polish, a woman with dyed brown hair that sits atop her head like chocolate icing swirled on a cupcake. When did I develop attention deficit?

Jess is always respectful even as people widely miss the mark with their suggestions. He aims for clarity and asks repeatedly if we understand before moving on. He couldn't be more patient and derives pleasure when we get something right. I notice the delicate way his hands hover above the cards, as if guiding a planchette over a Ouija Board. His fingers are large with trimmed nails, skin pale and smooth. All of his gestures emanate from his hands, and later I will learn (okay, google) that he is a jazz pianist. He approaches the cards like the keys on a piano, still, then ready to strike. I suspect Bridge and music form the double helix of his elegant mind. His teaching style is a combination of vaudeville, high noon, opera, and drama.

Now, in addition to teaching, Jess goes to the thrice-annual Bridge Nationals. Sometimes he comes back "humbled," sometimes happy. He has over 2,100 Master Points, which is the player-ranking system used by the American Contract Bridge

League. The highest ranking player in the country has over 80,000 points. You earn Master Points by playing in tournaments sanctioned by the league and advance according to the size and ranking of the tournament. Like the colors of karate belts that designate levels of mastery, bridge players climb the ladder from Rookie to Bronze Life Master, Silver Life Master, Gold, Diamond, Emerald, Platinum, and finally the highest title conferred: Grand Life Master. Bridge ranking rewards mastery and confers respect.

Jess is the first person I've spoken with who has both mastery of the game and exudes the enthusiasm of the brightest kid in the class.

"It's the most interesting, deep, and scientifically based game, and for me it's like music in that you're always a student. I find it wonderful and exciting and beautiful. I see it almost aesthetically as well. I love the cards. I even love the beautiful designs on the backs of cards." All of this tumbles out when we first sit down to speak. I quickly add that I love the beauty of the cards as well, and we start talking about them as if they were Picassos.

Jess started playing with his parents and grandparents. "We muddled through without really knowing the rules." Then he found a book on Bridge (William Root's *Commonsense Bidding*), and it was a revelation. "I discovered you can actually communicate—it's not a big guessing game." *It isn't?* He treated the book like a college course, writing what was in essence a paper on every chapter and quizzing himself afterward. Then he got the Bridge Baron app and began playing on the computer, which he describes as a crash course. He played social Bridge in college, and when he moved to New York he found his way to the Manhattan Bridge Club, and entered the competitive world of the game, entirely self-taught.

I notice that the man with the straw hat has changed his

eyeglasses to a pair with lilac-tinted lenses. The lady with the testicle necklace is checking e-mails. This is an unspoken no-no. The Wyoming-loving older couple appear to be very happy together, nodding at one another when they grasp a concept.

"Shall we?" The lesson concluded, Jess invites us into the main room with more card tables to start supervised play. I overhear some of the students asking about the future of the club; there are rumors that it's merging or moving or both. He tells us that it's true; the Manhattan Bridge Club is closing its doors in two weeks' time and merging with a club called Honors on the East Side. The location of the clubs, on either side of Manhattan, is representative of the club's personality or culture. The Manhattan Bridge Club is a West Side club, meaning the people are generally more down-to-earth, lots of teachers and social workers. You would never know who is a sharp player by the casual way he dresses. The women wear loose-fitting clothes and the men wear their slacks pulled up a bit too high. If someone is dolled up or wearing some kind of Brooks Brothers ensemble they are in the minority and stick out.

Honors, we are led to believe, is a bit more hoity-toity, just as the East Side of Manhattan is more moneyed and its people more status and appearance conscious. When I ask another teacher what the people are like there, she puts her hands to her face and pulls the skin back in imitation of a face-lift. When I eventually make my way over to Honors in the coming weeks I see what folks have been talking about. It's as if the Manhattan Bridge Club itself has gotten a face-lift. The decor is less like a community room and more like a country club. The signs around the place are laminated, and there are framed pictures of awards and fine-art posters from museums like in a fancy doctor's office.

A few more people show up for the supervised session, which

takes us to thirteen students. With three tables of four, one of us is odd man out. As we head over for the tables, it's clear to me as the newest student here that I am the odd man. The others either know each other or have come as partners. I am a big girl and I have to ask if I can join, pull up a chair, and rotate in. But I'm paralyzed. The table of women closest in age to me is engaged in conversation. The other two tables are filled; people are already shuffling. I get a strong vibe that none of the tables wants to adopt a rescue dog; playing with a fifth means less individual playtime. Standing there is also humiliating. Finally, Jess comes over and pulls up a chair to the corner of the table with the women and says I should sit there. No one looks too pleased. Marshaling all the maturity at my command, I say hi and introduce myself. The four women go around the circle and mechanically say their names.

The game begins and immediately the women at our table start calling Jess over for help. He stands behind each one, computes the value of the hand—the strength and length—in a few seconds and asks what they would do. As they point to the card they think they should throw or whisper bids from behind the fan of their cards, he shakes them off or nods yes. Sometimes he peppers you with questions: How many points do you have? How many do you need to bid or respond? What is your partner telling you with his bid? He wants us to think for ourselves and is not apt to supply answers. By the end of the two hours, I notice him blinking more rapidly or cracking his neck, the first signs of strain.

I become a semiregular at Jess's Tuesday-morning session, now located at Honors Bridge Club. I wish I had the time to go every Tuesday because it is the highlight of my week. There is a kind of theater surrounding Bridge that has me in its thrall. Though

I've been coming for a few months, I still feel like an outsider. Every week the same damn drill: tables of four are already deep in conversation, catching up, kibbutzing. Some tables only have one or two people sitting at them. Though often when I've shyly asked if a seat is free, I'd be met with the glare of the commuter who doesn't want to lift his bags off the seat next to him. Other times, a person apologizes: they are saving seats. I didn't have this much trouble in the high school cafeteria.

Still, I keep coming back. Each week, I'd eventually find a table with the stragglers and polecats. The two hours of play would fly by in a flash. I'd learn something with every hand. I began to understand how the finesse worked. I saw that losing a few tricks early could put you in a better position for winning more tricks later. And the cardinal rule: pull trump first. Listening to Jess each week, I began to focus more. It was his voice, his tone, and his wry sense of humor. One week a woman said she was too afraid to play a certain card.

Jess looked at all of us. "The cards don't have emotions, right?"

I was all emotion, terrified of my cards. Even though I was gaining confidence in some areas, discarding could still feel like facing a firing squad. I wasn't the only one who still got flustered. A tall blonde once turned entirely red while she played a hand, her chest, neck, and cheeks spread with color like spilled wine on a white tablecloth. Another woman had to run to the bathroom twice while playing. People called out a constant stream of questions for Jess, and he caromed from table to table like freshly broken billiard balls flying in every direction.

Then Jess said something that changed the whole way I approached the game. He was supervising the next table over from mine, but it caught my attention. He didn't say: listen carefully here is a key insight. He just offered it like any other advice or coaching he doled out on a regular basis. "You're telling a story," he said. "You and your partner are having a conversation through the language of bidding. You each have a story to tell."

Jess painted a picture for me that I hadn't grasped in the year I had been taking lessons. I'll never really get mathematical concepts; I can barely remember my own phone number. This was language from my world. *When the student is ready. . .*

♠

On a rain-filled morning I arrive early and boldly plop down at a table where two chairs are draped with coats. I'm sick of being such a *pisher.* When the two women return to claim their chairs they are friendly enough and introduce themselves. Yolanda, an elegant woman with a European accent, was someone I had played with before, but she doesn't recognize me (so much for making an impression). Esther, a woman who could easily be one of the Bridge Ladies, somewhere in her eighties, has bright red hair pulled back severely in a tiny ponytail, like the tip of a paintbrush. Then a woman who looks like she runs a Fortune 500 company barrels up to the table, claims a seat, and introduces herself as Bailey. She is a vision in camel with gold accents everywhere: the buttons on her blazer, earrings, four or five gold bangle bracelets, and a necklace with gold links that are nearly as big as belt buckles.

It appears after a deal or two that Bailey, Yolanda, Esther, and I are basically on the same level. Deal after deal, Yolanda gets all the good hands, full of honors or high-card points, and suits with six or more cards. Esther grows frustrated.

She and I continue to get garbage, all low cards, can't get into the bidding. We tease Yolanda that she is stacking the deck, not shuffling the cards.

"Watch," Esther says. "Next time she'll get all four aces."

When Yolanda gets her fourth great hand in a row, Esther throws up her hands.

In response, Yolanda says, "*Chance en jeu, malheureux en amour.*"

I ask her to translate.

"'Lucky in cards, unlucky in love.' I would rather be unlucky in cards," she says.

I look at her quizzically.

Yolanda explains that her husband had died not too long ago. She says this so quietly I think I may be the only one at the table who hears her.

"Oh, I'm so sorry."

"So you see why I would rather not have the cards."

"Would you say it again?"

"What?"

"The French."

Now she pronounces it even more slowly, sadly, "*Chance en jeu, malherueux en amour.*"

The next deal, I miraculously draw a big hand, lots of honor cards and points. I win the auction and become declarer. This is where the rubber meets the road. Winning the auction thrusts you into the spotlight. This is Wimbledon Centre Court, Fischer vs. Spassky. You are Shaun White and the table is your half-pipe. It's your moment to command the board, to finesse for kings, turn losers into winners, trump your opponents, and watch a lowly two of Diamonds take an ace of Spades if you play your cards right.

The contract is for four Spades, which means we must win ten out of thirteen tricks with Spades as trump. When my partner lays down the dummy, I see the strength of our combined hands; we have more than enough trump and high-card points to control the hand. I take two quick tricks (sure winners like the ace and king of a suit), and then start pulling trump. I know I need to try the finesse, but for the life of me I can't remember how to do that. Am I trying to force out a higher card or win a trick by ducking a higher card from swallowing mine? Jess happens to wander over just then and looks at my cards. I point to the one I think I should play and he lifts an eyebrow in approval. Have I ever felt this smart in my entire life? *The teacher appears . . .*

Jess announces that we should be wrapping up. Bailey is changing out of her shoes in favor of big rubber boots. Esther takes out her phone, flips it open like a Zippo. No one seems to care about the rest of the hand. In part, I suppose, because it's sure to win, the dummy filled with so many kings and queens. Then other tables start breaking up, people heading out. I move quickly, picking off the last few tricks like a rifle at a carnival game, and win the hand with two bonus tricks. There isn't time for praise or pats on the back. No "good job" or "well done," the way we usually flatter each other after we make our contract. The session is over, everyone dispersing. In truth, a monkey could have won the hand. I don't care. I head home a few inches off the ground.

And then I proudly call my mother.

CHAPTER 19

Ash

End of June, and still no Bette. Jackie is early as usual, sitting at
our regular table at the Country Corner Diner. The stout water
glasses are already beading with condensation. Jackie looks regal,
hair newly done, wearing a great tribal piece made of bone or
ivory plaques and tubes held together with black raffia string. I
notice she's wearing her signature ring with three prongs. When
I compliment her on it she says, "I'll leave it to you in my will."
I'm mortified. Of course it was a joke, but had I been coveting
it? What exactly do I want from the ladies? What have I taken?

A new waitress drops off menus. I wonder where the waitress
is whose beauty provided so much mystery in this plain country
diner.

Bea and Rhoda arrive at the same time.

"I'm on time!" Rhoda announces, pleased with herself. Bea
asks if she wants a gold star. Then my mother arrives, and the
table is complete. It's hard not to wonder: Will this be me in

thirty years? Is that a long time or no time at all? Will my hands be mottled, my face a walnut? Will I bury my husband or will he bury me? Will I wear purple, and resolve every year to be a better person, volunteer like Bea? Or will I run to concerts and lectures and Broadway shows like my mother, read the *New Yorker* cover to cover? Will I have any friends left?

Of all of the women, it's Rhoda who's kept up the largest network of friends. The first time we met, she had her high school yearbook already waiting on the kitchen counter. The cover embossed with a witch riding on a broom and named "The Witch" for Salem's famous trials.

"There I am," Rhoda said pointing to herself in this sacred high school relic.

Before Fran Kay, there was Rudie. Rhoda pointed to the picture of the girl next to her in the yearbook. Two girls appear nearly identical gazing out, heads tilted up, alabaster skin, and hairdos inspired by the film stars of the day. Not conjoined but nearly fused at the hip, the two girls with the same last name and the same spelling would go all the way from grade school through high school and then on to Russell Sage. Rhoda Belle Freedman and Ruth Helen Freedman: Rudie and Rho, Rho and Rudie.

"We'd walk from school to the beach, making up stories and singing songs the entire time."

"Are you still close?" I'd asked.

"Not as much as we once were," Rhoda admitted but proudly mentions that they still exchange birthday cards to this day.

"In fact, I have one right here I need to get in the mail." And sure enough there was a blue envelope on her counter with Rudy's name and address written in Rhoda's perfect script, a stamp already affixed.

Bette will tell me about Barbara, her roommate at Skidmore for all four years. She worshipped her bright and confident friend from exotic Brooklyn. It was Barbara who listened when Bette cried about Donald and set them up on dates with Dartmouth boys. And Barbara who encouraged Bette when she was distraught about not getting parts, her dream dissipating before her. "I love her to this day."

My mother hung out at the roller rink and boardwalk with Vivian and Sylvia, the other two points of a classic girl triangle. Vivian was the quintessential mean girl, the great beauty who ditched the girls when a fella came around. Sylvie was the loveable schlub, and my mother somewhere in between. They would each marry, go their own way. Bea had lots of friends, no one in particular to mention. Jackie was the president of her sorority though she won't admit to being popular. *(That is for other people to say.)*

I know my mother will order turkey dry on seedless rye. I know she won't have anything to drink. I know a few crumbs from her sandwich will fall on her chest and as she brushes them off she will scold herself for being messy. She looks lovely today, her hair recently cut and colored, just the right amount of makeup, and she's wearing some of her spring separates with a necklace made of tortoiseshell links I haven't seen before. She seems more relaxed today than usual.

When my father first died, I thought my mother was manically filling her time. Maybe she was. I hadn't understood how circumscribed her life had become, tethered to him and his disability. I said I gave her credit for taking care of him, but did I? Wasn't I always annoyed with her for not being nicer, or gentler, or just easing up a little on the sodium-free meals? How could I have not helped her more, how could I have been so judgmental? So shitty? In her eighth decade, she has taken up Hebrew lessons and fallen in love with opera. She has even taken herself several times to the Met. Maybe there some of her sorrow dissipates as notes in air.

Bea is quieter than usual. I notice she is wearing an oval-shaped gold ring with a dark green stone, a man's ring that swims on her finger. When I ask her where it's from, she says, having read my mind, "Sorry to disappoint you. There is no wonderful romantic story behind it." When I ask Bea where she got it, she perks up a bit, "Carl used to love to go to the antique stores on State Street. He loved picking up all kinds of odd things." Bea, I think, was his greatest find.

Today's headlines: a boy has killed his mother in Orange, a nearby town. It is the second matricide in this small town, which is coincidental, but sounds ominous, the premise for a Stephen King novel. In Milford, where Rhoda lives, a boy stabbed a girl to death after she turned him down for the prom. The ladies will never understand it.

Another friend has gone into the Whitney Center, an upscale assisted living facility in town, following a car accident. A New Haven widow who moved to Florida and swore she would never date now has a man friend! A neighbor no less!

Back at Jackie's, Bea and my mother are partners. Bea opens with a Club. It could mean that she has five Clubs or as few as three. I'm impressed with myself for knowing this. If my mother passes, it could leave Bea in the lurch if she is short on Clubs. My mother passes. The opponents also pass, so Bea is stuck with the bid. When my mother lays down the dummy, Bea threatens her, "You better have less than five points."

With more than five points my mother would have been forced to bid. However, she only has three points and has bid correctly. Bea is aggravated even though there was nothing my mother could do with that hand. "Sometimes you can't save your partner," a saying my mother is fond of.

Halfway into the hand, Bea makes an uncharacteristic mistake that costs them the game.

"I have the memory of a soda cracker," she says when she realizes her mistake, failing to keep track of trumps. When they go down, she shrugs it off. "What can I say, Betsy, we got squished."

After watching for a couple of hours, I start to drift as usual, yearn for my iPhone. I can feel my work in-box filing up with e-mails from the writers I represent, editors I work with, unsolicited query letters from people who hope I will take them on as clients. Many get in touch with memoirs about depression, eating disorders, mental illness, addiction, and suicide. When I was a young editor, I couldn't get enough of these personal stories and began to get something of a reputation for publishing them. A colleague once dubbed me the pain and suffering editor.

I knew that Jackie spent years volunteering at Clifford Beers, the first mental health organization in the country named for its founder, a man whose own suicide attempt and institutionalization led him to become a reformer in the field of mental health at the turn of the century. She volunteered and would eventually become the secretary, then the president, and finally a long-standing board member raising money, contributing, organizing benefits. When I once posited to Jackie that many people in the "helping" professions are seeking some sort of help themselves, much like Beers, she scoffed. I hypothesize that perhaps someone close to her needed help. Again, she rebuffs the suggestion. Surely, something fueled Jackie's passion for her work with the mentally ill. She insists there is no connection. I'm sure much is random in the universe, but I came to see the pattern in nearly all the books I worked on as an extension of myself: what I concealed, what I feared, and what I hoped for.

♠

One night, when my husband was away and my daughter off with her friends, I invited my mother to dinner and a movie. It was a little awkward at first, like a first date, as we are so rarely alone. But we're doing better. She attempts to stop herself from criticizing me (or offering suggestions, as she would say). I try not to let her get to me. When a zinger gets through, I feel like a catcher waiting for the pitch; will she throw her fastball or her curveball? Only now I'm ready for it, even looking forward to it, knowing I can handle it. I am also trying to be more attentive, more inclusive. I call my mother nearly every day. Whenever we hang up, she always says the same thing, "Talk to you next week."

"Mom," I say, thoroughly exasperated. "I call you every day! Why do you say 'talk to you next week'?"

I want the credit for calling as much as I do. How many people call their mom every day? Come on!

Spontaneity isn't my mother's strong suit either, and when we first moved back, it irritated her whenever I invited her for dinner at the last minute.

"Well, if I had known, I would have put it on the calendar," she would say. Or "I'm not dressed," or "I'm already undressed," and we would both get off the phone annoyed. Still, I kept inviting her same day or the day before, and sometimes last minute. Eventually she started saying "sure why not" or "yes, that would be lovely." Often she'd wind up treating us to dinner. If she already had plans, that would be okay, too. We'd get together another time. We've actually gotten good at it. Invitations tendered and accepted are more casual, less fraught. Sometimes she'll even show up in sweats and no makeup, apologize for looking like a mess but wanting to come. We don't care! It's just us! She still finds it unfathomable that we can throw dinner together at the last minute. "I don't understand how you people live," she'll say, as if we are Inuit, so strange are our customs.

At dinner she told me about a friend who had gone to the Whitney Center and swore by it. The people who love it become evangelical and want everyone to move there. Then she adds that the Whitney Center is having a 20 percent off sale. My mother had checked out the facility some months ago; she thinks about it a lot, but has yet to pull the trigger. I've never been and I'm curious if it's right for her. No matter how many people say they love it, no one really wants to go. Of all the Bridge Ladies, Bette is the most vocal. She has two reasons: the first is she doesn't want to be around old people exclusively. She wants to see middle-aged people, and children, and be in the mix of life. Once, Bette remarked how painful it was to see Maureen O'Hara accepting her lifetime achievement award at the Oscars.

"Why did she have to come out like that in her wheelchair?"

I thought O'Hara looked great and triumphant receiving the award at ninety-three. But Bette wants to remember her as the great beauty that she was. I imagine it's how she wants to remember herself.

Another reason Bette doesn't want to move is the move itself, dealing with sixty years of accumulation. "If I die in this house, the kids will have to clean it out. They'll throw it all away."

Originally, the Whitney Center had a very low percentage of Jewish occupants. The numbers have gone up considerably, and as a result it's where my mother now imagines she eventually might go. Plus, more and more of her friends are there. The apartments are spacious, the services extensive, the nursing care five-star. She continues to use the upkeep of the house as her excuse for considering the move.

"I can't take it anymore," she says, "this house is costing me a frickin' fortune." She never mentions health, mobility, or safety. She's just not there yet.

The movie was dark and slow. We both fell asleep early on and were awakened by a gunshot in the film. She leaned in and loudly whispered, "Should we leave?"

Driving home she told me to go slow multiple times. She instructed me to keep both hands on the wheel. She said aloud the name of almost every store we passed where she'd had a less than satisfying shopping experience, relaying stories about bad service and know-nothing salespeople.

"It's a good thing I save my receipts," my mother said, regularly returning a third of what she buys. And I know this to be true, as her pocketbook is home to receipts that date back to the Carter administration. She is always beseeching me to hold on to receipts, which may explain why I never do. When she accuses me of not returning things, like a shirt that doesn't fit or a bag of grapes that's half bad, it's like an indictment on my entire generation: the wasteful, the spoiled, the disposable.

I was about to make a left turn when my mother instructed me to make it wide.

"You never know when a curb or divider is going to pop up."

Then she confided that one night after making one of her trademark wide left turns, a cop pulled her over. "A big tall lady cop. Big!"

The cop asked her if she knew she had made a very wide turn.

"Oh, yes."

Then she asked her if she had been drinking.

"Oh, no, officer."

"Were you playing the age card?" I ask.

"So what if I did."

"Had you been drinking?" I know my mother occasionally likes a Stoli on the rocks.

"No, not that night. Thank goodness."

Hard to imagine the cop pulling my mother out of the car and making her walk a straight line if they still do that.

"You know who doesn't drive?" she asked rhetorically.

I never answer these statements, nor do I need to.

"Millie Klarik. She's in her nineties. I always give her a ride. She says I'm the worst driver she's ever driven with. But she still let's me take her. What do you make of that?"

I had no idea what to make of it. Does Millie have a death wish? Does sheer desperation compel her to take a ride from my mother? Was she insulted? She seemed to think it was funny. More pressing: Should my mother still be driving? She's commented once or twice that people are incredibly rude, constantly honking at her. This gives me pause: Why are they honking? Is she just going too slowly or perhaps taking one of her signature wide turns? At this stage, I know that losing one's license is like losing one's legs. It recommends the Whitney Center with its fleet of buses that take seniors to shopping, to downtown, to plays, doctor appointments, and New York! It all sounds great except it sucks after a lifetime of independence.

We make a date to visit the Whitney Center together. I want to see it for myself. We wait in the corridor for our guide. One wall is all glass, the other displays art from local artists and from the residents themselves. It has the air of an art show at a quaint town green, in other words vaguely depressing. The woman who greets us for our tour is everything you would imagine— warm, professional, knowledgeable. She's wearing what looks like an Ann Taylor summer shift and beat-up pumps she doubt- less keeps under her desk. After we introduce ourselves she says, "Shall we?" and we head off to a bank of elevators.

The first unit she is showing is called Ash. I know it's named for the trees, but instead I see a cold pile of ashes the morning after a campfire and a cremation urn. (Whenever my mother tells me she wants to be buried, I threaten to cremate her and scatter the ashes outside of Saks Fifth Avenue. She tells me to knock it off.) They really should get a better marketing team. I would name the units after Connecticut's famous figures: The Hale, The Twain, The Trumbull. Even Connecticut flowers would be nice: The Aster, the Daylily, or the Dogwood.

Once off the elevator we are led down a long hall with red carpeting. *Redrum. Redrum.* Inside Ash, I'm taken by surprise. It's all new and clean, and bright. Nothing in the hall would lead you to believe that the units would be so inviting. I can see my mother here. It looks a lot like Bea's and Rhoda's condos. I pull at a vertical door in the kitchen, and it's a pantry! My mother criticizes the design, saying that she wouldn't be able to reach the high shelves. I remind her that she can't reach the shelves at home either.

"Right," she says and starts scavenging in her pocketbook for something.

The woman walks us through the apartment. Both bedrooms share a small patio. The bathroom is new and the shower wheel-chair accessible. Pulls are mounted on every wall. My favorite feature is a walk-in closet with shelving and cubbies galore, storage for all my mother's Ferragamos.

We learn that you can hire people to pack you up and then furnish your apartment.

"All you have to do is turn the key. They'll even hang your pictures," the woman says this too eagerly. Of course, I also know that this is a luxury, options like these for a small handful of people who can afford it. But it seems creepy walking into your life that someone else has organized, like a blind person learning the contours of a new room. I also know that I would be fortunate if someone hung up my pictures, furnished my linen closet, mounted a flat-screen TV, loaded a fridge with diet Half 'n Half Snapple, and organized a regular Bridge game for me when I'm old.

My mother keeps asking questions about costs and insurance and maintenance and bundled vs. unbundled services. She has pulled out the sheet of paper she was looking for: a page of notes so convoluted Alan Turing couldn't crack them. She continues to take more notes while the woman betrays just the slightest whiff of impatience. She keeps telling my mother she has all the information on forms that she will give us at the end of the tour.

"I want to understand it in my head," my mother says. I look at my mother's paper, her familiar handwriting, graceful loops that drift into doodles when she gets bored. I know that no matter how hard she looks at this paper, it will never make sense, because moving here doesn't make sense.

The woman tells us that the units are flying on account of the special, and with that comment she shifts from soft sell to medium. Then she shows us the facilities: There are three dining areas, one with full restaurant service, a pub, and a café. You get a swipe card with points and they are good at all of the restaurants. I tell my mother that it's like college.

"Not my college."

There is a spa and beauty parlor. A gym and pool. There is a library with wooden bookcases. And in some of the open seating areas I see newspapers with magnifiers, chessboards, and against one wall a black, shiny grand piano that looks as if it hasn't been played in a long time. This big open room is empty save for one man sitting alone by a window. The whole thing feels like a funeral parlor to me. I ask the lady where everyone is, and she knocks out a list of activities like a director on a cruise ship.

The tour concludes and we wind up at the woman's office decorated with high school photos of her handsome sons, a

Garfield birthday card on the bulletin board next to some official papers, a large red button that says PANIC next to her computer, and other office bric-a-brac. Then the woman becomes more aggressive in her sales pitch. I figure she's got us pegged for window-shoppers and is going for broke.

"The thing is," she tells us, "a lot of people want to come here, only they wait too long and no longer qualify either financially or physically." She tells us about her in-laws who could have had a place but they waited too long, and now when they've had falls she has had to scramble to get them into nursing homes with two-star ratings. Even though I suspect this is all part of a prefabricated pitch, I'll admit it sort of scares me. And then she tells us that when people finally do come, they say they should have done it years ago!

"It's a worry-free place where you can maintain your lifestyle for you *and* your children." *And scene.*

The woman gives us the paperwork for the apartments she has shown us. My mother folds them into quarters and shoves them into her purse with a dismissive thank-you.

We sit there a bit stupefied. I feel the need to shake things up, fantasize about throwing her computer through the plate-glass window. Then I pull in close and ask one final question a little conspiratorially. "Is there hooking up here?"

"Excuse me?

"You know, hooking up?"

"You mean cable TV?"

She knows I'm not taking about Comcast.

"Do you mean romance? Yes, there are some romances that develop."

"Okay," I say, and get up.

I look over at my mother; she is thoroughly mortified, her head in her hand.

"Betsy," she says as we leave the office, "you go too far."

"Thank you," I beam, as if it's a compliment.

On the way out, my mother sees no fewer than seven or eight women whom she knows. All are widows except for one whose husband has Alzheimer's. They are all tiny Jewish women in their summer whites, with white hair, and white sneakers. They could be chess pieces clustered on a board. They all rave about the center and urge my mother to come. Most important, they all play Bridge. My mother speaks their language and falls easily into pleasantries and little jokes. They hug one another and say they look terrific or how happy they are to see each other. It's not hard to imagine my mother woven into this fabric.

The car is stifling. We open the windows, waiting to turn on the air conditioner. We don't say anything. I look over at her and she is far away. All the ebullience of meeting her friends has drained.

Finally I say, "Would you like my opinion?"

"Yes," she says. "I would."

"I think it's a nice option, especially knowing so many people, but you're not ready yet."

"Thank you," she says and turns on the air.

♠

Late June and the trees, once caterpillar green, have darkened into the color of dollars. Blockbuster movies dominate the big screens and farm stands are cropping up, soon to be bursting with fat tomatoes and piles of Connecticut corn. Arthur is in hospice now, and Bette and her family are keeping vigil. She must be terrified of losing him, uncertain of a future without him. Arthur was known for saying that the trick in life is never to take the last run, when the mountain is awash in incandescent blue and gold, when the lines and slopes are thinning out and it would be just a quick wait to get on the lift, when your body is spent but you yearn for one last run. This is the time to go home.

My mother calls on Sunday night, her voice rasping, she can't play Bridge. A recurring respiratory issue is dogging her. She wants to know if I will fill in. How can we play with Bette suffering? "We play," my mother says, "that's what we do." I hope knowing that the Bridge club is there waiting for her return is a comfort, though I'm also sure that Bridge is the last thing on Bette's mind.

The game is at Rhoda's. She has set her table on the deck and mentions that Bette above all loved eating on the deck. The view across the inlet is a landscape of industrial buildings to the right and mansions to the left. Motorboats congregate on the dock, their surfaces gleaming like white enamel. And a piece of driftwood or industrial steel juts out of the water like a broken Erector set.

Rhoda's rolled out a whole new set of matching place mats, napkins, and napkin rings with a summery theme. She serves iced tea and coffee in tall glasses with silver stirrers that double as straws out of which one can only demurely sip. Jackie looks like royalty, daintily holding the straw while she sips.

I had tried on three outfits before I settled on a long, gray linen dress in the shape of a column that I hoped forgave the extra pounds. I added a white cotton sweater and my gold watch. I even put on some makeup. Not much, just enough to cover the circles under my eyes, conceal the splotches on my chin. As I came in, Rhoda commented that I look nice, that I was wearing a dress. I realized that I have been scrutinized just as I have been scrutinizing them. Bea notices that my nails are done. (It's true

I got a manicure that morning and I picked the plum-colored polish for the name on the bottom of the bottle, "Just in Case.")

Bea points out five cormorants that have come to sun themselves on the jagged branch sticking out of the water. They are all black with the exception of one that has a gray chest. They are enormous birds and are engaged in various states of self-cleaning. Bea sees a pair of binoculars and gets the birds into view, advertising their strange beauty. Then she hands them to me. I see five detectives in black coats, five nuns out for some sun, five handsome ushers at a wedding, and five pallbearers at a grave. We all comment on the cormorants. Rhoda tells us they come every summer and that there are always five. Her comment, informational and offhand, makes me well up. The ladies don't see the symbolism: five old beautiful birds.

My partner is Bea and as always she is quick to point out when I make a mistake, and I make some doozies right off the bat. When I bid correctly, Bea gives me a slight nod, which I take as a huge pat on the head. After I settle down, I pretty much hold my own, which feels miraculous. Only twice does Bea point out that I failed to mention a strong secondary suit in the bidding. But she makes the hand both times. It's not a national disaster. When I am dummy, I go back on the deck. Four birds remain. Twenty minutes later when I am dummy again, I check again: three.

Today, the clock moves slowly. I'm worried about Bette. I'm worried about my mom. When the game ends, I go out to the deck and take one last look. The cormorant with the gray chest is left standing alone on the branch. She has spread her enormous wings, as if opening a kimono. Rhoda comes out and tells me this is how they dry themselves. Yes, I can see that. I feel the sun warm my face. Rhoda also tilts her face to the late-afternoon sun. Without warning the great bird takes off, flapping its great wings just above the water's surface in a straight line headed for another part of the cove. All five of the birds are now gone. I beg myself not to read too deeply into this tableau but it's too late.

♠

The next morning my mother calls to tell me that Arthur has died. She says he's at peace now and we both know she doesn't mean this. The end of suffering yes, but peace no. We are not sentimental about death. We don't think we will be reunited with our loved ones or anything like that. I start to cry; my mother remains quiet. Six months ago Arthur was grocery shopping, he and Bette were going to movies, out to dinner and to the JCC, where he walked on the treadmill and kibbitzed with the kibbitzers. When he first got sick, Bette consoled herself and anyone who asked that at least it wasn't life-threatening. All that unraveled in a matter of months.

My mother says it's okay to stop by Bette's; only when I do, there are no cars in the driveway. For a moment I think I'm in the wrong place or that this isn't a good time to come. I had imagined a crowd. When I ring the bell, Bette comes to the door where she has greeted me so many times for our talks and for Bridge. She looks tiny, gray, and when I hug her I can feel every bone in her back and I fear I will crush her. She ushers me inside. Outside on the deck her two-year-old twin grandsons are filling plastic watering cans and watering the flowers. The water mostly goes all over the deck and their comic relief is a small miracle. Bette is happy Arthur lived to see them.

We pass a half hour with small talk mostly. How I filled in for Bridge, any inane thing I could think of to offset my nervousness. Bette's daughter Amy is there and offers me a glass of wine. Bette's son Jack entertains his two boys, throwing a ball high in the sky, which makes them squeal and run in circles like puppies. When I finally ask Bette how she is doing, she flinches, shrugs; I'm not sure which. Then she tells me that they had to make arrangements earlier in the day—Arthur would be cremated—until then she had kept it together. Upon leaving the crematorium, the director said to Bette, "Don't worry, I'll take good care of him."

It was something he probably said by rote, a gesture, and that was all. But it set Bette off, "Who are you to take care of my husband? I'll take care of my husband."

Later, she will confide that she doesn't know what to do when people say "God bless," or when they say they are praying for Arthur. She knows they are well meaning but she doesn't know what God has to do with it. She wants to tell them to pray for themselves.

Everyone, including Bette, would say Arthur took care of her, lived for her, and that she was the center of his life. He spent a lifetime not complaining about a job he never liked or wanted. The only thing he kept from their fabric store is a glass-fronted case with brightly covered spools of thread in lockstep like a row of soldiers. That was Arthur, in lockstep with dutiful men of his generation. Bette's children worry about how she will manage on her own. Amy is the closest in Hartford. Davi, her middle daughter, lives in Paris. Her son, who lives out of town, is riddled with worry, wonders how she will make it through the winter, as if Woodbridge were Siberia and she had only a keep of apples to last her through the snows.

Sometimes a spouse will die shortly after losing a lifelong companion. It's known as broken heart syndrome and in some ways it has the same romantic appeal as when young lovers die together like Romeo and Juliet. Only most people outlive their spouses by more than five years and longer. Still, these stories, rare as they actually are, appeal to us. We want to believe that love can remain so strong that a person can't go on living without the other.

"Sixty years is a long time," Bette says when I leave. "How much more can you ask for?"

CHAPTER 20

The Bridge Ladies

The minute I see my mother in the parking lot, I regret the entire outfit I've concocted to wear for Arthur's memorial service. It's a black cotton dress that I cinch at the waist with a worn brown leather belt that in my mind's eye has a quasi–Ralph Lauren look. Only the fabric has attracted every thread and microbe of lint in the state of Connecticut and glows as if under a black light. The dress wanted a small heel, not the ballet flats that I've been wearing since last summer. Even my teenager suggested I change my shoes.

A week after Arthur died, the first named hurricane of the year touched down in North Carolina with hundred-miles-per-hour winds, with cyclone warnings and families evacuating along the coast. Cruelly or perhaps providentially, it was named Arthur. By the time it reached New England the storm was at its tail end: flash flooding, road closings, and power outages. Again, I tell myself not to read too much into it, and again it's impossible not to.

It's been a few weeks since Arthur died and it was unclear where Bette would hold a service—she and Arthur quit the synagogue years ago. She settled on our old country club, another landmark from my childhood that hasn't changed down to the hooks on the valet's pegboard where keys hang in clusters.

My mother and I kiss on the cheek. As usual, we are a study in opposites. She is wearing too much makeup, me not any. Her black patent leather Ferragamo handbag is the size of a kidney-shaped swimming pool; mine is as small as a kidney bean. Her hair is colored and fluffed into shape, mine is still wet and hanging limply. I know this also makes her crazy. *How could you go out with a wet head?* And while we're at it: *Don't you want to color those grays?* Only now, here, she won't say anything about how I look. We have come a long way, my mother and I.

Only then, she can't help herself and reaches out to pull a few of the more obvious threads from the dress. I don't want her de-linting me, or touching me for that matter, but I let it go. Nor do I insult her Eileen Fisher green cotton separates, which could easily double as surgeon's scrubs. This is supreme progress on both of our parts. Has proximity made friends of us? If we have learned anything I would say it is this, the first cardinal rule most of our mothers taught us: If you don't have anything nice to say, don't say anything at all.

At thirteen, at twenty-one, all through my thirties and for-ties, everything my mother said felt like a steel plate hurtling toward my head. Now, not so much. After three years with Anne, I felt ready to move on. When I told her I was ready to stop therapy, she nodded in agreement. She didn't suggest that I still had issues to work through, or make me feel insecure about my decision. Every shrink I'd ever seen tried to get me to stay, sometimes dragging out sessions for months. Still, it was hard to leave Anne and our weekly sessions, imagine someone else taking my place, my hour, sitting across from Anne looking to her for answers. *Good luck with that.* I'd like to think that she would miss me, and my fascinating life. Oh, how I admired her! Loved her! She never budged, never coddled or condescended. I didn't have to do anything, fix anything, or entertain anyone. There was no epiphany exploding like a chrysanthemum in a night sky of fireworks, no golden fields of barley. I didn't have to love myself first or embrace the journey I was on, which astonishingly led me to a 14-plex with my octogenarian mother on my arm. Unlike every other therapeutic relationship I'd ever been in, she actually helped me accomplish what I hoped to accomplish: she helped me care for my mother and by extension myself.

We see my older sister pull into the parking lot and wait for her before going inside. Nina has come from Boston, and my mother comments on how nice it was of her to make the effort.

"Mom." She sounds exasperated. "Of course I would come."

Our mother always claims ignorance about matters of the heart. "I didn't realize you felt that close."

My sister rears back. "Really, you don't know how I felt about Arthur? Or Bette?"

My mother remains oblivious. "I'm just saying it's very nice."

This response is yet more maddening. "Mom," my sister says, "I'm here, for you, too." Then she shoots me a look: *Can you believe her?*

It's Bette and Arthur's middle daughter Davi whom I first glimpse through the crowd backed up at the receiving line. Davi and I were in the same grade, are the same age, and are daughters of the Bridge Ladies. But we never really connected in high school. Then she went to Paris to live for most of her adult life. Had she followed a dream or was Paris anywhere but here? Did she become fluent and ride a bike with a baguette in the basket on her way home from work? Did she have many lovers? Like her mother, Davi is beautiful. When I see her I remember that she has a small white cloud in her right eye, just a fleck that always made her seem mysterious to me. Did she see the world through it? When I get up to her in the line, she says, "Isn't this bizarre? Why am I smiling?"

We laugh at the absurdity and I recognize the smile locked on her face. It's the one I wore to my father's funeral standing in that surreal receiving line.

I spot Bette in the center of the room, enveloped by people. She has some color again. I can't tell if it's rouge or if she's getting back some of the wind that was knocked out of her. She's wearing a pretty peach top and slacks with a matching peach and crystal choker around her neck. Was Bette able to manage herself or did Amy help her fix the clasp at the nape of her neck, the place where our mothers once held us, cooed and kissed our fat heads?

A slide show is projected against a wall, but sunlight streaming through the windows bleaches the pictures. Ghost images on a repeating cycle: Arthur in the Korean War, Arthur's college graduation, Arthur with Bette on the beach, her figure to die for. Arthur with his three babies, with his son hiking, with Bette on vacation. They are all handsome: this little band of Arthur's, the sailors on his ship. The images appear and disappear.

When Bette's son takes the microphone to welcome everyone, his voice sounds so much like Arthur's that it's scary, as if Arthur could come out from behind the curtain. *Just kidding. Still here.* But the curtains are still, the room quiet. Jack recalls a day at the beach when he was six or seven.

"There is a very brief window in a boy's life when he can hold his father's hand," Jack says.

Every one of us gathered knows about brief windows: the ineffable smell of a newborn, childhood, your first kiss. And windows that refuse to close: the first shame, the first betrayal, saying something you wish you'd never said.

Amy reads from some pithy letters Arthur sent her when she first went away to college. They are nonsensical and hilarious, capturing his slightly absurdist humor. But beneath the humor you could hear a father's longing to tell his girl he missed her, loved her, and hoped she was thriving. I marvel that she has held on to these letters all these years, as if she knew she would need them now. Davi speaks, too, the middle, like me, full of conflict, full of woe. She doesn't have a story, or a memory that anchors her speech as Jack's and Amy's did. She unfolds a piece of ruled paper from an ordinary notebook that looks like the kind you would pass to a friend in junior high, her voice losing strength as she starts to read, "I want to thank my father."

Later, Bette will tell me that Davi was extremely close to her father. She is also a nurse and was extremely helpful at hospice. It's easy to see how: She moves through the world slowly and with great care. "He wanted his binoculars," Davi told me. "Everyone thought it was silly since he couldn't get out of bed." Davi brought the binoculars. Then he wanted his nail file and she brought that, too. I like to think that Arthur was planning to break out, take his last run, more likely he wanted to keep his family safe, as he had always done.

When Jack invites the assembled to share stories, an old friend of Bette's from high school and college stands up first and introduces herself as Sis Levine. I immediately like her. Great gravely voice, wide smile, the kind of person who makes everyone feel welcome, or so I imagine.

"Bette was always an actress," Sis says, "I saw her in all of her plays."

Later Bette tells me that it was Sis who sent her flowers after her first performance at Skidmore. "I never forgot that, can you imagine doing such a thing?"

Bette once showed me an eight-by-ten photograph of herself as Lady Bracknell in a long dark Victorian-style dress and a black bonnet from that final performance at Skidmore. She was twenty, maybe twenty-one, completely in character. During our first visit I asked Bette what she loved so much about acting. Characteristically, she gave it some thought before answering.

"Well, I'd get very, very uptight before going onstage. The whole day of a performance, I'd be uptight. The minute I would walk out on the stage the nervousness would leave. It was as though I had a need to be somebody different—to not be Bette Cohen. And then I would relax because I wasn't me anymore."

I'm certain this is how she must feel today, would give anything to shed her widow's costume.

My husband joins me at our table. He arrived late and will leave early, but I am hugely touched that he has taken time out of his busy workday to come. He wanted to be here. He has shared many holiday meals with Bette and Arthur and has always felt warmly toward them. Still, I wouldn't have asked him to come. We are not a couple from the Eisenhower era and I am not a 1950s wife. It's not how we run our show. Independence trumps obligation.

When John and I were newly married, I fell into one of my worst depressions. Like my mother's postpartum, it seemed inconceivable that this could happen in the wake of something I had hoped for so deeply. I was barely functioning, unable to make simple decisions. Every beautiful thing turned menacing: the roots of trees, the distant whistle of our morning train, and when John took me for a walk near the ocean, hoping it would make me feel better, the sun appeared as a circle of paper punched from a hole, and the ribs of sand gently carved by the waves like a ghostly carcass of animal remains. I was terrified of being fired from my job, and all throughout pushing John away with my unwashed hair, stale breath, and clothes I could barely change out of. One night I heard him talking on the phone, keeping his voice low.

Later, he told me it was my mother.

"What did you tell her?"

"I said I was scared."

"What did she say?"

"She told me to hang in."

"What else?"

"She said you were worth it."

When John gets up to leave, I walk him to the door. I thank him for coming.

"Of course," he says.

The points on the collar of his shirt are curled up in the summer heat and I smooth them down. I don't want to let him go.

Two ladies at the table behind me are the Siskel and Ebert of memorial services. They narrate the entire proceedings while friends and family continue paying tribute to Arthur. They aren't even subtle about it, loudly croaking their opinions: "Too long," "Too rambling," "Is that Arthur's cousin?" "Is she sick?"

Last, a family friend gets up and starts to read from what looks like a few pages. *Groan.* His cadence is a mix of politician and preacher. His oration is a mix of clichés and homilies. Time moves slowly. The slide show clicks through again and again. Arthur, Arthur, Arthur. Finally, he asks all of us if we know what "the dash" is. No one seems to know what he's talking about. He surveys the room.

"The dash? Anyone?"

Finally, when no one wagers a guess, he enlightens us. It's the dash on a gravestone. It's what's between your birth year and death year. "The dash," he says, "is the way you lived your life. It's what you do between those years that's important."

Siskell, from behind me, pipes up, "What did he say, the gash? What's the gash?"

Then, from Ebert, "I can't hear anything."

It's like sitting in front of hearing-impaired Jews at the movie. Actually, I *am* sitting in front of hearing-impaired Jews.

No one else gets up to speak and it looks as if the testimonials are over.

People start to stand, head toward the buffet lunch. Only then does Bette stand up with the help of her daughters. She has something to say.

"I want to thank everyone for coming," she starts. "Arthur would have been surprised to see so many people, but I'm not."

Before we leave, I make my way around the room to say good-bye to Rhoda, Jackie, and Bea. They are camped out in the corners of the room like sturdy legs of a table. Bea is sitting closest. She is wearing black. It makes me long for her purples and lime greens.

"Hi, sweetie pie," she says and squeezes my hand and I smile at the few people sitting with her. It's hard to know what she is feeling today. She lost Carl a decade ago after a series of strokes. He was in a wheelchair and unable to communicate, but he stayed home with a full-time aide. "It was rough" is all Bea will ever say.

"Bea, you're amazing." I've told her this more than once. And she always says the same thing in response. "Betsy, it's amazing what you get used to."

Every time we talked, Bea loved to shock me with tales from Carl's days as a young ophthalmology resident.

"You want to know how they learned surgery, Betsy?"

"How, Bea?"

"On a cadaver's head, no, half a head," she corrected herself, and then wound up for the big finish. "They went right in for the eye and eye socket!"

Bea and Carl were married for sixty years. At Bridge, she brings out cocktail napkins with their initials monogrammed on the corners. The plates on her car still say MD. She tells me that when Carl died, she left a golf ball on his grave instead of a stone. When she went back some time later, of course it was gone.

Across the room Jackie and Dick are sitting with three other couples. They all must know how lucky they are. The odds are against them in marriages of over sixty years, with both spouses still in relatively good health. Every year, Dick and Jackie exchange anniversary cards. This year, their sixty-third, they picked out the same card for each other of a lion and a lioness. I nearly swoon; how romantic is that? Jackie brushes it off.

"Come on, don't you think it's incredible?"

Both of them independently cruising the racks at Walgreens or CVS and picking out the same card.

She shrugs.

"What do you think it means?" I urge her for an insight.

"That we're on the same page?"

Once Jackie told me that the secret to marriage was that she accepts Dick for who he is. It struck me as a completely radical concept. Was I supposed to accept my husband for who he is? Was I supposed to accept myself? On good days, we considered ourselves works in progress. Our parents didn't wonder what they would be when they grew up, or for that matter *if* they'd grow up. They were grown-up!

I notice Jackie is wearing her three-pronged ring. She told me some time ago that it was her lucky ring.

"Lucky for what?"

"Flying at first. I got it when we started flying and always wore it."

"And now?"

"For life, I guess."

♠

Rhoda has come alone, but she mentions that she's seeing George later. He comes over every weekend, and she cooks a Shabbat meal for him on Friday night. More than once Rhoda has mentioned that George loves her cooking and he's always grateful.

"You can make him an egg and he loves it!"

They go to the movies, lectures, and plays. They socialize and travel. They go on cruises together! (The ladies believe they share a cabin.)

"George is a gentleman," Rhoda says, and then to illustrate, "a gentleman in the truest sense of the word. He always opens doors and pulls your chair out." They've never gone Dutch on anything!

It's clear that George meets Rhoda's high standards, and that's saying something. He even meets with Beth's approval. Rhoda naturally felt some trepidation the first time the two of them met. But the day went exceedingly well and Beth sent an e-mail that night: "I love him. He's a keeper!" Her son was also happy for her, happy for the companionship.

Once, when Bridge was at Rhoda's, Bette asked if George brought the flowers on the coffee table.

"George always brings flowers," Rhoda said, a little cocky, and who can blame her: finding love in her eighties.

"Why don't you get married?" Bette asked.

"Then there'd be no flowers!" Rhoda laughs loudly at her own joke.

"It must be nice," Bette said, "to have a companion, someone to watch TV with."

"Don't be so naïve, Bette," Rhoda shot back.

Rhoda and George have been together for three years. When I asked her if she was in love, she blushed. Then she said yes, very much so.

♠

They are all here, the Bridge Ladies. If you didn't know them you would never guess that they've been together in a club for over fifty years, thousands of lunches, many more thousands of hands of Bridge. All the bowls of Bridge mix, the disputes over bad bids, the number of tricks taken, tricks lost. Their club has more staying power than most marriages. Children born, schooled, launched into the world. A tidal wave of worries, a string of happy days, a family singing together in a station wagon on a long ride home. The nest emptied. Husbands buried. *Sunrise, sunset.*

I had assumed the Bridge Ladies' bond was inviolable, enviable. I imagined they confided their deepest secrets, confessed their worst fears, worried about their children, and groused about their husbands. You know: what happens at the Bridge table stays at the Bridge table. I often wished the ladies tasted some of our freedom to sleep with different guys before committing to one. My mother once said all cats are gray in the dark. As far as I know she didn't have a control group. I wished the ladies felt that they could have pursued careers: Bette on Broadway, my mother an author, Jackie her own travel agency, and Rhoda a rabbi. Bea, well, she could have done anything: feed the hungry, start a social media company, or become a Grand Life Master at Bridge. I wanted them to confide in each other and draw comfort from doing so. I wanted them to hug!

Their periods never aligned like girls in a dorm, they never got high and drove through the winding roads of Woodbridge with the windows down, the volume up on a Bruce Springsteen ballad or a Bob Marley beat. They never did anything really stupid, rocked any boats, or went out very far on any limbs. They haven't fought any wars or even picketed any causes. For the most part, they upheld the conventions they were raised with. Mostly, they've hung in. They meant their marriage vows when they said them. They raised their children and they continue to help them into adulthood when they falter, meet with life's rough breaks: loss of jobs, divorce, health problems, money problems. When I stumbled out of the starting blocks of my life, my mother said she believed in late bloomers. And when I stumbled again, she repeated it. I never thought I would say this, but I think the Bridge Ladies are brave.

♠

Driving my mother home from the memorial, my mother mentions a piece about the poet Edward Hirsch that she just read in the *New Yorker* (for the record, she is the only person I know who is up-to-date on her *New Yorker*s).

"Do you know him?"

"I don't know him but I've read him."

"Really?"

"Mom, I have an MFA in poetry."

"Oh, yeah."

"Why?"

"There's a piece on him in the current *New Yorker*, have you read it?"

"What about it?" *I'm like a year and half behind.*

"Well, he lost a son and he's written a book about it. Something in there really touched me."

"What about?"

"You'll read it, you'll see."

"Just tell me."

"It's about suffering."

The conversation ends there. I go home and look up the article. I see it right away, the verse near the end of the piece:

> Look closely and you will see
> Almost everyone carrying bags
> Of cement on their shoulders
> That's why it takes courage
> To get out of bed in the morning
> And climb into the day.

"My life is over," Bette confides in my mother when they are back on the trail a week or so after Arthur has died, their sensible shoes crushing the leaf rot as they turn the corners.

"It's not over, Bette," my mother says. "It's shattered."

How many times has my mother's life been shattered? Her father a tyrant, her coat in flames, pushing a sad carriage with a blank face. And what of our chapel, its shards of stained glass—yellow, orange, burnt orange—soldered together like an antique map. What is it like for my mother to return to this place? Her young life shattered; the pieces here?

Sometimes, when we were young and winters more brutal than they are now, ducks would come to our half-frozen pond, fooled into thinking they could rest a while only to die, trapped beneath the encroaching ice. We'd beg our father to go out on the ice and save them. He'd tamp at the edge with his boot, attempt to take a step, only then you would hear it: ice cracking almost like electricity beneath the surface. We'd all step back then, both roused and relieved. Then we'd go back inside. *Empty-handed.*

♠

Bette finally returns to Bridge after a few more weeks. She says she feels as if she has lost half of her brain. She can't focus, can't concentrate. I don't imagine for a moment that returning to Bridge marks an actual turning point, rather some desire for camaraderie, some need to put on lipstick and pearls or to feel something familiar like a deck of cards with its elegant symmetry and iconic suits: Clubs, Diamonds, Hearts, and Spades.

Lunch is at The Woodbridge Gathering, a very low-key deli with no emphasis on decor. A very sweet waitress brings over menus. The front pieces of her ponytail have come loose and swing back and forth in front of her glasses like windshield wipers. Bette is late. There has been some miscommunication between her and my mother; they were going to meet at a gas station for a tutorial. In the midst of this confusion, Bette slips in like the cat whose been missing for days. She pulls up a seat, and that's it: No royal welcome. No hugs or kisses. No one says anything.

I'm shocked. Bette has been gone for more than six months. She has lost Arthur. Am I living in a parallel universe where the expression of emotion is punishable by death? Couldn't they just once step down from Mount Rushmore and give someone a hug? Instead, talk meanders from topic to topic. Jackie's granddaughter is getting married in Maine. She likes the young man very much. A conversation about paperless invitations ensues. Spoiler alert: the ladies do not like them.

When I see Bette next, I don't want to call attention to the fact that no one made much of her return, but I feel indignant on her behalf.

"Aren't you surprised there wasn't more of a welcome?"

"No, not really."

"You mean you weren't upset when no one brought up Arthur? The memorial?"

Bette thinks more deeply now before answering. "No, I really wasn't. I would have brought it up if I needed to. I think they were being respectful of my feelings. Anyway, I didn't want to talk about it. It was nice to take my mind off it and just play Bridge."

Epilogue

My mother and I take the plunge. We decide to go as partners to the Tuesday game at the Orange Senior Center, where we had taken Bridge lessons and where I played with Jonathan and nearly collapsed from anxiety. It's October and I haven't been able to get into New York to play at Honors, I haven't been able to find a peer group to play with in New Haven, and I'm worried that I will forget everything. We goad each other on and finally find a Tuesday to play. I've been studying my Bridge books more, playing on my app, and have told myself to relax. I can handle it this time. It's my mother who is intimidated and a little freaked out, as if she's getting into bed with someone new after being with the same person her whole life. She knows her way around the Monday game with the ladies, but the players here are known to be fierce; some play every day of the week.

I have newfound respect for how my mother has managed since my father died nearly a decade ago. She never asks for help with the big things, finances and house repairs, and has a handyman do everything else: change lightbulbs, install a new mailbox, and clean the gutters. I've always thought of her as completely dependent, somewhat bumbling even. That was the dynamic between her and my dad. He was the person who got things done. As he declined, it was left to her to take care of everything, gradually then completely. When I ask her how she did it, she said, "Dad had taken care of everything. After he got sick, I'd push myself out of bed every day and say, 'You're up. It's your turn. You're at bat.'"

I have a newfound respect for the seniors at the Orange Senior Center, too. The place is lousy with hearing aids, walkers, accessories that could make a drag queen weep. The men come with flip phones attached to their belts in leather cases like Eagle Scouts. But they're fierce. They know their way around a hand of Bridge and I suspect a whole lot more. How many collective compromises, broken hearts? How many in safe marriages, or worse, unsafe? Some have cheated on their spouses or never loved them; some have broken their children's spirits; doubtless some were broken themselves. How many bags of cement?

Inside, the room is filling fast, and it's that same old feeling of musical chairs. My mother and I nab seats with a man and woman though it's not clear if they are a couple. Only when the man makes a mistake, the woman rips him a new one, which leads me to think they are married. I can't tell if we've been dealt fairly straightforward hands that are easier to bid, but we bid and make three out of four hands. Next we play with Bea and her partner. She introduces us and we exchange chitchat, but when the bell rings, it's all business. It's my deal and when I open my hand I have exactly thirteen points and five Spades, including the Ace, King, Queen in honors.

"One Spade," I say, confidently.

"A Spade, you say," my mother replies conspiratorially, running her fingernail against the fan of cards worthy of a Liberace glissando.

We will make that hand and more before moving to the last table, where my mother recognizes a woman whom she knew a hundred years ago and they exchange pleasantries. She whispers that she'll fill me in later, implying that the woman is a real piece of work.

Overall, we win half the hands we play and feel very positive about our partnership. Bridge made a team out of us. Three hours later, no worse for wear, we leave the center.

"We weren't the worst," I say.

"Far from it. You were really good, Betsy. You're a lot better than you think you are."

"Would you play again?"

"Definitely," she says.

It's still light out, but cooler now. As we head across the parking lot, my mother looks at me, "Aren't you going to button your coat?"

First and foremost, my deepest thanks to the Bridge Ladies: Bette Horowitz née Cohen, Jackie Podoloff née Brody, Beatrice Phillips née Bernstein, Rhoda Meyers née Freedman, and Roz Lerner née Cohen. They welcomed me into their club, invited me for lunch and Bridge every Monday, sat down with me for multiple conversations, and let me play at their table. It was a great honor.

I am also grateful to the Bridge daughters who spoke with me about their memories of the Bridge club: Lisa Podoloff Boles, Davi Horowitz, Amy Horowitz, Nancy Phillips Meredith, and Beth Meyers Stubenhaus. And to Dick Podoloff, who was always an enthusiastic participant.

My sisters, Gail Lerner and Nina Palmer, generously shared their time and memories with me. They have both been incredibly supportive of this project, reading multiple drafts and giving comments and encouragement. Thank you both so much.

Colleagues and friends to whom I am also deeply grateful include Amy Williams, Caron Knauer, Leah Hager Cohen, Sylvie

Rabineau, Georgina Morley, Mizzi Vander Pluijm, Erin Hosier, Jennifer Carlson, and Henry Dunow. I am indebted to Rosemary Mahoney, who once again generously applied her sharp mind and pencil.

My interns Casey Blue James, E-Lynn Yap, Arielle Datz, and Ana Barros helped me tremendously over the years. To my teachers who all moved the needle of my fledgling game a little further: Ellen Friedman, Al Pol, Barbara Bayone, Jeff Bayone, and Wendy Frieden. My greatest debt goes to Jess Jurkovic, who offered his expertise, his friendship, and his gift of description in parsing the complexities of Bridge.

To my Bridge buddies: Barbara and Bernard Barkin, Anne Dailey, Jack Hitt, Rick Prum, Tina Pohlman, Dan Greenberg, Simon Lipskar, Eamon Dolan, and Matty Goldberg. Thank you for playing with me. ;)

I am enormously grateful to my agent, David Black. As a fellow agent, I can only say that his guidance in this process has been inspiring. His friendship, support, stamina, expertise, and intensity continue to astonish me from the first phone call on. My thanks to the wonderful people at the Black agency: Susan Raihofer, Sarah Smith, Jenny Herrera, and Sarah Paolantonio.

Karen Rinaldi: thank you. Even when I wanted you to tire, you didn't! You pushed and challenged and prodded and I am so grateful for your editorial eye and publishing savvy. We, too, made a good team. Thank you for believing in the ladies, and me. I must also mention Hannah Robinson, assistant extraordinaire—aka The Slayer—and soon to run a major corporation. Thank you for everything. The entire Harper team has been incredibly supportive and creative. Thanks to Victoria Comella, Brian Perrin, Penny Makras, Tina Andreadis, Kathy Schneider, Virginia Stanley, Milan Bozic, Bill Ruoto, Nikki Baldauf, Jonathan Burnham, and Michael Morrison.

Acknowledgments

Last and most, I thank my daughter, Raffaella Sweet, who has set a very high bar for going big or going home. And my husband, John Donatich, who read every single draft and never stopped pushing me to do better, offering advice that always turned out to be exactly right. And for all that I mostly wanted to kill him.

extracts reading groups
competitions books new
discounts extracts extracts
competitions events
books new extracts
new events discounts
events books
extracts reading groups
new titles reading groups
interviews
books events extracts events
discounts events books
new books events
events new interviews
discounts extracts discounts books
www.panmacmillan.com
extracts events reading groups
competitions books extracts new